The Dominican Intervention

THE DOMINICAN INTERVENTION

Abraham F. Lowenthal

Harvard University Press / Cambridge, Massachusetts / 1972

Preface

I regard the U.S. military intervention in the Dominican Republic as a tragic event, costly to the Dominican Republic, to the United States, and to inter-American relations.

I have spelled out some of the costs elsewhere.* In this work, however, I am examining what happened and trying to explain why, not evaluating the results or speculating on what might have been done. I aim not primarily to judge the Dominican intervention, although some judgments may be deduced, but to analyze how it occurred.

No one can live through an upheaval like the 1965 Dominican crisis and feel himself wholly dispassionate. I know that my own views on the Dominican intervention must be influenced by my perspective as an American citizen, by my close friendships with some of the participants in these events, by the kinds of access I was able to obtain to relevant people and information, and by my personal and political prejudices. Despite and in part because of my biases, however, I have done my best to obtain many different views and weigh them carefully. Now I can only hope that my account will be read and criticized by

* See Abraham F. Lowenthal, "The Dominican Intervention in Retrospect," *Public Policy* (September 1969), 133–148.

those who may be able to supply additional information and other viewpoints upon which future writers can draw.

Writing on so recent and controversial a foreign policy occurrence as the 1965 Dominican crisis involves serious problems of research and presentation. Much of the information needed for conclusive analysis is not now available, and a good deal of the data a persistent investigator can find may not yet be documented.

My working premise, however, has been that—despite the difficulties—I should try to take advantage of the special research opportunities which came to me because I was living in the Dominican Republic when the 1965 crisis erupted. Diplomatic historians a decade or two from now will be able to cite documents now restricted and they may also have access to papers not available to me. But they will probably not be able, as I was, to question the men who drafted the documents and who presumably know why they said what they did and omitted what they did not say. Official documents are very likely to blur differences in perceptions and perspective among various actors in the foreign policy-making process; sometimes, particularly in this age of telephone calls, they are meant to obscure and even to deceive. I believe, therefore, that the chance I had to conduct extensive interviews with many principal participants after the heat of crisis subsided but before their memories had completely faded provided me special advantages in preparing this account.

One of my two main sources, accordingly, has been a series of almost one hundred and fifty personal interviews I conducted from 1965 to 1969 (in English and Spanish) in the Dominican Republic, Puerto Rico, and the United States. All but eleven persons, almost all of them American intelligence officers, agreed to allow their names to be listed alphabetically in Appendix I.

Collecting reliable data through interviews is admittedly a tricky art based on an uncertain process of triangulation guided by inference. Personal rivalries and reputations, political convenience, psychological vested interests, memory lapses, and discretion combine to color what one can learn from talking with those who help shape policy, and there are always others with whom one cannot talk at all. To increase the likelihood that participants would meet with me and would talk freely, I chose very early in my research to conduct my interviews on a "background" basis, promising each person I would not attribute any statements to him.

I made a similar commitment in order to obtain access to my second most important source: a great deal of written material, and some tape recordings, not now generally available to the public. I have examined many hundreds of still-classified public documents, including virtually all the State Department's cable traffic between Santo Domingo and Washington from April through June 1965, various chronologies, studies, and histories done within or for the U.S. government, several memoranda of conversation and the like. I am also drawing on voluminous personal correspondence with Ambassador W. Tapley Bennett, Jr., and with General Bruce Palmer, Jr., on extensive personal files and correspondence made available to me by Theodore Draper, and on unpublished notes and manuscripts provided me by Barnard Collier, Jaime Benítez, Emmanuel Clarizio, the late Héctor García Godoy, and a number of other participants and observers who prefer to remain unnamed. I have also heard and taken notes on recordings made of conversations over open radio lines between U.S. defense attachés and Dominican military leaders. Some of this material I agreed not to quote directly, but only to paraphrase. The only other condition imposed on my use of these privileged sources was that the information thus obtained not be attributed.

Agreeing not to make attributions was the price for obtaining a great deal of previously unavailable information; it is a cost which the reader, unable to find citations for many of my statements, must share.

I have given much thought to the difficulties for scholarly practice posed by the preferential access and not-for-attribution procedures I agreed to accept; my sensitivity to these issues has been further heightened by Theodore Draper's essay "The Dominican Intervention Reconsidered," published in the *Political Science Quarterly* (April 1971) after the rest of this manuscript had been completed. Were I to begin this research project now, six years and an administration after the events in question, I might be able to hold out for more conventional and documentable access. In the circumstances in which I conducted my investigation, however, I made commitments regarding attribution which I am now bound to honor. I can do no more at this time than present my book as it stands and ask the reader to evaluate my argument with respect to its own integrity and coherence and with reference to all the information available from other sources. Perhaps the publication of my version will spur some participants to record and reveal their own memories; at least it should provide other scholars additional data with which to frame their further inquiries. I continue to hope, as well, that early publication of the testimony on the Dominican intervention presented to the Senate Foreign Relations Committee in 1965, and of other classified documents, may facilitate future analyses of the Dominican case and evaluations of my account.

The rest of the material is in the public domain. Published documents, books, and articles contain a surprising amount of data on American policy in the Dominican crisis. Leaks and counter-leaks abounded, and much previously classified information was consequently made available in one form or another. To help others make good use of the published materials, many of them not widely known, I have written Appendix II, A Guide to Public Sources for Study of the 1965 Dominican Crisis.

Finally, a word on my method of citation. No procedure is perfectly satisfactory, given my extensive use of unattributable sources, but I hope my adherence to the following procedures will be useful.

(1) Whenever my best (or only) authority for a statement is in the public record, the public source is cited.

(2) Whenever a public source exists but is not cited, this is because I believe the source I have actually used to be more authoritative than the public reference.

(3) Whenever I feel uncertain about the reliability of the source I have used, some qualifying word or phrase, such as "apparently," or "reportedly," is included in the text.

(4) Whenever the sources conflict or are unclear, or necessary information is unavailable, the text or a note makes this clear.

(5) Whenever I am going beyond the data to present a hypothesis or to advance a possible explanation, I have tried to make this clear.

ACKNOWLEDGMENTS

The debts I have incurred in preparing this study are too numerous to list individually, although each person who has helped me deserves my special thanks.

I wish to express my appreciation to several categories of friends: to those in the Ford Foundation and the Asociación para el Desarrollo, Inc. of Santiago, Dominican Republic, who made it possible for me to work in Santiago from September 1964 until August 1966 and to return there from time to time thereafter; to my fellow students of Dominican politics and U.S. policy who have shared their insights and data; and to my parents, my professors at Harvard, and many others who have stimulated my interest in international affairs and in Latin American politics. I also want to thank the Center for International Affairs at Harvard for sponsoring the 1966–67 "Seminar on U.S. Policy in the Dominican Republic," the members of the seminar for their helpful comments on an early draft of part of this essay, and the Brookings Institution, for awarding me a Research Fellowship which enabled me to complete this work.

I wish to record my special gratitude to the many individuals who granted me personal interviews and access to restricted materials. Their willingness to help me and their confidence in my judgment and discretion have been a continuing challenge.

I must make an exception to my decision not to list individual acknowledgments in favor of those who cheerfully undertook the sometimes painful mechanics of translating my scrawl into typed manuscript: Judith Sullivan, Peggy Bell, Graciela de Niezen, and Mónica Protzel.

Finally, I owe most to my wife, Janet, for so much that I cannot begin to say. To her and to our daughter Linda, born in the Dominican Republic, I fondly dedicate this work.

Abraham F. Lowenthal

June 1971

Contents

The Dominican Intervention

Introduction

On April 28, 1965, over five hundred U.S. Marines landed at Santo Domingo in the Dominican Republic. Armed and authorized to return fire, they were the first combat-ready U.S. forces to enter a Latin American country in almost forty years. Within a week, a rapid buildup had put nearly twenty-three thousand U.S. soldiers ashore. Almost ten thousand additional troops stood ready just off the Dominican coast and thousands more were on alert at bases in the United States.

The massive U.S. military intervention in the Dominican Republic surprised, even shocked, most students of U.S. policy in Latin America. After almost a century of repeated American military interventions in the Western hemisphere and particularly in the Caribbean area, the United States government had in the days of President Franklin D. Roosevelt forsworn this practice in Latin America. In 1947, under President Harry S. Truman, the United States had agreed to join with the other members of the Organization of American States in formalizing the proscription against unilateral intervention. Despite repeated involvements in Latin American politics—in Argentina, in Guatemala, and particularly in Cuba—the United States had, since 1928, always kept its actions short of overt military intervention.[1] Yet U.S. forces were now sent into Santo Domingo without specific consultation in the OAS, much less the members' prior approval. Observers of American policy began at once to ask whether President Lyndon B. Johnson was formulating a new "doctrine," one which would justify again the use of American troops in this hemisphere.

If the military intervention of April 1965 raised questions about the course of U.S. policy in Latin America, the events of the next few weeks underlined these questions and provoked many more. Having proclaimed first that it was landing its troops to protect the lives of Americans and other foreign nationals—although not a single American or other foreign citizen had been hurt—the U.S. government then added that it was acting also to preserve the Dominican people's right to a free choice of government. Soon it seemed, however, that the U.S. government itself was attempting to impose a regime on the Dominican people. It appeared that American troops were actually aligning themselves with Dominican forces who were taking lives, even committing atrocities, who had deprived the Dominican people of their freely chosen government by overthrowing it in 1963, and whose determination to thwart the attempted restoration of the 1963 constitutional regime accounted for the 1965 crisis.

When the Dominican intervention was first announced, administration spokesmen, emphasizing the danger to American lives and the general aim of stopping bloodshed, had explicitly disclaimed U.S. political objectives. Within a few days, however, official statements revealed that the troops' primary mission was to prevent a "Communist takeover" in Santo Domingo. Requests from journalists and others for evidence of alleged Communist influence in the Dominican revolt elicited firm statements that although such evidence existed, it could not be made public. But soon the administration released the names of fifty-eight supposed Communist activists, said to be participating in the uprising. Then it turned out that the "fifty-eight" were really only fifty-five (three had been double-listed), and that even the reduced roster was full of ambiguities and errors, including the mention of persons who were ill, out of the country, in jail, or otherwise unavailable for revolutionary pursuits.[2]

Poor coordination and extraordinary haste might well explain the inconsistencies revealed by this numbers' game, but many other apparent contradictions of U.S. policy during these weeks were more difficult to understand. Having declared, at last, that its troops had been sent in both to stop the bloodshed and to prevent a Communist takeover, the U.S. government then deployed its forces in such a way that they actually protected Dominican Communists in one section of Santo Domingo and permitted bloodshed to continue in another part of the city.

The political stance the U.S. government adopted was even more baffling. The United States seemed to back first one Dominican faction and then another while proclaiming its continuing neutrality, and to call one group "rebels" and another "loyalists" while professing not to favor either. Something beyond mere duplicity appeared to be involved, for the actions taken by the U.S. government seemed just as inconsistent as its public pronouncements. U.S. officials helped establish a military junta under Colonel Pedro Benoit, invited it to issue a written appeal for U.S. military intervention, and then—having sent in the Marines—refused to recognize the Benoit junta as the legitimate Dominican government. American officials then insisted that the U.S. government had no candidate for the leadership of a new Dominican government, nor any wish to suggest one, even as former Ambassador John Bartlow Martin worked in the home of Dominican General Antonio Imbert to help him form a regime. No sooner had the Imbert regime been announced and supported by an immediate recommendation from U.S. Ambassador W. Tapley Bennett, Jr., that it be granted diplomatic recognition by the United States, than Washington seemed determined to ignore or even undermine the Imbert government. High-level U.S. officials, including top presidential aide McGeorge Bundy, next engaged in detailed negotiations with Juan Bosch, Antonio Guzmán, and others to establish another regime, in place of the Imbert junta. Yet at the very point when formation of a U.S.-backed government under Guzmán seemed imminent, the U.S. government suspended negotiations with Guzmán, Bundy returned to Washington, and Ambassador Ellsworth Bunker flew to Santo Domingo to establish a new regime under Héctor García Godoy, presumably unconnected with either of the two groups with which the United States had up to then been dealing.

The impression of overwhelming confusion which American policy conveyed during the first weeks of the Dominican affair was heightened by the proliferation of efforts to deal with the crisis. At one point in May 1965 Santo Domingo claimed the presence, aside from the usual American embassy team, of a former U.S. ambassador to the Dominican Republic on one presidential assignment; one Undersecretary of State, the Undersecretary of Defense, an Assistant Secretary of State, and the Special Assistant for National Security Affairs on a second mission; and another Assistant Secretary of State plus a Deputy Assistant Secretary of Defense on a third. The task of seeking peace in Santo Domingo, meanwhile, was also being pursued by the OAS Secretary General, a five-man OAS special committee, a special observer from the United Nations and his military and political advisers, as well as the papal nuncio.

A variety of U.S. government agencies also operated in uncertain relationship to one another. While members of the U.S. Armed Forces shot Dominicans, volunteers of the U.S. Peace Corps manned Dominican hospitals to care for the wounded, many of them taking every opportunity to express dissent from what they took to be the U.S. government policy. Units from the Central Intelligence Agency, the Defense Intelligence Agency, and the Federal Bureau of Investigation—plus a large team from the 82nd Airborne Division—queried and requeried local sources in search of useful information. Psychological warfare specialists from the 82nd Division, the CIA, and the U.S. Information Agency engaged in a wide variety of operations, including not only extensive publicly acknowledged activities but also such covert measures as jamming radio broadcasts by one Dominican faction, facilitating the publication of a newspaper for another faction, and even transmitting clandestine broadcasts designed to discredit the Dominican group they purported to represent.

And while the intelligence agents snooped, and the information specialists informed and misinformed, and the would-be peacemakers struggled, the nearly twenty-three thousand American troops and small contingents from Latin American countries stood aside while one Dominican armed faction routed another in the northern sector of Santo Domingo, despite a formally signed and internationally endorsed cease-fire agreement. Many events in this Caribbean imbroglio seemed to defy rational explanation.

As reports from Santo Domingo accumulated, James Reston reported in the *New York Times* that Washington was gripped by a "feeling of uncertainty about how policy is made."[3] The Johnson administration seemed to be floundering badly. Each passing week brought an apparent change in the U.S. strategy for dealing with the Dominican situation, or at least a switch in the U.S.-preferred candidate for the Dominican presidency. A newspaper cartoon showed a Martian space explorer reporting to his colleagues after returning from the Dominican Republic: "And then they took me to their leader, then another leader, and another leader, and another."[4] Russell Baker, the satirical columnist of the *New York Times,* termed the administration's policy a "confuse-in." The only logical explanation for U.S. actions in the Dominican crisis, Baker suggested, was that the president hoped to create enough confusion to guarantee himself a free hand.[5]

This study is primarily a search for other explanations of the U.S. government's response to the 1965 crisis in the Dominican Republic. Its specific focus is on the first week of the crisis, from the first request that American forces proceed toward Dominican waters until the definitive deployment of U.S. troops in a fixed line dividing the city of Santo Domingo. My main aim is to help account for one particular set of occurrences, comprising the massive U.S. armed intervention in Santo Domingo. I hope, however, that this detailed analysis will contribute to clarifying the entire Dominican episode and that it will also help generally to illuminate the process by which U.S. foreign policy is made.

1. The United States and the Dominican Republic to 1965: Background to Intervention

The history of U.S. relations with the Dominican Republic, indeed with the Caribbean region generally, is a tale of mutual frustration. Perhaps in no other country has the influence of the United States been so long and so continuously exerted as in the Dominican Republic, yet in few places have the limits of America's power to transform foreign realities been more evident. Three times within sixty years—in 1905, in 1916, and in 1965—the United States sent the Marines to Santo Domingo, but these military interventions are only the most dramatic episodes in a record of extraordinary American involvement in Dominican affairs, involvement which preceded the first intervention and survives the third.

Events in the Dominican Republic, for instance, occasioned the Roosevelt corollary to the Monroe Doctrine, the initial U.S. interest in customs receivership, and undisguised American efforts to dictate policies of the Dominican government—all before the U.S. military occupation of 1916–1924. More recently, in the five years before the 1965 intervention, the U.S. government undertook a wide variety of activities in the Dominican Republic, including: implementing OAS-approved sanctions against the brutal Trujillo dictatorship; using the threat of military force to stabilize a volatile situation after the dictatorship's sudden end; expending foreign aid for immediate political purposes; helping to organize and assure free elections under OAS supervision; assisting the elected government through the Alliance for Progress; strengthening some groups through political development programs and reinforcing others through military assistance and training; attempting to deter and then to reverse an unconstitutional change of government by threatening to withhold recognition and suspend aid, and then by doing so; pressuring for a return to constitutional procedure through national elections; and eventually aiding the unconstitutional regime in many ways—funding its development programs, training its police, even providing it tactical political advice—although the promised elections were not held.

Review of this troubled history suggests that the United States has long been deeply, pervasively, but somewhat reluctantly involved in Dominican affairs. The extent of American involvement in the Dominican Republic has almost always been extraordinarily great. Its nature has been mainly preemptive and its principal motivation has been the protection of U.S. security.

Although the landing of American troops at Santo Domingo in 1965 shocked even knowledgeable observers of U.S. policy in Latin America, the action should not really have been so surprising if viewed in the context of previous American relations with the Dominican Republic and the rest of the Caribbean. Earlier American involvements in the area did not make inevitable the 1965 military intervention, but they did help shape the attitudes both of Dominican politicians and of American officials, thus making what occurred in 1965 more likely than it would otherwise have been. An analysis of this history and its effects on American attitudes and assumptions will make the events of 1965 easier to comprehend.

II

Although nominally sovereign and independent since 1844, the Dominican Republic has never been able to exclude the predominant influence of the United States. As early as 1849 one

Dominican president approached Washington to request that the Dominican Republic be annexed.[1] This particular overture was rejected, but the American government's special interest in conditions on the island of Hispaniola (which the Dominican Republic shares with Haiti) due to the "proximity of that island to the United States" was noted by President Millard Fillmore in his Annual Message to Congress a year later.[2]

Several times during the second half of the nineteenth century, American officials negotiated with Dominicans on proposed annexation agreements. Even more often, U.S. and Dominican representatives discussed proposals to grant the U.S. government special rights and concessions, particularly for use of Samaná Bay. None of these discussions ever produced lasting agreement, but one annexation proposal—strenuously backed by President Ulysses S. Grant—did reach the floor of the Senate in 1870; half of the fifty-six Senators present at the vote supported the plan.[3]

Available scholarly analyses of successive periods in Dominican-American relations reveal the deepening U.S. involvement in Dominican affairs from 1870 to 1915. During the last quarter of the nineteenth century, "relations were necessarily of an intimate nature," as American engagement increased with the expansion of U.S. private interests and the broadening of U.S. strategic horizons.[4] At the turn of the century, the establishment of the San Domingo Improvement Company—organized to collect the Dominican government's debts to foreign bondholders—climaxed "two decades of steady advance toward American commercial and economic dominance of the Dominican Republic."[5] The U.S. government's support for the San Domingo Company, another analyst concludes, "marked the beginning of a more active participation by the United States in the Dominican Republic—leading to closer control of the country's economy" as the twentieth century opened.[6] During the first two decades of this century, a fourth scholar notes, "In no Latin American country were the economic and political intervention by the United States more in evidence nor carried farther towards their logical conclusion than in the Dominican Republic."[7]

Step by step the U.S. government involved itself more deeply in Dominican affairs. Having supported the claims of the San Domingo Improvement Company on the Dominican government's resources, the U.S. government next—under President Theodore Roosevelt—asserted the right to collect customs charges at Santo Domingo and other Dominican ports in order to guarantee that the Dominican government would pay its debts. Once established, U.S. control of Dominican customs' collection paved the way for American demands to exercise final authority on the Dominican government's expenditure of revenue collected by the customs' receivership. Soon the United States government demanded, as well, the right to dictate specific policies to the Dominican government. American officials were particularly eager that the Dominicans disband their armies and establish a national constabulary under U.S. supervision, and also that Dominican factions agree to hold U.S.-supervised elections and pledge to respect the results. When the Dominican government balked at these and similar demands, the stage was set in 1916 for President Woodrow Wilson to send in the Marines.[8]

Once the Marines landed, U.S. officials thought it necessary to establish an outright military government in the Dominican Republic. For eight years American military and civilian personnel ruled the Dominican Republic directly, taking over every branch of public administration. American troops attempted to impose order, American officers trained and commanded a Dominican constabulary, American revenue agents collected taxes, American engineers built roads and bridges, American bureaucrats set up a civil service system and reformed the post office, and American educators revamped the Dominican Republic's schools.[9]

The occupation period marked the height of American intervention in Dominican affairs, but strong U.S. influence was assured even after the Marines withdrew and an elected Dominican regime took office in 1924.[10] The United States–Dominican Republic Convention of that year reserved several rights to the U.S. government, and it appears that American officials considered the threat of renewed military intervention a legitimate means of assuring that these rights would be respected.[11] Even after the Franklin Roosevelt administration formally renounced unilateral intervention as a policy instrument, the U.S. maintained its customs receivership officially until 1941 and retained other fiscal controls over the Dominican government until 1947.[12]

U.S. entanglement in Dominican affairs decreased somewhat during the long Trujillo period, from 1930 to 1961. General Trujillo assiduously maintained his contacts with American Marine officials and subsidized extensive lobbying operations of various types to advance his personal and political interests, but by and large the U.S. government was less interested and involved in Dominican affairs from 1930 to 1960 than it was before or has been since. Trujillo's regime presented the United States with no real difficulties during this period, and the Dominican Republic offered the United States the support Washington considered appropriate during World War II and then the Cold War.

The last years of the Trujillo era, however, brought renewed American involvement.[13] The U.S. government's decision in 1960 to go beyond diplomatic and economic sanctions the OAS had voted against Trujillo by imposing a special fee on the purchase of Dominican sugar served to strengthen the will of Dominicans opposed to Trujillo and thus brought the U.S. government back into Dominican politics as a key actor.[14] American officials in Santo Domingo identified and encouraged a group of anti-Trujillo Dominicans, assuring them that the United States government would cooperate with them should they gain power. According to some reports, U.S. agents may even have materially aided the Dominican plot which culminated in Trujillo's assassination on May 30, 1961.[15]

Whatever the accuracy of the rumors about American complicity in Trujillo's death, it is clear that by the time Trujillo died the U.S. government was prepared once again to participate actively and directly in Dominican affairs. The extent of American involvement soon became extraordinary; from mid-1960 through 1962, writes Jerome Slater, the "United States in the Dominican Republic engaged in the most massive intervention in the affairs of a Latin American state since the inauguration of the Good Neighbor Policy."[16] Employing a wide variety of instruments, American officials sought to help the Dominican Republic move through the difficult transition from tyranny through disorder to constitutional democracy.

In the very first days after Trujillo's death, a U.S. Navy Task Force composed of nearly forty ships patrolled the Dominican coast, ready, if necessary, to implement a presidentially approved contingency plan providing for armed intervention in Santo Domingo.[17] The order to land never came, but U.S. forces remained near the Dominican Republic for several months more. In November 1961—during a crisis caused by the sudden return to Santo Domingo of two of Trujillo's brothers, apparently bent on regaining control of the Dominican Republic—the proximity of the U.S. fleet enabled the U.S. government to play a dramatic, probably decisive, role in Dominican politics. Secretary of State Dean Rusk's warning on November 18 that the U.S. would not "remain idle" if the Trujillos tried to "reassert dictatorial domination" and his statement that the U.S. was "considering the further measures that unpredictable events might warrant" gained credibility when U.S. warships appeared within hours in clear view of Santo Domingo. By the next day, U.S. military attachés were encouraging key Dominican Air Force officers to oppose the Trujillos, and U.S. Navy jets were seen flying over Santo Domingo. On the following day, both the *New York Times* and the *Wall Street Journal* reported that the U.S. government was prepared to land the Marines, if necessary.[18] That night the Trujillo brothers and a planeload of relatives and close associates left the Dominican Republic, and Dominican crowds chanted pro-American slogans.[19]

Once the almost universally despised Trujillo family was gone, the U.S. government turned to means short of the threat of military intervention to influence Dominican politics. First, American officials (particularly Deputy Assistant Secretary of State Arturo Morales Carrión) encouraged, and even actively participated in, detailed negotiations among Dominican political factions seeking to establish an interim Council of State. American pressures—including private bargaining, public statements, the conditional offer of aid, and even the movement to new positions of U.S. naval units—affected the negotiations at several key stages. Successful conclusion of the talks late in December elicited a personal statement from President Kennedy announcing that the U.S. government would soon renew diplomatic relations with the Dominican Republic and increase sugar purchases from Dominican producers, and would dispatch a high-level economic assistance mission upon the formal installation of the Council.[20]

Next, when an attempted coup led by Air Force General Pedro R. Rodríguez Echavarría threatened to unseat the new Council in mid-January, a strong American response helped reverse the coup. Official spokesmen in Washington quickly let it be known that the U.S. government might suspend diplomatic relations anew, rescind the sugar quota increase, and withhold economic assistance unless the Council of State were reinstalled. In Santo Domingo, American representatives made it clear to Dominican civilian and military leaders—including General Rodríguez Echavarría himself—that the United States would welcome a countercoup to restore the Council to power. Within two days General Rodríguez Echavarría was arrested by fellow military officers and exiled to the United States, and the Council of State resumed office.[21]

From the definitive installation of the Council of State until the inauguration of an elected government fourteen months later, the U.S. government forcefully sustained the Council against opposition (and despite the repeated threat of its disintegration) and helped the Council perform its primary task: to hold national elections. An emergency AID loan of $25 million rescued the Council from a severe reserves' shortage at the start, and increased American sugar purchases and additional economic assistance kept the Dominican government solvent thereafter. The pesos generated by the $25 million loan and other U.S. aid were used to implement projects designed to cut unemployment and otherwise gain quick public support for the Council's efforts. American officials repeatedly showed their backing of the Council, or even of specific policies, by public statements and speeches, journalistic leaks and inspired articles, photographs of the U.S. ambassador with some or all members of the Council, and even by ostentatious port calls and receptions for Council leaders aboard U.S. warships. U.S. police officers trained Dominican forces in "public safety" methods, thus enabling the Dominicans to quell a series of riots and demonstrations. An American military assistance advisory group (MAAG) taught counterinsurgency techniques to Dominican Army units. American advisers helped determine the Dominican government's policies on numerous matters, including the disposition and management of the former Trujillo enterprises, programs for agrarian and tax reforms and housing development, and ambitious plans for improvements in education.[22]

Finally, the U.S. government undertook, both directly and through the OAS, to arrange and facilitate the 1962 election. An OAS mission helped draw up new election laws and procedures while American advisers prepared an intensive press, radio, and television campaign to teach Dominicans the new procedures and to encourage them to vote. Then an OAS team observed the elections throughout the country, thus inhibiting any possible fraud or other disruptive procedures.[23] Behind the scenes, meanwhile, U.S. embassy officials drafted and secured formal agreement in advance by the two leading candidates to a declaration that each would respect the outcome of the election and that the loser would recognize and congratulate the winner.[24] Ambassador John Bartlow Martin's efforts to facilitate the election sometimes exceeded what the State Department could endorse. When Martin called in newspapermen on the eve of the election to state for direct attribution that "the United States Government would support whoever won," the department rebuked the ambassador, cautioning him "to say 'assist' rather than 'support' next time."[25] Indeed the embassy's activities to assure that the elections would be held without incident or delay, to prevent either major candidate from withdrawing, and to guarantee that the results would be accepted went so far that at one point the President of the Council of State complained to Ambassador Martin: "You make me feel that I am no longer President."[26]

The election of Juan Bosch in December 1962 and his accession on February 27, 1963, brought into office a Dominican regime with its own mandate, eager to assert its sovereignty.[27] American participation in Dominican politics during the seven months that Bosch presided, accordingly, was more circumspect than it had been during the Council of State's tenure.[28] It is not true, however, that the "active role of the United States temporarily ended."[29] From Bosch's triumphant preinaugural visit to the White House until his exile to Puerto Rico less than ten months later, the U.S. government continued its direct entanglement in Dominican affairs. Ambassador Martin functioned during these months, as one fellow U.S. diplomat put it, "much as would the authoritative coach of a rather backward football team."[30] Martin extended to President Bosch insistent advice on matters as sensitive as the designation of Cabinet officers and military commanders, the advisability and even the constitutionality of specific legislative proposals, and general political strategy; once he actually offered Bosch his considerable talents as an experienced speechwriter.[31]

U.S. economic and military assistance to the Dominican Republic continued at high levels during the Bosch period, and the high-priority Peace Corps program was reinforced.[32] Special efforts were intensified to help the Dominican government establish an effective countersubversion agency.[33] New programs were instituted, designed in part to camouflage the extent of American participation in Dominican affairs. U.S. government-sponsored experts—operating through an ostensibly private entity called the Centro Interamericano de Estudios Sociales (CIDES)—undertook to perform key functions of the Dominican government, including preparing budget estimates, compiling statistics, conducting surveys, formulating plans, and drafting legislation.[34] Other specialists, also apparently linked to the U.S. government, worked to organize Dominican labor and peasants and to train cadres of political activists.[35]

The most extraordinary American involvement in Dominican politics during these months arose from Ambassador Martin's continuous attempt, right up until the last night of Bosch's tenure, to shore him up against domestic opposition. Although Martin's vivid memoir, *Overtaken by Events,* clearly reveals that the U.S. government's willingness to commit itself to Bosch's regime was limited, Martin also documents the intense efforts he and his staff made to help Bosch. Martin issued statements in Santo Domingo and encouraged articles and speeches in Washington by influential U.S. leaders backing Bosch. He sponsored dinner parties and other social functions to build ties between Bosch and Dominican business leaders, announced actual and proposed economic assistance to bolster Bosch's prestige, pressed for mediation efforts to conciliate Bosch and opposition leaders, and repeatedly engaged in feverish efforts to head off a coup.[36] When the coup finally came, only Bosch's refusal, in fact, prevented Martin from accompanying Bosch to confront the military leaders who overthrew the Dominican president.[37] The U.S.-sponsored "showcase of democracy" in the Dominican Republic was quickly smashed, but not for lack of American involvement.[38]

The U.S. government's response to Bosch's overthrow further reveals the extent of American entanglement in Dominican affairs well before the 1965 crisis. Beginning on the very morning of the coup—when Ambassador Martin invited José Rafael Molina Ureña (the Speaker of the Dominican House and constitutional successor) to breakfast in the embassy and suggested to the Minister of the Armed Forces that Molina be recognized as president—American officials encouraged initial efforts to bring to power a constitutional successor to Bosch.[39] To implement this policy, the U.S. government quickly recalled to Washington Ambassador Martin and the heads of the AID and MAAG missions and soon made it known that it was withholding recognition of the newly installed Triumvirate.[40] A week later Secretary Rusk announced not only the immediate suspension of all economic and military assistance to the Dominican Republic but also the U.S. government's plans to reassign all the personnel involved. The United States seemed publicly committed to the principle of "constitutionality." U.S. embassy officials in Santo Domingo consulted with a number of Dominican figures in an attempt to find an acceptable political solution, and at least some of those Dominicans working actively to restore "constitutionality" thought that the embassy was supporting their cause. The climax of American involvement in the postcoup imbroglio came on October 14 when the U.S. chargé d'affaires and the chief U.S. political officer went so far, under instructions, in pressuring the Triumvirate to consider a "return to constitutionality" that the Dominican regime officially complained to the OAS about American intervention and also asked that the political officer leave the country.[41]

Perceiving that its leverage and influence were severely limited, the U.S. government felt itself reduced over the next few weeks to suggesting a variety of different political and constitutional schemes, none of them acceptable to the Triumvirate. U.S. support for an immediate return to "constitutionality" was attenuated and then abandoned. When the U.S. government finally extended diplomatic recognition to the Triumvirate on December 14, 1963, the only concession secured by the United States was the Dominican regime's agreement to hold national elections in 1965.[42]

Following the reestablishment of normal diplomatic relations with the Dominican Republic, the U.S. government appointed a new ambassador, W. Tapley Bennett, Jr., an experienced foreign service officer who had served in the Dominican Republic early in his career.[43] Bennett was neither inclined by temperament nor instructed by Washington to play the active role which Ambassador Martin had fulfilled in Santo Domingo. Like most career officers, Bennett welcomed the switch in Washington's orientation (reinforced by the change in administration but already evident in the later Kennedy period) back to an avoidance of what had come to be regarded as counterproductive ideological posturing and undue involvement in Latin American politics.

Nevertheless, the U.S. embassy continued to be a major focal point of Dominican politics. Despite Bennett's wish not to be drawn into internal Dominican struggles, the new ambassador and his staff soon found themselves helping to resolve almost weekly crises on very diverse matters: economic and fiscal policies, sugar marketing, labor difficulties, trouble with Haiti, political jockeying among individuals and groups, and frequent rivalries among Dominican military cliques. Characteristically, one group after another sought support of one kind or another from the embassy.

Nor were the U.S. government's activities confined to the embassy's political and diplomatic efforts. Economic and military assistance programs were resumed early in 1964, and a new AID mission began to assemble by March. By early 1965, a U.S. Army Special Forces team was again training Dominican counterinsurgency units, sizable new aid commitments were being announced, U.S.-financed political development specialists were establishing a school to train *campesino* leaders, the CIA was sponsoring secret polls of Dominican's political preferences, and U.S. agents were even preparing to give covert political advice and organizational assistance in case the U.S. government were to choose to back a candidate in the scheduled national elections.[44] Once more, the United States government was very much involved in the affairs of the Dominican Republic.

III

Although deep and pervasive, the U.S. government's involvement in the Dominican Republic, and in the Caribbean area generally, has rarely, if ever, been positive and wholehearted. The tension in Dominican history between the desire for protection, even for annexation, and the demand for full sovereignty has been mirrored in the United States by the conflicting pull between the urge to control foreign events and the ideal of national self-determination. Strong currents of opinion favoring respect for Dominican sovereignty have influenced U.S. policy time and again.

In the nineteenth century, the U.S. government several times resisted proposals put forth by Dominican politicians that the United States should annex the Dominican Republic. When President Grant finally sought to win the Senate's approval of annexation, vigorous opposition led by Senator Charles Sumner defeated the plan. More recently, the U.S. military interventions of 1916 and 1965 offended many American opinion leaders almost as much as they inflamed Dominican passions; both interventions were affected by domestic American opposition.[45] All through the history of American relations with the Caribbean runs a thread of unwanted engagement. The U.S. government has been much more concerned about how to withdraw and decrease its involvement in the Caribbean than with how to intervene there. Periods of especially intense American participation in the Caribbean (and in the Dominican Republic specifically) have characteristically been followed by years in which American officials attempt to refrain from overt involvement.

If the United States has not sought to annex the Dominican Republic, has rejected several obvious opportunities to do so, and has tried periodically to reduce its involvement in Dominican and Caribbean affairs, why then has it continuously become so engaged in Dominican politics? What explains the U.S. government's persistent entanglement in the Dominican Republic over the years?[46]

Many discussions of American involvement in the Caribbean stress the supposed importance of positive U.S. interests, primarily economic.[47] The whole record of American involvement in the area, however, suggests that the main interest of the U.S. government has not been economic. Security concerns and traditional axioms, not simple conquest or profit, have motivated American involvement in the Dominican Republic and the rest of the Caribbean for many decades.

Private economic interests—mainly of dubious adventurers at first, later of banks and investment houses, and in this century mainly of sugar and fruit producers—have been important in drawing the U.S. government's attention to the Dominican Republic. Undoubtedly they have influenced American policy on occasion, especially through personal relations with U.S. diplomatic representatives in Santo Domingo.[48] But by and large, the pressure of existing business interests on American policy toward the Dominican Republic does not appear to have been substantial or effective, particularly in recent years, beyond the highly specific business-related issues on which it has concentrated.[49]

Nor does it seem that prospective trade and investment opportunities have importantly affected American involvement in the Dominican Republic, for the country's size and resources have not been sufficient to attract significant U.S. commercial interests. Far from being embroiled in Dominican affairs to protect existing or proposed U.S. private interests there, the U.S. government has actually attempted to spur American investment in the Dominican Republic in support of government policy. The initiative for much recent U.S. investment, like that of the "dollar diplomacy" of another era, has come from Washington, not from the business community.[50]

Elsewhere in the Caribbean, where the United States has established and maintained important military facilities, these have undoubtedly been a cause of continuing American interest. The military advantages the Dominican Republic could offer the United States have never been of major significance, however. The United States has never established a permanent military base in the Dominican Republic. The missile tracking station set up there in 1951 was never of vital importance and was abandoned by 1962. A century ago American authorities were interested in the possibilities of using Samaná and Manzanillo bays for coaling stations or naval bases, and some interest in Samaná continued into this century, but the main reason for continuing American concern about Samaná seems to have been to assure that the bay would not be used by Germany or any other European power. Moreover, MacMichael argues, "After 1877 it was not so much American desire to secure a naval base at Samaná as it was a Dominican conviction that the U.S. still desired the bay and would pay well to obtain it that kept the naval base project alive."[51]

Positive economic and military interests, then, do not account for the history of intense American involvement in Dominican affairs. The chief goal of U.S. policy, rather, has been pre-emptive. The means used by the U.S. government have varied, but the fundamental U.S. aim in the Dominican Republic and the entire Caribbean has always been the same: to assure that no situation actually or even potentially damaging to U.S. security has a chance to develop. The main concern has been to prevent the introduction into the Caribbean of any new foreign influence which might oppose the United States. Proclaimed as policy by President James Monroe in 1823, the U.S. aim to keep new foreign influence out of the Caribbean has ever since been considered "doctrine" with the force of axiom, if not of international law.[52]

Ever since the Dominican Republic achieved formal independence in 1844, the U.S. government has tried to prevent any external power from gaining influence there. President James Polk in 1846, for example, expressed his fear that a European power might exert control over Santo Domingo, and for the next several decades one of the chief concerns of "successive Secretaries of State was that some foreign nation might secure Samaná Bay as a naval base."[53] Later in the century, increased U.S. participation in Dominican affairs was "motivated at least in part by the fear of foreign intervention, especially German, in the Caribbean area."[54] Measures taken to assure the payment of bondholders were intended less to satisfy private American claims than to preclude European intervention to obtain repayment; the U.S. sought to stem the Dominican Republic's economic deterioration and "to prevent this weakness from becoming a threat to American security" by opening the way for the introduction of European influence.[55] "Far from being an attempt to enslave the Dominican economy," another scholar argues, the 1907 Customs Convention was "designed to set it free from foreign shackles," that is, to minimize European influence.[56]

At the turn of the century, after the local superiority of the U.S. force over any European power had been established by the Spanish-American War, U.S. concern in the Caribbean came to focus on the possibility that political turbulence among or within the countries of the region might somehow permit the quick introduction there of extracontinental power. To prevent this eventuality, the U.S. government undertook both to promote mechanisms for settling intraregional disputes and to foster political stability within the countries of the region.[57] The means chosen by the United States to promote internal stability, as well as the intensity of American interest in this aim, have varied as the actual possibilities of extracontinental exploitation of local turbulence have ebbed and flowed, and as the presumed causes of instability have been analyzed and re-examined. But the basic aim—to assure local political stability in order to exclude possible opportunities for the introduction of extracontinental power—has been the keystone of U.S. policy in the Dominican Republic and the rest of the Caribbean throughout this century.[58]

It was partly the search for stability, together with the claims of U.S. bondholders and the fear that Europeans would make efforts to secure payment of their loans, which led the U.S. government to take over the Dominican customhouse early in this century. Because customs revenue appeared to American officials to be the main booty of Dominican politics, they hoped —by controlling the customs apparatus—not only to forestall European actions but also to remove what they regarded as the prime cause of continued Dominican strife.[59]

When it became clear (after Dominican President Ramón Cáceres was assassinated in 1911) that an American customs receivership alone would not provide political stability, other means were sought. President Woodrow Wilson, imbued with a moralistic concern for teaching Latin Americans how to govern themselves, favored U.S. supervision of Dominican national elections, full U.S. support for the elected president, and an announced U.S. policy not to tolerate further insurrections in the Dominican Republic. When this approach also proved inadequate, the United States demanded control of major Dominican government expenditures to assure that they would be spent on public works, sanitation improvements, schools, and other programs American officials thought were likely to promote stability. American officials tried, moreover, to establish the right to organize the Dominican Armed Forces, hoping thereby to remove another presumed source of instability by replacing competing local armies with a central national constabulary. And when Dominican authorities rejected these American demands, the U.S. government threatened to withhold diplomatic recognition, and therefore customs payments, to compel acceptance. Dominican officials continued to resist, and political strife went on unabated. The United States became more preoccupied with the war in Europe, and concern intensified over the possibility that the Caribbean might become part of the conflict. When the persistent struggle within the Dominican Republic seemed likely to produce the accession of Desiderio Arias, a caudillo reported by concerned American officials to have pro-German sympathies, U.S. military intervention was ordered in 1916.[60]

The ensuing eight-year U.S. military occupation of the Dominican Republic saw repeated demonstrations of American concern for political stability. Often the approach adopted was touchingly naive, as when the Dominican War and Marine departments were merged with that of Interior and Police so that "in the absence of a Department for the conduct of hostilities, the thoughts of Dominicans might be diverted from warlike measures to peaceful pursuits."[61] Sometimes the American approach was tragically simplistic: the attempt to disarm the Dominican population and to establish a nonpartisan constabulary responsible to the national civil government actually facilitated the rise to power of the brutal Rafael Trujillo.[62] But the chief aim of U.S. policy—evidenced also by measures to improve the Dominican Republic's roads, communications, schools, and agricultural techniques, and to adjust the country's administrative and legal systems—was always to promote political stability (conceived of as following from economic development) and thereby to avoid the need for renewed U.S. intervention.[63]

Largely because of the difficulties experienced in attempting to disengage from the occupation of the Dominican Republic, Haiti, and Nicaragua, American officials in the late 1920's made conscious efforts to reduce the degree of American participation in Caribbean affairs. As Henry Stimson and others drew non-interventionist conclusions from the experience of an interventionist decade, a new period of reduced American involvement in the Caribbean began.[64]

The U.S. government's attitude toward the possibility of Rafael Trujillo's rise to power in Santo Domingo typified the new American approach and its results. When the U.S. minister in Santo Domingo, fearing Trujillo's likely accession, asked Washington to authorize a formal declaration that the United States would not recognize a Trujillo regime because Trujillo had previously agreed not to be a candidate, the State Department refused, arguing that "through scrupulously avoiding even the appearance of interfering in the internal affairs of the Dominican Republic our relations with Santo Domingo have been put on a very sound basis in the 6 years since the withdrawal of the military occupation."[65] Washington did not wish to involve itself in Dominican affairs to the extent necessary to prevent the accession of the admittedly distasteful General Trujillo, who soon took the presidency and began his prolonged rule.

American concern with the Dominican Republic's stability and with the overriding aim of precluding the introduction into the Caribbean of extracontinental power continued during the thirty-one years of Trujillo's regime.[66] During the late 1920's and the 1930's, when no European power was capable of threatening the United States, the U.S. instituted toward Latin America what came to be known as the Good Neighbor Policy, under which the United States renounced the practice of military intervention and announced its intent to refrain from participation in the internal politics of nations in the hemisphere.[67] Consistent with this general policy, and later with the policy of supporting Latin American allies in World War II and then the Cold War, the United States maintained normal diplomatic relations with the Dominican Republic under Trujillo for three decades and even extended some economic and military assistance throughout the period.[68] Given the continuing American aims, the U.S. stance was understandable, despite Trujillo's flagrant departures from the principles of the Atlantic Charter, the Act of Chapultepec, and the Charter of the United Nations. However illiberal, Trujillo did bring a temporary end to Dominican turmoil and to the immediate possibility that foreign power could be introduced into the Dominican Republic, and his continuing opposition to the Axis powers (and then to the Communist bloc) seemed to be assured. As President Roosevelt is said to have remarked, Trujillo may have been an S.O.B., but "at least he's our S.O.B."[69]

Only when events elsewhere made Trujillo seem more a threat to than a source of stability in the Caribbean did American support for Trujillo end. The U.S. government's belated realization that Castro's easy displacement of Batista in Cuba might augur ill for Trujillo and other Caribbean strongmen, together with mounting evidence that Trujillo's regime was becoming increasingly repressive and also that his inter-Caribbean enmities might exacerbate the region's problems, induced the U.S. government in 1959 to reexamine its policy toward the Dominican Republic. Spurred also by pressures from Venezuela and Costa Rica to oppose right-wing dictatorships as a prelude to possible actions against Castro, the United States began then to disassociate itself from Trujillo and even to press for changes within the Dominican Republic (even though these pressures led to attempts by Trujillo to court the Soviet Union).

Dropping its previously unreserved support for the nonintervention doctrine, the U.S. government began in 1960 actively to support proposals in the OAS aimed at inducing liberalization in the Dominican political structure.[70] Both in concert with OAS members and on its own, the U.S. government undertook measures designed to bring an end to the Trujillo regime and to facilitate a transition to a new government with a better prospect of providing lasting stability. To head off a Castro-type movement in the Dominican Republic—with its potential for introducing extracontinental power into the Caribbean—the U.S.

sought out and began to aid moderate anti-Communist opponents of Trujillo. Among those in the group which assassinated Trujillo in May 1961 were men whom the U.S. government had encouraged to organize.

The objectives of American policy during the period of transition after Trujillo's death were mixed. The newly installed Kennedy administration was committing itself in 1961 to encouraging economic development, social reform, and political democracy throughout the hemisphere. President Kennedy, in presenting the Alliance for Progress proposal in March, specifically mentioned his hope that the Dominican Republic—then still under Trujillo—could soon be included.[71] Some in the administration—particularly the Puerto Rican group to whom Kennedy had turned for help in formulating and implementing his Alliance program—hoped to transform the Dominican Republic into a special "showcase of democracy," a demonstration of the efficacy of development under democratic auspices.[72]

But the primary emphasis of U.S. policy toward the Dominican Republic, even in the early days of the Kennedy administration, was the traditional aim of preventing any security threat from arising there, now cast with new urgency in terms of the need to prevent a "second Cuba." Part of the reason for regarding the Dominican Republic as a potential "second Cuba," no doubt, was Castro's announced interest in extending his revolution to Hispaniola, evidenced concretely by his support for the June 1959 invasion of the Dominican Republic by anti-Trujillo Dominicans. More important was the simple fact of perceived analogy, however faulty. The Dominican Republic, like Cuba, was a sugar-producing island nation in the Caribbean ruled for many years by a corrupt praetorian dictator. Differences between the two islands—which were at very different levels of economic and political development and had very different histories—were obscured as American officials focused their attention on the supposed similarities. Unprepared to analyze Santo Domingo in terms of its own past, American observers attempted to interpret the complicated swirl of Dominican events by referring to the experience of neighboring Cuba, with which they were more familiar and which was salient in their minds. The fact that Foreign Service officers who had failed to predict Castro's turn to the Soviet bloc had found their careers blighted undoubtedly made U.S. government personnel especially sensitive to the possibility that Santo Domingo would go the way of Cuba.

IV

Whatever the reasons, it is clear that by 1961 American officials regarded the Dominican Republic as a potential "second Cuba." Just days after the Bay of Pigs, President Kennedy personally approved a contingency plan for landing troops in the Dominican Republic which stressed as the principal policy guideline that the United States could not afford and would not permit the imposition in the Dominican Republic of a pro-Castro or pro-Communist government. This theme was repeated time and again in presidential instructions to U.S. officials concerned with the Dominican Republic. President Kennedy reportedly felt that his first year in office would be successful if neither the Dominican Republic nor the Congo were lost to international Communism.[73] He is said to have believed that there were three possibilities in the Dominican Republic "in descending order of preference: a decent democratic regime, a continuation of the Trujillo regime, or a Castro regime." "We ought to aim at the first," Kennedy reportedly concluded, "but we can't really renounce the second until we are sure we can avoid the third."[74]

The aim of preventing a "second Cuba" shaped American policy toward the Dominican Republic at every stage after Trujillo's death in May 1961. The dispatch of a Navy Task Force to the vicinity of Santo Domingo in June, immediately after Trujillo's assassination, was meant specifically to preclude any possible pro-Communist movement and to prevent possible Cuban involvement. President Kennedy's instructions to Consul General John Calvin Hill in July emphasized his keen interest in the progress of anti-Communist laws and other measures designed to exclude Communists and Castroist exiles from the Dominican Republic and to oust Dominican Communists already there. The ambiguous stance the U.S. government adopted later that year with respect to the Balaguer regime reflected conflict between the desire to prevent immediate Communist subversion by strengthening Balaguer's hold and the belief that Communist prospects over a longer period might better be countered by providing the Dominican people an early opportunity to choose a new government through national elections.[75] The eventual decisions to press for the removal, first of the Trujillo family and then of General Rodríguez Echavarría and of Balaguer himself, stemmed from the U.S. view—forcefully presented to the embassy by the Unión Cívica grouping of prominent Dominican figures—that these steps would best foster stability and thus make it easier to exclude Communist influence. And throughout this period, and the years that followed, conscious American efforts were made to strengthen the Dominican Armed Forces as a bulwark against possible Communist encroachments.

U.S. activities during the Council of State's tenure in 1962–63 —including massive economic aid used for tactical expenditures, assistance to strengthen the National Police, to establish a "public safety corps" for riot control and to train a counterinsurgency unit in the National Army, programs to strengthen the democratic labor movement, and the general emphasis on holding free elections—were primarily aimed at curbing the presumed Communist threat. Each time the Council of State suffered a reverse, Ambassador Martin reflected on the danger that "Castro-Communists" would gain strength.[76]

This focus on precluding a possible "Communist takeover" continued after Juan Bosch took office on February 27, 1963. During the very week Bosch was inaugurated, Ambassador Martin found himself preoccupied by the reported presence in the Dominican Republic of eight Communist agents. The ambassador's first duty after Bosch became president was to ask him to accept U.S. assistance to strengthen the Dominican government's security apparatus. From then on, Martin continuously stressed to Bosch the need to protect the Dominican Republic from "Castro-Communist" subversion both genuinely to prevent possible Communist gains and to preclude predictable

Dominican and American criticism of Bosch for weakness on this score. Among the specific measures Martin recommended to Bosch were that he close a supposedly Communist school, ban travel to Cuba, propose a law permitting deportations, and even "enact something like our Smith Act."[77]

In internal communications with his staff in Santo Domingo and with his superiors in Washington, Martin stressed the need to guard against Communist subversion.[78] Recording his own retrospective regret that his embassy had spent so much time and effort reporting Communist activities, Martin explained: "But we had to, a Castro-Communist takeover was the one thing the United States government, and the American people, would not tolerate."[79]

Some prominent U.S. officials, including Alliance for Progress Coordinator Teodoro Moscoso, had begun dealing with the newly elected Bosch early in 1963, full of hope that they could help this recognized member of Latin America's social democratic circle. Their expectations were disappointed, however, for the Dominican Republic's problems were much more intractable than they had realized at first. Bosch himself, who alienated one Dominican group after another by his statements and actions, turned out to be a much less skillful politician than they had presumed, although it is fair to observe that any leader would have had great difficulty coping with Trujillo's political, economic, and social legacy. By the summer of 1963, some officials in Washington were ready to write Bosch off as a failure, although Ambassador Martin, Alliance Coordinator Moscoso, and a few others sought frantically to sustain him. Moscoso went so far as to leak word that the United States was considering massive assistance for a comprehensive river valley development scheme in the Dominican Republic and even to plan a personal trip to Santo Domingo in this connection, but Bosch fell before the announced visit could be held.

Since the fundamental American objective in the Dominican Republic was never primarily tied to Bosch's democratic experiment but rather to preventing a "second Cuba," the U.S. government's reaction to Bosch's overthrow was not surprising. When

Ambassador Martin asked the State Department late in September whether Washington would send an aircraft carrier to the Dominican Republic to show U.S. support for the badly faltering Bosch regime, the department refused unless a Communist takeover was threatened. Bosch's fall was assured.[80]

The overriding American concern for anti-Communist stability in the Dominican Republic continued after the 1963 coup. Despite President Kennedy's strong statement condemning the coup, the withholding of recognition, and the suspension of all American aid, it soon became obvious that the U.S. government's support for the principle of "constitutionality" was somewhat ambiguous.[81] American officials were much more interested in keeping Communists out of office than with helping Bosch or a constitutional successor get in. Immediately after the coup, rumors and reports circulated that, despite Ambassador Martin's efforts, the U.S. government had not been united in supporting Bosch against opposition; it was even said that the embassy's military attachés had helped encourage the coup, or at least had not discouraged it actively.[82] Within a few days Martin himself confirmed to President Kennedy that the United States did not want Bosch back "because he isn't a President."[83] Martin's own exasperation after months of dealing with the mercurial Dominican leader seems to have been very influential —together with the disenchantment of leading Latin American social democratic leaders with Bosch—in establishing a consensus view within the U.S. government that Bosch's own return should not be encouraged, a view that was to have an important effect on the 1965 crisis.

Washington's subsequent interest in a "constitutionalist" solution—that is, the continuation of Bosch's regime under someone other than Bosch himself—ebbed and flowed for a few weeks, affected most of all by varying assessments of the Triumvirate's durability and of opposition to it. Pressure for a return to "constitutionality" was eased, and then dropped altogether, when it seemed likely to produce turbulence, and President Kennedy reportedly decided early in November to extend recognition to the Triumvirate when suitable agreements were reached on when national elections would be held. At last, in December, rumors of flickering attempts to promote a countercoup—together with the Triumvirate's own indication that continued nonrecognition might undermine its position and strengthen the hand of leftist opponents—speeded President Johnson's decision to recognize the Dominican regime without further delay. A week after U.S. recognition had been granted, Dominican Army patrols executed sixteen guerrilla leaders, their usefulness having been outlasted.[84]

The basic thrust of U.S. policy toward the Dominican Republic from the recognition of the Triumvirate up to the outbreak of the 1965 crisis remained the same: to prevent any threat to U.S. security by promoting immediate stability and guarding against "Castro-Communist" gains. The U.S. government's approach to Dominican politics continued to focus on the presumed danger from the left. Embassy officers reporting on the activities of Bosch's PRD concentrated on the alleged relations between members of Bosch's group and those farther to the left; reports highlighted cases of extreme leftists joining the party, and tabs were kept on who was meeting with whom. Apparently fearing that the PRD, excluded from power, might become so thoroughly committed to cooperation with the extreme left (in opposition to the Triumvirate) as to lose its own freedom of action, American officials came to treat Bosch's party as if it had a permanent burden of proof that it was not seeking or even accepting "Castro-Communist" support. From the time the U.S. recognized the Triumvirate until after the U.S. intervention in 1965, "the only official U.S. personnel who talked with Juan Bosch were FBI agents who wanted him to inform them about Communists in the Dominican Republic."[85] Talks with PRD officials in Santo Domingo, as well, focused more often on the party's knowledge of Communist activities and plans than on its own program.

The U.S. government's involvement in the Dominican Republic in 1964–65 was in many ways less active than it had been during the period of very intense American participation from 1961 to 1963. Just as the occupation period in the Dominican

Republic and elsewhere in the Caribbean in the early 1920's brought about a period of American restraint in the area, so the extraordinary activity of Martin's tenure in the Dominican Republic (and of the dynamic activism of the early Kennedy administration) was followed by an attempt to reduce the scope and depth of American involvement in Dominican affairs. Ambassador Bennett's personal attempt to limit his participation in Dominican politics, the reduced level of AID expenditures in the Dominican Republic, and Washington's support for the economic austerity program (see Chapter 2) were all aspects of a conscious attempt by American officials to deal with the Dominican Republic less intensely. The U.S. government was now trying to treat the Dominican Republic as one of many nations with economic and political problems, which would not become a matter for priority attention in Washington unless American security appeared directly to be threatened.

American policy toward the Dominican Republic in 1965, as almost always before, was keyed not to opportunity but to threat. The Dominican Republic was approached no longer as a possible "showcase for democracy," but still as a target of "Castro-Communist" subversion. American concern was focused on preventing a "Communist takeover," on precluding a "second Cuba," and events were seen through this lens. Juan Bosch and the PRD were viewed not as possible partners in the Alliance for Progress but as ineffectual reformers and politicians and, even worse, as likely dupes of Communist organizers. Dominican Communists, in turn, were seen not mainly as weak and fragmented groups of dissidents, but as potential agents of extracontinental power. The Dominican Armed Forces were conceived not primarily as rival bands of plunder, but as an institution opposed to instability and to Communist advance. As for the overall role of the United States, positive commitments to assist desired Dominican changes were publicized, but the emphasis of American officials was on avoiding renewed entanglement in Dominican politics and on keeping the Dominican Republic "off the front burner." Largely because of these attitudes and assumptions, events in Santo Domingo in 1965 which might otherwise have passed unnoticed—by the U.S. government, at least—had they occurred in some other area or era were to become instead the background to intervention.

2. The Origins of the 1965 Dominican Crisis: Setting the Stage

Political instability has characterized the Dominican Republic since the assassination of Rafael Trujillo in 1961. Political parties, labor unions, student groups, and military factions have formed, split, realigned, and split again. Constant turnover has occurred at top levels of every government department, even in the supposedly autonomous agencies established to insulate development administration from political turmoil. Shifting groups of "outs" have arrayed against equally temporary alignments of "ins" in a continuous political kaleidoscope. There has been almost no institutional continuity, very little consistency by political leaders with regard to program or ideology, and not even much loyalty to personal caudillos.

Perhaps the key characteristic of Dominican politics in the years after Trujillo's death has been the predominance of direct confrontations among groups in conflict. Contending forces in the Dominican Republic have increasingly employed undisguised and unrefined displays of power, directed more often at replacing the government than at forcing it to take specific actions. Students and university politicians have demonstrated, rioted, marched on the National Palace, and clashed with police and army units. Labor unions have demonstrated, carried on strikes—including several national general strikes—disrupted traffic, and even engaged in sabotage. Businessmen have staged general strikes of their own and have organized paramilitary groups for self-defense and for terrorism. Even the Church has often exerted its political power, directly through pastoral letters and other public appeals and indirectly through the personal influence of individual priests.

Since Trujillo's death, competing Dominican factions have also engaged almost incessantly in conspiracy and subversion, encouraging their military counterparts to coup and counter-coup. Various military cliques have suppressed opposition, prevented governments from executing specific policies, overthrown regimes and established others. Even before the 1965 crisis, internal struggles within the Dominican Armed Forces led to strafings and less violent demonstrations of strength—troop movements, tank deployments, and airplane maneuvers—by one side against another.

Events that were to be crucial (and surprising) in April 1965—the swift collapse of the Dominican government under Donald Reid Cabral, the initial uncertainty as to who actually had ousted Reid, the quick division and subsequent rapid disintegration of the Dominican Armed Forces, the sudden escalation of the conflict from a colonel's coup to a civil war—all are easier to comprehend when viewed in this context of political chaos. Examination of the Dominican political background of the 1965 crisis also permits retrospective analysis of matters which were misinterpreted by American officials in April 1965: the degree of cohesiveness of the Dominican Armed Forces, the locus of power within the pro-Bosch groups, and especially the role and strength of Dominican Communists and their relation to the pro-Bosch movement. By identifying the key actors in the Dominican drama and understanding what they were doing when the 1965 crisis erupted, it may be possible to discern not only what American officials thought was occurring during the first days of the crisis, but also what actually was happening. The gap between Dominican realities and American perceptions, owing largely to established American attitudes and assumptions, was a major cause of the 1965 intervention.

I have tried elsewhere to analyze the general causes of the instability which characterized Dominican politics after Trujillo's death and established the preconditions for the 1965 crisis.[1] This chapter, therefore, deals only with the specific origins of the April 1965 uprising in the Dominican Republic.

I

The immediate causes of the 1965 Dominican political crisis may be traced directly to the events of 1963, particularly to the overthrow of President Juan Bosch on September 25 of that year.[2] The loose coalition of forces which joined the attempt in April 1965 to restore "constitutional government" under Bosch was already forming in 1963, even before and especially after the September coup. And the deep divisions and intense distrust which made Dominican politics in 1965 so volatile, which made violence so easy to spark and agreement so difficult to reach, were largely precipitated by Bosch's overthrow.

Some of the elements of what was to become the "constitutionalist movement" of 1965 began to come together before the 1963 coup. During the summer of 1963, at a time when rumors of an imminent coup were circulating, a number of influential Dominican professionals, mainly lawyers, publicly avowed their opposition to any overthrow. Many of these figures had supported the major opposition party, the Unión Cívica Nacional (UCN), in the 1962 elections, and very few were affiliated politically with Bosch. Now, however, they declared their support for the principle of "constitutionality" and their consequent rejection of any coup. Other groups, too, lined up in advance against any effort to oust President Bosch. Leaders of Bosch's own party, the Partido Revolucionario Dominicano (PRD), announced they would defend the government, if necessary by means of a general strike, against any would-be successor. Spokesmen for the Partido Revolucionario Social Cristiano (PRSC) also expressed their party's support for the Bosch regime against any possible overthrow, and leaders of the militant leftist Catorce de Junio movement (1J4)—despite earlier grave differences with Bosch and the PRD—now vigorously advocated sustaining the constitutional government. Within the Armed

Forces, too, some officers reportedly moved to support Bosch against opposition; the head of the Military Academy, Colonel Rafael Tomás Fernández Domínguez, is said to have organized a group to oppose by force any attempted coup.[3]

When the confrontation finally occurred late in September, however, the various groups pledged to defend the Bosch government proved to be ineffectual against an opposing coalition comprised of powerful segments of the Dominican Army and Air Force (spearheaded by Colonel Elías Wessin y Wessin), leading elements of the Santo Domingo business and commercial community, and a host of unemployed politicians. Never purposefully led by Bosch, who did not act effectively to preserve his own power, those committed to "constitutionality" hardly reacted when the coup took place.[4] No general strike was called, Colonel Fernández's supposed force was not employed, the lawyers and other professionals confined themselves mainly to signing manifestos, and the PRD leadership—disorganized and rent by division—stood by helplessly. Only high school and university students, many of them members of the Catorce de Junio movement, immediately displayed their intense opposition to the coup, and their demonstrations were quickly curtailed.

Yet efforts to reverse the coup began almost immediately. Within days of Bosch's arrival in San Juan to begin his exile, two top PRD leaders—House Speaker José Rafael Molina Ureña and José Francisco Peña Gómez, the party's leading radio propagandist—flew to Puerto Rico to consult with the ousted president and to discuss a possible countercoup.[5] Bosch's former Minister of Industry and Commerce, Diego Bordas, joined other PRD figures in New York in forming a "Committee for the Restoration of Constitutional Government in the Dominican Republic."[6] Within the Dominican Republic, PRSC leaders denounced the coup and began talks with PRD representatives, high military officers, and U.S. embassy officials about measures to restore "constitutional government. Disgruntled ex-military officers and even a group of rebellious enlisted men also groped for ways to oppose the new regime, as did several officers and a number of civilian politicians tied to another exiled former president,

Joaquín Balaguer.[7] All of these—together with some leftist activists, especially university students and labor leaders—were joined in their pleas for a return to "constitutionality" by assorted adventurers and hangers-on.

The initial acts of this loose collection of individuals and groups opposed to the 1963 coup took several forms, none of them particularly effective at the time: public statements and manifestos against the coup, marches and demonstrations, clandestine negotiations, attempts to start various strikes, the election by a secret congressional session of Senate President Juan Casasnovas Garrido as the constitutional successor to Bosch, and even several abortive plots aimed at ousting the post-coup regime by force. But though none of these tactics succeeded in 1963, these first steps did provide important antecedents for the "constitutionalist movement" of 1965. The participation of several military officers, particularly Colonel Fernández Domínguez, and of some enlisted men in these futile efforts to reverse the coup indicates that Bosch had already cultivated some support within the Armed Forces, a fact of great importance in 1965.[8] The role of some of Balaguer's key supporters in the attempt to establish Casasnovas Garrido as president and then in the attempted countercoup staged at the Santiago Air Base was also significant, for cooperation among supporters of Bosch and Balaguer was to be central to the background and evolution of the 1965 crisis. Another continuing strand was the participation in these early efforts to reverse the coup of disgruntled military officers and former officers, including ex-General Santiago Rodríguez Echavarría and others, who joined the inchoate movement more because of personal rancor or ambition than from political commitment. Finally, a very important aspect of the 1965 movement evident already at this early point was that political figures of various leanings could agree on the goal of reestablishing "constitutionality," a vague formula which allowed all elements opposed to the makers of the September coup to cooperate. PRD members committed to Bosch personally, other PRD figures willing and some even eager to accept a return to power without Bosch, PRSC leaders hoping to join in a coalition regime of some sort, 1J4 activists wishing to regain the legal guarantees of which the new regime had deprived them, backers of Balaguer seeking early elections in which their exiled leader could participate, as well as those few committed by ideological principle to "constitutionality": all could join in opposing the illegal, "unconstitutional" regime which had overthrown Bosch.

The groping, uncoordinated efforts in 1963 to reverse the coup and to restore "constitutionality," although apparently encouraged and even assisted for a time by the United States government, never got very far.[9] Divisions between pro-Bosch and anti-Bosch groups within the PRD, between the PRD and the PRSC, and between these groups and those associated with Balaguer caused problems from the outset; but the decisive difficulty was the lack at this stage of any really substantial support for a countercoup within the Armed Forces. By the time the U.S. government formally recognized the postcoup regime in December, Dominican opposition to the new government was clearly faltering. Some of those who earlier had opposed the coup were by now making their peace with the regime. Others remained in opposition, open or clandestine, awaiting a better opportunity to launch a countermovement.

II

The military officers who had imprisoned President Bosch in the National Palace on September 25 hastily transferred power to a civilian Triumvirate, which in turn established a coalition Cabinet including representatives of all six parties which had actively supported the coup.[10] The pro-coup alliance, however, was even less solid than the loose coalition opposed to the coup, for its components were bound together only by dislike for Bosch and by a desire for power and the spoils of office. With Bosch in exile and power theirs, the coupmakers almost immediately began to differ and their movement quickly disintegrated. The continuing kaleidoscope of Dominican politics, fueled by personal ambition and virtually unchecked by program commitments or mediating institutions, moved on to a new constellation. The Triumvirate—which was eventually transformed by a series of resignations and replacements into a two-man regime dominated by Donald J. Reid Cabral—was soon struggling to retain office.[11]

The circumstances under which Reid Cabral tried to govern were exceptionally difficult. A deepening economic crisis— caused mainly by the very low prices then prevailing for the Dominican Republic's principal export crops: sugar, cacao, and coffee—arrayed most of Dominican society against the regime.[12] By December 1964, the country's commercial balance had fallen to its lowest point in forty years.[13] Farmers, day laborers, merchants, and small businessmen especially felt the pinch of the 1964–65 depression. The crisis was worsened by an unusually severe drought (which also increased unrest in the water-starved capital city) and by the effects of a prolonged U.S. dock strike, which slowed Dominican exports and customs receipts. Each distressed group looked to the National Palace for relief, but the Dominican government itself was in severe financial straits. Deeply in debt, the Reid regime had to stall on its payments to creditors, including businesses, provincial governments, autonomous public agencies, schools and hospitals, university personnel, and even day laborers.[14]

The measures Reid adopted to fight the economic crisis further undermined his political standing. Implementing an "austerity" program (supported by the International Monetary Fund) to tighten credit in order to limit imports and restore the country's payments position nearer to balance, Reid came under fire from nearly every side. Merchants complained bitterly, while passing the increased costs on to irate consumers. Labor leaders claimed that the program would further increase unemployment, already estimated at over 30 percent of the available work force.[15] Economists, members of professional associations, and other opinion leaders alleged that Reid's program was not only economically restrictive but also socially regressive, for it tended to put large businesses, which can more easily obtain credit, in a stronger competitive position. Some charged, moreover, that Reid's economic policies—particularly his acceptance of the IMF standby credit and of major loans from the U.S. government and private commercial banks—would only exacerbate the Dominican Republic's problems of economic and political dependence.[16] Reid's announcement early in April 1965 that his government would issue special bonds to pay creditors was particularly costly in political terms, for it not only failed to satisfy the creditors but also strengthened the widespread impression that Reid was saddling the government with increased debts.

Attacks on the Triumvirate, increasingly frequent and vociferous, came from all shades of the Dominican political spectrum. The extreme left, which instigated student demonstrations within a week of the September 1963 coup and attempted a guerrilla uprising in the country's northwest region from October to December of that year, kept up unrelenting opposition in 1964–65, employing propaganda, strikes, and sabotage. Prolonged leftist-inspired strikes by Santo Domingo taxi drivers and dock workers hurt the regime badly in 1964, and constant unrest among sugar workers at the U.S.-owned La Romana complex was even more costly. Leftist agitators scored a particularly telling blow in March 1965 when labor troubles at La Romana forced the Triumvirate to send in troops and even to fly over a squadron of P-51's to quell the disturbances.[17]

The Dominican left was by no means united during this period. Bitter disagreements, both personal and ideological, divided the far left into three major factions: the Castro-oriented Catorce de Junio movement (itself rent by division), the Moscow-line Partido Socialista Popular (PSP), and the more violent Movimiento Popular Dominicano (MPD). In 1963 these groups had differed on such issues as the feasibility of guerrilla warfare in the Dominican Republic, and major disagreements persisted up to (and through) the 1965 crisis. But the political context of 1964–65 did produce unanimity on the one important count: support for the reimposition of the Bosch regime. Each of the three extreme left organizations, repeatedly harassed by the Triumvirate, adopted as its chief tactical political objectives the aims of toppling the Triumvirate and restoring the "constitutional government" of 1963.

Apart from the extreme left, the sector most vigorous in its criticism of Reid by early 1965 was the set of established Santo Domingo politicians whose strident opposition to Bosch in 1963 had made them appear then to be far rightists.[18] Although many of these leaders played important parts in ousting Bosch, they apparently felt their influence in the postcoup regime to be insufficient, especially after Reid purged many members of the original coalition Cabinet and took personal control. Frustrated by their continued exclusion from power, figures like Rafael F. Bonnelly, Severo A. Cabral, Luis Amiama Tió, and Horacio J. Ornes—among the principal leaders of the anti-Bosch movement in 1963—unleashed repeated attacks on Reid Cabral in 1964–65.[19] Many of those who had actually participated in the Triumvirate's original Cabinet of 1963 were busy undermining Reid's government by 1965.

Attacks on Reid were not limited to the political extremes, however. The most important sectors opposing Reid were the two major parties: Bosch's PRD and Balaguer's Partido Reformista (PR), each led from abroad by an exiled former president hoping to regain power. The ultimate interests of these two popular leaders conflicted, for each sought personal vindication, but the circumstances of 1964–65 brought them together in opposition to Reid Cabral.

Balaguer and his followers wished to participate in national elections, officially scheduled to take place in September 1965, since they expected to win a competitive poll. Pro-Balaguer leaflets were already beginning to circulate in the spring of 1965 and campaign organizations were beginning to form. June 1 was the date legally established for the start of the scheduled election campaign, and as that date began to approach, Reformista leaders intensified their pressures for assurances that the elections would actually be held on time and that Balaguer would be permitted to return from New York to campaign. Reformista leaders, particularly party Vice-President Francisco Augusto Lora, warned repeatedly that the only alternative to free elections was violence.[20] Pressures on Reid Cabral mounted to allow Balaguer to enter the country, ostensibly to visit his reportedly ill mother but obviously to assure that he would be able to campaign.

Many of Bosch's partisans, on the other hand, favored a "return to constitutionality without elections," an openly avowed objective which seemed to mean the simple reimposition of Bosch's 1963 government. They argued that the Dominican people's freely expressed choice in the 1962 elections should be respected, and that calling new elections would undermine constitutional procedures.[21] Some PRD leaders, however, seemed ready to accept the possibility of returning to "constitutionality" (and to power) through the electoral process, provided that guarantees for their participation in truly free and competitive elections could be assured.[22] Bosch himself—still in Puerto Rico —spoke occasionally of the legitimacy of his elected regime and of his party's aim to restore "constitutionality without elections," but he did not publicly disclaim the intense efforts some PRD figures were pressing to obtain assurances that the scheduled elections would be held, would be open for the PRD to participate, and would be impartially run.

III

Bereft of acknowledged legitimacy or substantial popular support from the beginning, the Triumvirate found its position increasingly shaky during 1964 and early 1965. Originally its main sources of power were the business community, particularly importers and merchants, the Armed Forces, and the United States government. None of these sectors, however, maintained undiminished support for the Triumvirate in 1964–65, and none could or would sustain the Reid Cabral government against attack in April 1965.

Reid Cabral lost favor in Dominican business and commercial circles not only because of the effects of the economic crisis and of the measures he was taking to fight it, but also because of the regime's apparent toleration of widespread corruption and contraband, some of which hurt the sales of established import firms. Criticism focused for a time on the government's failure to close the Cantina Nacional, CxA, an enterprise which imported goods duty-free and sold them at a markup for the benefit of high officials of the National Police; some merchants in Santiago even tried a brief strike to protest. The appearance of substantial quantities of contraband merchandise for sale at Christmas-time in 1964, and especially published reports that Dominican military planes were being used to import toys and other items from Puerto Rico, brought new outcries. The head of the Santo Domingo Chamber of Commerce, although related to Reid Cabral by marriage, blasted the prevalent contraband trade as a "national calamity" and political commentators picked up the theme.[23]

Reid Cabral's tolerance of flagrant corruption by high military and police officials, and then his belated efforts to curb these much-criticized practices, were closely linked to his marked loss of support within the Dominican Armed Forces. The Triumvirate began with strong military backing at the time of Bosch's overthrow, but this was progressively eroded as the months went by. A few officers, including Police Colonel Francisco Caamaño Deñó among others, expressed outrage at the prevailing practices of the entrenched military-police leadership.[24] They found widespread sympathy among junior officers and among enlisted men for their attacks, which were aimed not only at the top officers but also at the Reid regime itself; some argued that the overthrow of Reid would be necessary to reform the Armed Forces.

Paradoxically, however, Reid's own success late in 1964 and early in 1965 at weeding out some of the retrograde military and police leaders further undermined his power within the Dominican Armed Forces. Exploiting personal rivalries within the military-police leadership and capitalizing on American support, Reid removed from their positions a number of previously powerful figures, including Air Force Chief of Staff Miguel Atila Luna Pérez, Navy Chief Julio Rib Santamaría, Army Chief Salvador Augusto Montás Guerrero, and Police Chief Belisario Peguero Guerrero. Reid successfully survived a series of crises—several of which he provoked to remove individual officers—but he emerged from each fight with additional enemies. In February 1965, when he removed Secretary of State for the Armed Forces Víctor Elby Viñas Román and personally assumed Viñas's Cabinet post, Reid increased his immediate control but lost even more support. And when rumors surfaced that Reid did not view as necessarily permanent his convenient alliance with General Wessin y Wessin, whose backing had helped him remove the aforementioned officers, the beginning of Reid's end was close at hand.[25] When the crisis came to a head in April, no one in the Dominican military establishment, not even General Wessin, was willing to exert himself to defend the Reid regime.

The Triumvirate's third source of support, at least after obtaining diplomatic recognition in 1963, was the U.S. government. Once the Triumvirate had consolidated its hold and especially after Reid Cabral joined it, the U.S. government actively and openly supported the Dominican regime. Several American officials had been favorably impressed by Reid's performance in 1960–1962—first in the clandestine anti-Trujillo movement and later as second Vice-President of the Council of State—and they welcomed his accession to the Triumvirate and then his domination of it. Ambassador Bennett and other U.S. officials admired Reid's businesslike approach to public affairs and were gratified at his receptivity to their suggestions on a number of issues. The U.S. government was especially pleased by Reid's decision to implement the recommended "austerity" measures, by his reorganization of the state-owned sugar corporation, by his avowed support for the "civic action" programs the U.S. military assistance group was promoting, and particularly by his decisive actions against the corrupt military chiefs. Ambassador Bennett hailed Reid's ouster of key military and police officers in January 1965 as the greatest step forward in the Dominican Republic since the departure of the Trujillos in 1961, and he repeatedly urged Washington to take note of Reid Cabral's accomplishments.

The favorable U.S. government attitude toward Reid Cabral was very much influenced by the opinions Ambassador Bennett and his colleagues in Santo Domingo and in Washington had of the other major participants in Dominican politics. Ambassador Bennett himself was particularly concerned about the potential harmfulness of the retrograde military establishment, which he considered more dangerous for Dominican society than any sector other than the "Castro-Communist" left. He was also disturbed by the possibility of a return to power by Joaquín Balaguer or his supporters, whom he believed to be justifiably discredited because of their long associations with Trujillo, influential Dominicans who had participated in the Unión Cívica movement against Balaguer in 1961 did all they could to reinforce the ambassador's views. As for Juan Bosch, whom he had never met, Ambassador Bennett shared the contemptuous attitude of his Washington superiors. The PRD, and Bosch personally, were viewed as dismal failures at their "unfinished experiment" in the Dominican Republic. Bosch himself was considered an erratic figure, skilled at agitation but incapable of governing, whom the PRD continued to support only for lack of a unifying alternative. On several occasions, in fact, Ambassador Bennett sought to persuade Washington to consider ways of limiting Bosch's political activities in Puerto Rico, hoping thereby to reduce the exiled leader's continuing influence.

Given these likely alternatives to Reid Cabral, the U.S. government identified itself with Reid's government and even began considering whether and how Reid's tenure might be extended beyond the elections scheduled for September. The embassy view in February was that U.S. interests would be served by the continuation of Reid Cabral's term well beyond 1965. During an extended term, embassy officials thought, Reid could continue to implement sound economic policies and could reduce the burden of the Dominican military establishment. The embassy felt that Reid's position would be strengthened if he were to hold legitimizing elections and it wished him to do so. But the embassy also advised Washington that its position would have to be reconsidered if the risks posed by elections were to become greater than the risk of trying to prolong the existing state of affairs.

For his part, Reid Cabral assiduously cultivated not only extensive American backing but also the unmistakable appearance of it. Rejecting nationalistic political criticisms, Reid took every opportunity to declare his regime's partnership with the United States through the Alliance for Progress. So many photographs appeared of Reid with Ambassador Bennett that the U.S. envoy came to be known in some Dominican circles as "el otro Triunviro," the other member of the Triumvirate.

Ambassador Bennett apparently tried, especially from late 1964 on, to avoid creating such an undiluted image of support for Reid's regime, but he did continue—in private discussions with Dominicans and Americans alike and in his dispatches to Washington—to identify himself with Reid's accomplishments, to defend Reid from criticism, and even to rally support for the Triumvirate. Believing that most observers would concede that Reid was doing an honest job in a difficult situation, Bennett pointed out privately to influential Dominicans that the Triumvirate was more capable than any Dominican government since Trujillo's death and as effective as any foreseeable regime. To Washington, in turn, Ambassador Bennett argued that Reid needed and deserved additional American support. Again the opposition of those, including Assistant Secretary of State (for Economic Affairs) Anthony M. Solomon, who wished to hold the Dominican regime to strict compliance with the IMF's austerity recommendations, Bennett urged less stringent requirements in view of the Dominican political situation. Much of Bennett's time and energy was spent, moreover, in attempting to convince Washington to authorize increased sugar purchases from the Dominican Republic and also to extend additional economic assistance. Reviewing the general situation early in April 1965, Bennett contended that bad luck—low world prices for sugar and cacao, trouble with the coffee quota, problems in the banana industry, and especially the severe drought —had tended to obscure and undercut Reid's accomplishments in the economic sphere and with respect to the military structure. Bennett reported that Reid's hold was weakening as a result and that a further worsening of the Dominican economic situation would result in additional political deterioration. "Little foxes, some of them red, are nibbling at the grapes," the ambassador warned; inattention might result in sour wine. Bennett urged Washington to grant increased aid and to reconsider the possibility of authorizing a substantially increased sugar quota for the Dominican Republic. Action now, Bennett suggested, was required to avoid a possibly precipitate decline, for the Dominican economy was—in Bennett's phrase—"on the ropes."

Various measures were already being implemented by American officials in an attempt to help bolster Reid's popularity. Aid agreements were announced in March and April 1965 for community development programs, agrarian reform projects, and the construction of access roads—all designed to cut unemployment and to produce quick political impact. The embassy asked Washington for information on Peru's Cooperación Popular program and on its possible suitability as a device for Reid Cabral's use. The CIA station, meanwhile, began planning ways to help Reid build a campaign organization, in case the U.S. government should decide to back him secretly in an election bid.

By April 1965, however, questions were being raised within the U.S. government about the wisdom of tying American prestige to the unpopular Reid Cabral regime. Reid and his American backers had apparently expected his initially small personal following to increase with time, exposure, and accomplishment, but the opposite was occurring. Reid's public personality—his image as a practiced manipulator from the Dominican moneyed class, governing by croneyism and by condoning corruption—undermined his efforts to gain public favor. His barnstorming trips backfired, for many Dominicans found cynical these quick helicopter trips to open highways and agrarian reform projects or to distribute baseball equipment or other toys.

Indeed the very fact that Reid seemed to be campaigning cost him possible support; Dominicans increasingly resented Reid's apparent desire to parlay a purportedly temporary regime into a full-fledged government. Far from exploiting the latent divisions among his opponents—not only between Bosch and Balaguer, but even within Bosch's party among those favoring elections and those opposed—Reid Cabral drove his enemies closer together by indicating his own desire to extend his rule beyond the scheduled elections. From late 1964 on, Reid dropped various hints that he would try to perpetuate his regime, either by postponing the elections or by running as a candidate and barring potentially more popular figures, including Bosch and Balaguer.[26] In a televised interview on February 27, 1965, Reid put both exiled presidents in the same category, first by disparaging their respective performances in office and then by stating that permission for their return to Dominican soil would be contingent upon the state of public order; this was a policy which left Reid free to judge any pressure demanding the return of the exiled leaders as sufficient reason to keep them out.

Reid's ambitions thus effectively united a series of very diverse opponents. Harassed leftist extremists and frustrated right-wing politicians; corrupt military chieftains, ambitious young military officers, embittered ex-officers and disaffected enlisted men; the urban poor and the relatively prosperous commercial sector: all joined the two major political parties in rejecting Reid's continuísmo, his aim to stay in office. By April 1965, very few Dominicans remained loyal to the Reid Cabral regime.

The increasing feeling—even within the American embassy, especially among junior political officers—that Reid's days were numbered and that it was illusory to expect him to be elected president was reinforced early in April when preliminary results from a secret CIA-sponsored public opinion poll became available to the embassy. The survey indicated that only about 5 percent of the potential Dominican electorate supported Reid Cabral; five times as many favored Bosch, and ten times as many preferred Balaguer.[27] Arguing that this poll and other evidence showed that Reid could not win the scheduled election, the CIA station chief and others argued that the facts should be brought forcefully to Reid's attention so as to dissuade him from attempting to run and to prepare the way for some sort of political understanding acceptable to a majority of Dominicans, and especially to Balaguer and his followers. The station chief even took his case to Washington and argued this position in an interagency meeting early in April, chaired by Assistant Secretary of State Jack Hood Vaughn. The result of that meeting was the State Department's decision to recall Ambassador Bennett to Washington for consultations; the ambassador, too, was anxious to return in order to persuade the department to respond favorably to his appeals for additional assistance to the Dominican Republic, or else to canvass alternative measures.

It is not certain how the State Department would have responded late in April to Ambassador Bennett's recommendation that the U.S. government increase its assistance to the Dominican government under Reid. Undoubtedly the department would have reviewed the overall political situation with the ambassador, and some discussion would have focused on the future of the Reid regime and on the scheduled Dominican elections. Had the issues of U.S. policy toward these elections ever been posed in unequivocal terms—whether or not the U.S. government should exert pressures to have the elections held as scheduled or postponed, whether or not Reid should be encouraged to run as a candidate or to withdraw, and whether or not the U.S. government should pressure for permission to let Balaguer and/or Bosch participate—the already latent conflicts within the American government might have emerged more clearly. Some officials would have favored U.S. pressures on Reid to hold free elections in which Bosch and Balaguer could participate as the only way they saw to defuse a potentially explosive situation. Some would have viewed another national election in the Dominican Republic as destabilizing, partly because they considered the probable contenders and likely winners unacceptable; they would have urged that Reid be spared U.S. pressures and helped to strengthen his position.[28] Others, perhaps, would have sought an alternative solution: a possible agreement among Bosch, Balaguer, and Reid Cabral, a formula for separating the congressional and presidential races, or some other scheme designed to gain time.

The issue had not really been defined, however, by April 23, 1965, when Ambassador Bennett left Santo Domingo, intending first to visit his seriously ill mother in Georgia and then to proceed to Washington for consultations. Since the date for opening the scheduled election campaign was June 1, no deadline had forced the U.S. government to define its attitude toward a possible attempt by Reid Cabral to continue in office; presumably the planned consultations would have aimed for a U.S. government position on the issue. In the meantime, U.S. policy as of April 23 continued to support the Reid regime.

The extent of American backing was open to question, however. When the coup against Reid Cabral began the next day, the prevailing U.S. government assessment of Reid's weak political position virtually precluded any significant American action to sustain him against attack.

The basic tactic Juan Bosch and his associates adopted to reverse the 1963 coup was straightforward. Just as sectors of the Dominican Armed Forces had removed him in 1963, so Bosch counted on other sectors of the Armed Forces to be instrumental in bringing him back. Beginning early in 1964, Bosch and a few of his most trusted associates began to lay the groundwork— within the Armed Forces and outside—for an eventual attempt to restore him to power.

Perhaps the first external indication that Bosch planned a comeback was his successful effort in 1964 to reassert and consolidate his personal control of the PRD by ousting those in the party who were prepared to have the PRD reenter Dominican politics without insisting on Bosch's own return. Bosch's rival, Angel Miolán, was read out of the party and Miolán's erstwhile supporters within the PRD lost influence, while Bosch's closest associates, particularly Molina Ureña and Peña Gómez, gained additional stature.

Bosch's move to begin constructing a vehicle for returning himself to the Dominican presidency was also signaled by a concerted campaign to attract middle-class professionals into his ranks. Bosch and his partisans worked deliberately to establish closer ties with what they called "la clase pensante," the thinking class. Several prominent Santiago lawyers, mostly former leaders of the UCN—including Salvador Jorge Blanco, José Augusto Vega, Miguel Angel Brito Mata, Pedro Manuel Casals Victoria, and Aníbal Campagna—were brought into personal contact with Bosch by his long-time friend Antonio Guzmán, Minister of Agriculture in the 1963 regime. In Santo Domingo, meanwhile, Molina Ureña's close friend Leopoldo Espaillat and several other PRD-affiliated lawyers, physicians, engineers, and architects (including Enriquillo del Rosario and Emilio Almonte) organized a working group of leading professionals which met frequently in Almonte's home.[29] Many of the same persons also helped organize two major receptions—one in Santo Domingo in December 1964 and the other in Santiago in January 1965—to which hundreds of opinion leaders from various sectors of Dominican society were invited. These receptions were calculated to suggest PRD leadership of the mounting opposition to Reid Cabral, and many individuals joined the PRD after these well-attended meetings.

Another step designed to prepare the atmosphere for Bosch's attempt to regain power was the publication in December 1964 of Bosch's account of his own regime and its overthrow: *La crisis de la democracia de América en la República Dominicana*. A powerful tract, the book contained in every chapter references calculated not only to elucidate the past but also to affect the events of 1965. Bosch's longstanding emphasis on the class division of Dominican society and on the need to overcome the rigid hold of established interests took special shape in this book as Bosch focused on the vital role the middle class would have to play, inside the Armed Forces and outside, in making a revolution.[30] Hundreds of copies of Bosch's volumes were sold within a day of its appearance, and Bosch's standing as the leader of the antigovernment opposition gained dramatically.[31] Similar efforts were undertaken, meanwhile, to renew international interest—particularly in U.S. liberal circles—in Professor Bosch and his cause. Bosch's criticisms of unfavorable accounts of his regime were privately but widely circulated, arrangements were made to translate Bosch's own book into

English and publish it in the United States, and Bosch's ties with Puerto Rican leaders were fortified by a visit to San Juan in March of some thirty PRD leaders who came ostensibly to express their thanks to ex-Governor Muñoz for his hospitality to Bosch.

Another step to establish a framework for the "return to constitutionality" was the Pact of Rio Piedras, a formal agreement between the PRD and the PRSC committing the parties to cooperate to restore "constitutionality." The pact, signed by Bosch and PRSC President Antonio Rosario in Puerto Rico on February 1, 1965, proclaimed the unity of the moderate left on the goal of restoring "constitutionality" without specifying the means. Some PRSC leaders may have regarded the pact as a preelectoral coalition, but nothing in the text precluded a "return to constitutionality without elections" and Bosch continued to pursue that goal, apparently with the explicit acquiescence of Rosario and several other PRSC chiefs.

The most important step Bosch and his supporters undertook to facilitate their return was to strengthen their ties with dissident elements of the Dominican Armed Forces. The key development which shaped the early phase of the 1965 Dominican crisis was the success of Bosch's confederates at stimulating some military plots against Reid Cabral and infiltrating others, while building up a cadre of officers loyal to Bosch.

The way the pro-Bosch cadre developed and organized itself is not wholly clear.[32] Members of this group—among them some of the country's ablest young officers, trained at U.S. installations, as well as some chronic troublemakers—were apparently inspired by a number of motives: genuine belief that a reversal of the 1963 coup was necessary to cleanse the honor of the Armed Forces and to make possible the development of a respected professional institution; frustration at the permanent flux and factional struggle which had followed the removal of Trujillo's authority in the Armed Forces; jealousy at the personal profits enjoyed by those in high military office or disgust at the flagrant corruption of senior officials; even, in some cases, simple zest for conspiracy and love of conflict.[33] All, however, shared deep dissatisfaction with the incumbent military leadership and were willing to cooperate with Bosch and his supporters to remove what they regarded as the causes of their unrest.

Both their degree of dissatisfaction and their willingness to work with Bosch were reportedly very much influenced by Colonel Fernández Domínguez, who continued to support Bosch after the 1963 coup. Trusted emissaries from Bosch reestablished contact with Colonel Fernández early in 1964 in Madrid, where he had been sent as a military attaché two weeks after the 1963 coup, exiled (in effect) by the Triumvirate because of his known opposition to the overthrow and his incipient activities to reverse it.[34] From his post in Spain—and later from San Juan, Puerto Rico, and finally from Santiago, Chile, where he was reassigned—Fernández kept in close touch with several colleagues in the Dominican Republic, including some active military officers and others who had been cashiered for one reason or another. Some of these officers, in turn, met with various PRD civilian leaders (Molina Ureña and Peña Gómez among them), who gave them continuing political orientation, and a few also retained contact with a group of recalcitrant enlisted men within the Army.

Lieutenant Colonel Miguel Angel Hernando Ramírez, a close friend of Colonel Fernández, was apparently picked late in 1964 or early in 1965 to lead the active military group within the Dominican Republic; he met repeatedly with Molina Ureña and at least once flew to Puerto Rico to see Bosch himself. Ex-officers, including some who had been removed from the Armed Forces in 1961–62 and others who had been dismissed after the 1963 coup, gathered principally around former Army Captain Héctor Lachapelle Diaz and ex-Air Force General Santiago Rodríguez Echavarría; the latter, employed as a commercial pilot in the government-owned airline, still retained considerable influence among a group of active Air Force pilots who were enlisted for the proposed overthrow of Reid.

The decisive event in the slow development of the pro-Bosch movement reportedly came when Colonel Fernández himself secretly visited the Dominican Republic in December 1964, and consulted his colleagues about specific plans for a coup attempt to be launched in January. The January plan was never executed, probably because it was partially discovered by Dominican authorities, but Fernández's visit rallied the spirits of the various military subgroups, who continued to plot during early 1965. At several points in February, March, and early April the plotters apparently came close to attempting a coup, but no definitive move to topple Reid was made. The decision to oust Reid on a specific date appears not yet to have been taken as Holy Week of 1965 (April 11–18) ended and Dominicans turned their attention once more from religious devotion and family reunions to conspiracy and rumor.

Intrigue permeated Santo Domingo by mid-April 1965. Rumors of an impending coup were freely reported in the daily press; such reports are relatively infrequent even in the coup-prone Dominican Republic. Although it is still difficult to sort out the various conspiracies, it appears that most or all of the plotters can be fitted into three main groups: those aiming to return Bosch to the presidency without new elections; those favoring the establishment of a junta effectively pledged to hold prompt elections in which Bosch and Balaguer could run; and those working simply to replace Reid by establishing a junta without any particular political preconditions. Not all who pursued any one of these goals were actually cooperating with one another, but groups with very distinct objectives and tactics found that their immediate aims coincided temporarily. Nor were the plotters bound in any way to seek only one of these objectives; many of Bosch's supporters, in particular, pursued simultaneously the goals of returning to "constitutionality" either through elections or without them, rather than commit themselves definitely to one tactic or the other. The fact that some plotters participated in more than one scheme at a time, or jumped easily from one to another, made it impossible for anyone—in Reid's government, in the U.S. embassy and its intelligence services, or among the plotters themselves—to have a complete grasp of all the conspiracies and their interrelations.

This helps account for the widespread confusion which followed the overthrow of Reid Cabral on April 24, and for the inability of either Dominican politicians or American officials to discern at first exactly what was happening.

The sector committed to restore Bosch directly to power was spearheaded by the pro-Bosch cadre which had been forming since the 1963 coup. Although their objective—"return to constitutionality without elections"—was proclaimed publicly, members of the group managed to obscure their specific plans by aligning themselves with various other groups working to topple Reid. Peña Gómez's radio speeches illustrate these tactics. Peña used his daily program to praise, as the occasion demanded, such diverse groups within the Armed Forces as the corrupt Generals Belisario Peguero and Atila Luna, pro-Balaguer plotters like Colonel Neit Nivar Seijas, noncommissioned officers and enlisted men, as well as the "young and honest" officers dedicated to constitutionality, while he and other supporters of Bosch also worked closely with ex-officers in the Dominican Republic and outside.

Such efforts to camouflage the pro-Bosch movement within the Armed Forces were largely successful, for neither Reid's government, nor pro-Balaguer conspirators, nor extreme leftist plotters, nor American officials feared a significant military movement committed to Bosch.[35] It was known that PRD leaders maintained contact with some military officers and ex-officers. At least one CIA report in February 1965 even discussed a reported plot of Bosch and a number of his colleagues with Colonel Fernández Domínguez and General Rodríguez Echavarría, and another intelligence report on April 16 specifically named Colonel Hernando Ramírez as a leading pro-Bosch conspirator. Such items received little attention, however, amidst a welter of rumors and reported plots, most of them involving Balaguer's supporters in the "San Cristóbal" Army clan. Ambassador Bennett reported in March that the attachés knew of no serious disaffections within the Armed Forces due to the PRD efforts, and even the April 16 report on Colonel Hernando was specifically discounted by the U.S. Army attaché.

The possibility that followers of Bosch would actually come

to dominate the Dominican Republic through the Armed Forces was not taken seriously by American officials, who regarded the leadership of the Dominican military as united in its opposition to Bosch. Virtually the entire top officer corps of the Dominican Armed Forces had joined to oust Bosch in 1963 and only a handful of individual dissidents were believed to harbor pro-Bosch sympathies.

A second grouping favoring the immediate reinstallation of Bosch but independent of the PRD-PRSC movement, was made up of the various extreme left parties. The spring of 1965 was punctuated by intense squabbling on the left, as the Communist parties vied with each other and with the PRD and the PRSC for influence in the anti-Triumvirate movement. Spokesmen for the PSP, the MPD, and the 1J4 repeatedly called for the establishment of a "united front of all democratic forces" committed to restore Bosch and the 1963 Constitution, but PRD and PRSC leaders deliberately excluded them from formal adherence to the Pact of Rio Piedras and from participation in the pro-Bosch conspiracy within the Dominican Armed Forces. Far from cooperating closely with the PRD (as some American officials were later to suggest), the Communist parties all attacked the PRD and the PRSC for rejecting the popular front strategy and excluding them from the Rio Piedras agreement, for allegedly vacillating about whether a return to "constitutionality" *through* elections would be acceptable, and even for seeming to consider the possibility of approaching the American embassy to seek guaranteed elections. The main theme from the extreme left was sounded by a PSP manifesto on March 16, rejecting "the way out of the crisis through elections" and insisting that the return of Bosch and the 1963 Constitution should be accomplished by "mass actions," not through elections nor via intrigue.[36]

Among themselves, however, Dominican Communist groups differed bitterly about the precise role of mass actions in securing the return to "constitutionality," about the relative importance of Bosch's own return as distinct from the mere restoration of the 1963 Constitution, and about the immediate and long-term significance of the restoration of "constitutionality." Clandestinely published newspapers and leaflets stressed clarifications and counterclarifications to indicate each party's distinct position.[37] All agreed that the return of "constitutionality without elections" should be sought, but none was in a position to do much more than proclaim the aim and wait for a better opportunity to achieve it. Because they dismissed the possibility of significant support for Bosch within the Dominican Armed Forces, extreme leftists discounted the prospect of an immediate return to "constitutionality." They continued their propaganda efforts, however, hoping to increase the chances that a popular revolution could eventually be stimulated.

Support for the simple replacement of Reid's regime by a new junta, not necessarily pledged to hold elections, came primarily from members of the previously established military leadership, especially from the so-called "San Cristóbal" group of Army officers. Many officers and ex-officers from this group maintained contact with pro-Balaguer figures working to establish a junta pledged to hold prompt elections. Although all these officers had participated in the anti-Bosch coup in 1963, some now also had ties with those plotting for Bosch's return; a few were even to declare their backing for the pro-Bosch movement when it seemed about to prevail on April 25. Such flexibility was symptomatic of the fact that the major participants in this group were not loyal to ideology or to personal leaders. Some were out to protect their financial interests in the face of Reid's crackdown on military graft. Others, sensing that Reid would soon fall, were simply maneuvering to keep their military positions.

None of the plots discussed by these officers was ever executed. Their opposition to Reid Cabral, however, left the Triumvirate with very little support within the cliques which make up the Dominican Armed Forces against the conspiracies launched by supporters of Bosch and Balaguer. Reid's almost total lack of military support was to become very important and very evident when the crisis broke on April 24.

The sector wishing to set up a junta pledged to hold prompt

and free elections included two major subgroups: those committed to Joaquín Balaguer and those favoring the return to power through new elections of Juan Bosch personally or of the PRD. Balaguer, exiled in New York since early 1962, still retained (or had reacquired after the 1963 coup) a number of avid followers in Dominican political and military circles, and rumors of an impending pro-Balaguer coup circulated from time to time throughout 1964 and early 1965. Balaguer himself insisted, however—both in numerous public statements and in private remarks to intimates—that he wished to return to the Dominican presidency through free elections, his personal reputation thereby vindicated. By February and March of 1965, as indications mounted that Reid might postpone or otherwise interfere with the scheduled elections, leading Reformista figures pressed for action against the Triumvirate. Meeting with sympathetic military leaders, party vice-president Lora and others worked out some of the details of a coup plan, execution of which Balaguer would presumably have authorized only if and when it became absolutely clear that Reid would not hold free elections in September. The plot was being organized primarily by two long-time intimates of Balaguer, ex-Army Colonels Neit Nivar Seijas and Braulio Alvarez Sánchez, senior officers whom Reid Cabral had relieved of their battalion commands earlier in 1965.

Preparations for Reid's overthrow seemed to Reformista leaders to be proceeding satisfactorily in early April. Then, on April 12, Reid Cabral suddenly deported Colonel Nivar to Puerto Rico and closed in on several other members of the pro-Balaguer plot. Other Reformista plotters, apparently, decided to lay low temporarily.

Since he knew Nivar Seijas to have considerable influence within the Army, to be committed to Balaguer's return, to have had continuing contacts with Peña Gómez of the PRD, and also to have been plotting a coup, Reid Cabral may well have thought that by exiling Nivar he was eliminating the major source of active military conspiracy against him; this, in any case, was the U.S. embassy's view. It turned out, however, that other plots kept on developing even after Reid ousted Nivar and Alvarez.

Indeed, Reid's removal of these key pro-Balaguer officers, first from command of the two main Army battalions garrisoned just north of Santo Domingo and then from active service in the military, significantly facilitated the execution of the pro-Bosch conspiracy. One of the newly appointed battalion commanders, Lieutenant Colonel Pedro Augusto Alvarez Holguín, turned out to be part of the pro-Bosch cadre. The other, Colonel Giovanni Gutiérrez, had plotted with several groups in the past. When the pro-Bosch coup finally was attempted on April 24, Gutiérrez's decision to throw in his lot with the coupmakers was to be crucial to the development of the crisis.

The second sector favoring the junta-and-elections formula included many PRD and PRSC supporters—some of them backers of Juan Bosch and others opposed to him personally—who desired a return to "constitutionality" but did not insist that this be achieved *without elections.* Those opposed to Bosch, mainly backers of Angel Miolán, wished the PRD to return to power by running a candidate other than Bosch in new national elections.[38] Even among those in the PRD loyal to Bosch, there was considerable uncertainty about the wisdom of launching a countercoup against Reid.[39] Hoping to break the cycle of violence, several PRD leaders suggested that the party should try first to pressure Reid into overseeing free elections as scheduled in September. Some, including several military figures, contended that Reid should be given every opportunity to define his intentions before a coup should be considered.[40] The official deadline for entering the campaign was to have been June 1, and some discussion apparently focused on attempting a coup at that time if free elections had by then still not been effectively guaranteed.

Most PRD leaders, it appears, were more concerned about reaching power again than about the precise avenue used to get there. A few believed a new popular mandate through elections to be indispensable, many thought new elections an acceptable route, and only a small cadre insisted on the immediate "return to constitutionality without elections." Most were extemporizing —waiting to see how the situation developed and which means of restoring the PRD to office would be most likely to succeed—

while attempting to improve the chances for their eventual comeback.

Neither Bosch nor any of the PRD plotters seem to have planned or expected a "revolution," involving civil strife. Each group, like the sector supporting Joaquín Balaguer, believed it would achieve its objective through its influence within the Dominican Armed Forces.

IV

By April 1965, then, almost all politically active Dominicans opposed the Reid Cabral regime. Probably most would have favored prompt elections, in which former presidents Bosch and Balaguer could participate, as the best means for replacing Reid's government. There was no agreement, however, on whether and how elections could be assured. Reid Cabral, far from guaranteeing the widely desired elections, was hinting that they might be postponed, or that Bosch and Balaguer might be excluded from participation.[41] Sentiment for a coup to open the way for the return of Bosch or Balaguer gained, therefore, among supporters of each leader. The American embassy, very anxious to avoid a coup, with all its uncertain consequences, concentrated on sustaining Reid. Noting the obvious American support for Reid, Dominicans were unconvinced that the United States government would exert its pressures to assure free elections in September. Consequently, the incentive for an early coup increased still more.

It is impossible to say how the different currents of opposition to the Reid regime might have worked themselves out had the June 1 electoral deadline approached and presumably forced attitudes to crystallize. Before the elections issue could be resolved, and before any significant U.S. pressure to find a solution to the impasse had been exerted, Reid learned about the secret pro-Bosch conspiracy.

On April 22, just ten days after he had exiled Colonel Nivar Seijas, Reid announced that seven junior Air Force officers were being fired. Since all seven had connections with the pro-Bosch cadre, leaders of the group feared that their conspiracy had been discovered, especially because ex-General Santiago

Rodríguez Echavarría was that same day suddenly fired from his job with the government-owned airline and because Reid that same week had personally asked Colonel Hernando Ramírez what he was planning. Apprehensive that any delay would permit Reid to deal with the rest of their number, Hernando and his colleagues met that evening and set April 26 as the date for their coup attempt.

Early on the morning of Saturday, April 24, however, the 1965 Dominican crisis began. Acting apparently on the basis of new information, General Marcos A. Rivera Cuesta, the Army's Chief of Staff, personally advised Reid that several influential Army officers—including Lieutenant Colonels Hernando and Alvarez Holguín—were definitely involved in the pro-Bosch conspiracy. Since Rivera earlier had been willing to vouch personally for the loyalty of these two officers, Reid was quickly convinced by the new report. Reid ordered General Rivera immediately to cancel the commissions of Hernando, Alvarez Holguín, and several junior officers believed to be part of their group.

General Rivera Cuesta left at once for his headquarters at the nearby 27th of February camp, prepared to carry out his charge. But when Rivera confronted several of the pro-Bosch military plotters at about noon on April 24, he soon found himself under arrest. Unsuspected members of the pro-Bosch group, led by Captain Mario Peña Taveras, imprisoned Rivera and his chief aide, thus initiating the split in the Dominican Army and the fall of Reid.

Captain Peña Taveras called Peña Gómez, about to broadcast his daily program, to let him know what had transpired. Within minutes Peña Gómez announced on the air that Reid Cabral's regime had fallen, and that a return to "constitutionality" was under way. The Dominican government's radio-television station immediately began broadcasting announcements denying that a coup was occurring and denouncing rumormongers, but the regime's hold began to slip away. Within hours, opponents of Reid from every part of the political spectrum—as well as the American embassy—were actively trying to find out exactly what was happening, and how they might influence events.

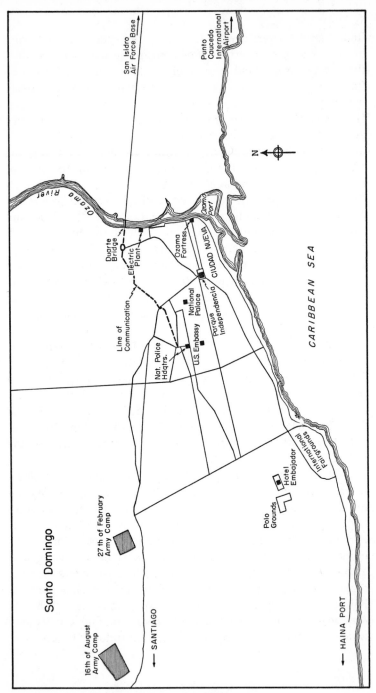

Strategic Points in Santo Domingo, Spring 1965

3. The Decision to Intervene

At noon on Saturday, April 24—while pro-Bosch plotters were imprisoning General Rivera Cuesta and his chief aide—Ambassador Bennett was in Georgia visiting his mother. Chargé d'Affaires William B. Connett, Jr., in Santo Domingo less than six months, was beginning what he expected to be a leisurely weekend. Carter Ide, the AID Mission Director, was in Washington, as was Public Safety Adviser Anthony Ruiz. Public Affairs Officer Malcolm McLean had just returned to Santo Domingo from an exhausting day touring the Dominican Republic with the University of Michigan Jazz Orchestra. A key member of the embassy's CIA contingent was playing golf on the Hotel Embajador's course. Another CIA officer was on his way downtown to buy shoes; the Station Chief—just recently returned from Washington and still catching up—was at his desk. The naval attaché, Lieutenant Colonel Ralph Heywood, was out shooting ducks with one of his primary contacts and best friends in the Dominican Republic, Brigadier General Antonio Imbert Barrera.[1] Eleven of the thirteen members of the Military Assistance Advisory Group (MAAG), the U.S. personnel with the closest and most continuous contact at junior levels of the Dominican Armed Forces, had left twenty-four hours earlier to attend a conference in Panama.

This embassy was not expecting imminent trouble. In its routine weekly report of April 20, the embassy had mentioned rumors of continued pro-Bosch plotting within the military but had explicitly discounted their significance. The Reid regime was believed to have the various conspiracies within the Armed Forces under surveillance and control.

The U.S. government in Washington was even less prepared to deal with a sudden crisis in the Dominican Republic. The Central Intelligence Agency was just switching directors; Admiral William Raborn was not to be sworn in as the new director until the following Wednesday. Assistant Secretary of State for Inter-American Affairs Jack Hood Vaughn, appointed to his post a few weeks before, was attending a conference of Western Hemisphere intellectuals in Mexico. His deputy, Robert B. Sayre, Jr., had taken up his job earlier in the week, as had the White House staff specialist on Latin America, William Bowdler. The acting Dominican Republic desk officer in the Defense Department's office of International Security Affairs was also new to his job. The Defense Intelligence Agency's specialist on the Dominican Republic, a veteran of several years' work on Dominican affairs, was out of town for the weekend and unable to return to her desk until Sunday evening. President Johnson himself was at Camp David, hoping to relax.

I

The radio announcement by José Francisco Peña Gómez of General Rivera Cuesta's arrest opened the curtain on the 1965 Dominican crisis. Immediately after Peña Gómez's announcement on Radio Comercial, Radio Santo Domingo—the government station—officially denied reports of a coup. Soon, however, Radio Santo Domingo proclaimed a 6:00 P.M. curfew, while continuing to dismiss rumors that Reid Cabral had been overthrown. But just a few minutes later, Peña Gómez, Manuel Fernández Mármol, Miguel Soto, and other PRD leaders burst into one of Radio Santo Domingo's studios and used the official channel itself to declare that a movement of "young and honest" officers dedicated to "constitutionality" had overthrown Reid; one speaker called for the return of Juan Bosch.

Chargé Connett, sending out the first of several "CRITIC" messages that were to come out of Santo Domingo that week, informed Washington of the rumors about a coup and of the takeover of Radio Santo Domingo.[2] He noted that the Reid government might be in serious difficulty but that there was no solid evidence it had actually been overthrown. The capture of Radio Santo Domingo, he reported, appeared to be an isolated incident; at least it had not yet been accompanied by attacks on other important installations.

Enthusiastic demonstrations which had begun around the country—mostly for Bosch, some for Balaguer—quickly ended later in the afternoon when members of the National Police retook the Radio Santo Domingo studio, arrested Peña Gómez and the others, once again denied that the regime had been overthrown, and repeated the earlier announcement of a 6:00 P.M. curfew. Although some disorders continued (crowds sacked one of Reid's personal businesses and several other enterprises), the Reid government seemed now to be dominating the situation. Strategic points in Santo Domingo were reinforced, including the Ozama Fortress, the National Police Palace, and the military police barracks. Police riot control squads dispersed unruly crowds at a number of points.

Connett now told Washington that the situation appeared to be calming down. Although the rebellious officers and men still had control of Army headquarters at the 27th of February camp, the attachés reported that the uprising seemed to be confined to some junior and noncommissioned officers in the Army; elements from other services did not appear to be participating. Air Force Chief of Staff General Juan de los Santos Céspedes and Navy Chief Commodore Francisco J. Rivera Caminero had assured the embassy that they were backing the Reid regime. General Wessin's position was not yet clear but it was believed that he would join the service chiefs in opposing the insurgency within the Army.

The embassy at this point was still trying to ascertain the

political ties and intentions of the coupmakers. So far the embassy was not sure of anything beyond the fact that the group which had appeared at Radio Santo Domingo was from the PRD; it was not clear whether they were attempting to restore Bosch immediately or to guarantee elections, nor was it even certain that they were closely tied with the military group which had arrested General Rivera Cuesta. The Army attaché reported that the rebel camp was in command of Lieutenant Colonel Jorge Leonidas Cheng Contreras, who said the rebel plan was to establish a military junta under Lieutenant Colonel Miguel Angel Hernando Ramírez.[3] Captain Mario Peña Taveras, the man who had actually imprisoned Rivera, told a U.S. attaché, however, that the movement aimed to restore Bosch to the presidency. The situation was generally confusing, but the insurgency did seem to be confined to a few Army officers. By nightfall, the embassy thought it probable that Reid's regime would maintain control.

Thus assured by the embassy, the Dominican desk officer at the State Department in Washington briefed Benjamin Read, the department's Executive Secretary, at 6:30 P.M.; Read decided that it was not necessary to alert Secretary Rusk about the crisis. At 6:35 P.M., the desk officer went home, feeling that the Dominican situation was probably in hand; he arranged to keep himself in touch with the department just in case things should change.

In fact, Reid Cabral's regime was crumbling. The First Battalion under Lieutenant Colonel Pedro Alvarez Holguín and the 16th of August camp under Colonel Giovanni Gutiérrez had both joined the uprising during the day. Two-thirds of the Dominican Army units in the vicinity of Santo Domingo were now in revolt, and were being reinforced by groups of ex-officers who were reporting to the camps in accord with prearranged plans. There were indications that some of the rebellious troops would attempt to enter the downtown area that night. Reid Cabral now asked General Wessin to prevent the rebels from taking over the city. But Wessin gave no immediate response; his loyalties and his intentions were unclear.

Faced with the need to subdue the two rebel camps, Reid Cabral appeared on Radio Santo Domingo's television channel at about 8:30 P.M. to tell the country that the attempted coup was being put down, to emphasize that only two camps were resisting the government, and to threaten military actions against the camps if the men there did not surrender by 5:00 A.M. on Sunday. Perhaps Reid was confident at this point that his ultimatum would succeed; the embassy apparently assumed for a time that it would. But Reid's broadcast alerted the whole country to the fact that the two major Army barracks just north of Santo Domingo were still in revolt. The rebel movement now gained added force.

The next few hours were full of intricate, almost incredible, maneuvering by a number of Dominican figures, all anxious to emerge from the uncertain situation at the top of the heap. General Imbert's day, for instance, reads like fiction. Shooting ducks with Colonel Heywood, Imbert had first been informed of the attempted coup when a message was received over his car's special two-way radio connection with National Police headquarters. Imbert called Reid Cabral in the National Palace, who told him that the challenge was not serious and asked him to make sure that the provincial Army garrisons at La Vega and Santiago supported the government. Accompanied by Colonel Heywood, Imbert visited the two installations and urged the troops there to remain calm and loyal.

Imbert and Heywood then hurried back to Santo Domingo, Heywood to don his uniform and report to the embassy, Imbert to visit Reid Cabral. Informed by Reid of the split within the Armed Forces, Imbert reportedly offered to help unite the military and put down the revolt if Reid would name him Secretary of State for the Armed Forces. But Reid had already decided to name General Wessin to this post, hoping thereby to assure Wessin's loyalty and to make his support obvious to all. Imbert nevertheless agreed then to visit the rebellious camps and to sound out the position of the movement's leaders.

By the time Imbert arrived at the 27th of February camp, it was clear that the challenge to Reid's government was indeed severe. Sizing up the situation anew, Imbert now offered to support the coup and to arrange for the establishment of a new junta under his leadership which could hold elections. But rebel military leaders rejected Imbert's suggestion, informing him that their movement was committed to restoring Juan Bosch to the presidency.

Next, General Imbert contacted the American embassy again, informing U.S. officials that the rebels seemed determined to bring back Bosch. He warned the embassy that troops from the 27th of February camp would enter the city, apparently prepared to fight.

Imbert's reports confirmed what the embassy was learning from other sources. Colonel Hernando Ramírez had told a Dominican journalist that his group was fully committed to Bosch's return. Captain Peña Taveras, responding to a call from Reid himself, refused to negotiate and confirmed the movement's aim to restore constitutional government under Bosch. Some troops from the 27th of February camp did enter the city, which buzzed with reports that the coup was gaining ground. At 2:00 A.M. on Sunday, rebel sympathizers took over Santo Domingo's fire station and sounded its sirens, as if to herald the triumph of their movement.

II

In the first hours of Sunday, April 25, the embassy informed Washington that Reid's hold was fast deteriorating. It appeared at about 4:00 A.M. that General Salvador Augusto Montás Guerrero, who had been removed as Army Chief of Staff just a few weeks earlier but was still serving as Reid's Minister of Interior and Police, had thrown in his lot with the rebel movement. The Operations Center (the State Department's twenty-four-hour communications complex), now fully alerted to the crisis in Santo Domingo, recalled the Caribbean desk officers to work. At 6:15 A.M. a "Dominican Republic task force" was established in the Operations Center.[4]

By 5:00 A.M., the line between the Army rebels and the Reid government had been clearly drawn by the insurgents' refusal to heed the regime's ultimatum. It was also obvious by now that

Reid could not count on his military chiefs to subdue the uprising. Undoubtedly hoping to gain evidence of American backing, Reid asked the U.S. air attaché to find out whether the Dominican Air Force would comply with an order to act against the rebels. The attaché inquired, but General De Los Santos—under pressure from pro-rebel pilots and himself sympathetic to Balaguer's return—told him that the Air Force officer corps had met and decided not to accept any such order; they wished instead to work for a solution to the crisis which would avoid bloodshed.

Reid next called Wessin and asked again for his assistance. Wessin demurred, explaining (according to one report) that "he could not use his tanks without air support."[5] Whatever his reasons, Wessin declined to act.

Reid now turned once more to the American embassy, informing U.S. officials of his concern about the situation. He noted that rebel soldiers had taken up positions in the city overnight, reported that arms were being distributed, and claimed finally that Communist activists were at work. Given these circumstances, Reid asked Colonel Heywood, would the United States be willing to intervene?

Additional information coming to the embassy made it clear that Reid's situation was desperate. Several military leaders earlier ousted by Reid—including General Belisario Peguero Guerrero, General Atila Luna Pérez, and Commodore Julio Rib Santamaría, each with his own clique of supporters—had all joined the revolt; Peguero had even used his continuing influence with the National Police to free Peña Gómez and his colleagues from custody. General Montás Guerrero, tied to the ousted generals but still in Reid's Cabinet, was busy trying to set up a provisional military junta to which Reid could transfer power, a task in which he was reportedly joined by retired Generals Manuel Mario García Urbaez and Renato Hungría Morell. The active military chiefs—General De Los Santos, Commodore Rivera, and General Wessin—were obviously standing aside, letting Reid fall. If Reid's regime were to be saved, the U.S. government would have to act.

In Washington, meanwhile, the U.S. government began gearing for action. The Dominican desk officer, back on the job, had awakened Undersecretary of State Thomas C. Mann at 5:00 A.M. to confer with him by telephone. President Johnson received a staff briefing on the Dominican situation before 7:00 A.M. An hour later, Caribbean Country Director Kennedy M. Crockett gave telephone briefings to Secretary of State Dean Rusk and Deputy Assistant Secretary Sayre, and to Ambassador Bennett in Georgia; Bennett asked for the department's help in securing an early reservation on a commercial flight from Atlanta to Washington. At 8:45 A.M. Sayre asked Vaughn to return to Washington from Mexico. Crockett—operating on a contingency basis, that is, without consulting the president—was meanwhile asking the Department of Defense to order the Navy's Caribbean Ready Group to move toward the Dominican Republic, out of sight of land, ready to evacuate U.S. citizens if necessary.[6] Procedures were already being set in motion which within four days would culminate in military intervention.

Informed of Reid's inquiry or apparent request, Connett decided to tell Crockett at the State Department to ask for guidance. Crockett suggested that Connett meet with Reid, ask him precisely what kind of assistance he was asking, and explain that there was little the United States could do. Connett and Crockett agreed that the immediate alternatives for U.S. policy were either to back Reid Cabral forcefully or to favor a move by the established Dominican military leaders (who were abandoning Reid but opposed Juan Bosch) to form a temporary military junta. Although Connett and Crockett recognized that such a junta might at this stage be unacceptable to some of the pro-Bosch rebels, they felt it would afford a better chance of avoiding bloodshed than a last-ditch stand in support of the unpopular Triumvirate; accordingly they now decided to support the creation of a junta.

The idea that the embassy might encourage the leaders of the Dominican Armed Forces to accept Juan Bosch's return was never considered. To an indeterminate but undoubtedly important extent, this was due to the strong preexisting attitudes within the U.S. government about Bosch and the PRD, which made it unlikely that U.S. officials would ever actively favor Bosch's return. The U.S. government's failure even to consider backing Bosch's return stemmed as well from the immediate perceptions—both in Washington and in the embassy—of exactly what was happening in Santo Domingo. American officials had believed for months that only a few military officers and members of the PRD left wing were actually committed to Bosch's immediate return and that this minority could not possibly obtain power in the face of the prevailing military opposition to Bosch. Nothing had happened so far to challenge this belief. Since the essential conflict seemed to be within the Dominican Armed Forces, with a few junior officers from two Army battalions pitted against all the rest of the military establishment, it seemed likely that the majority faction would agree to establish a provisional junta. And since it was thought that a junta pledged to hold the scheduled elections would be favored by all non-Communist parties except a minority faction of the PRD, it was expected that an agreement to establish a junta would be reached fairly easily. No direct American participation in the conflict was envisioned, nor was it thought likely at this point that Dominican force would have to be employed to produce agreement. Certainly no American official, in Santo Domingo or in Washington, was yet contemplating U.S. military intervention, although the Caribbean Ready Group's standard operating procedure for evacuation operations was already bringing Marines toward Santo Domingo.

Connett's hope as he entered the Palace to talk with Reid, therefore, was to secure Reid's approval to transfer power to the group which General Montás was already forming. Reid was unenthusiastic about this suggestion, however. Connett then mentioned Reid's earlier conversation with Colonel Heywood and pointed out that the United States could do little to help Reid. Reid, agreeing that time was short, suggested that the embassy might still be able to persuade the rebels to desist. Connett expressed doubt that such an attempt could be successful at this stage and asked Reid to reconsider the proposal for establishing a military junta as a way of avoiding bloodshed.

Connett now returned to the embassy and again called Crockett at the Operations Center. He informed Crockett of his conversation with Reid, and of the prospect that General Montás Guerrero might assume power temporarily, pending negotiations to form a junta. He also told Crockett that Manuel Fernández Mármol—a PRD leader who had participated the day before in the brief takeover of the Radio Santo Domingo station had just called the embassy, claiming that Reid was willing to turn his office over to a PRD group but that PRD leaders would accept power from Reid only in the presence of a U.S. representative. Connett was dubious of the truthfulness of Fernández's story (Reid had told Connett nothing of the sort) but he was not sure that it was false.[7] Crockett told Connett to "steer completely clear of anything like this," stating that under no circumstances should the embassy become involved in such a scheme, which might tie the U.S. government to an impermanent and not necessarily advantageous formula. The two agreed that Fernández Mármol and his colleagues of the PRD left wing were probably trying to use the embassy to achieve a fait accompli, and that the embassy should not let itself be used in this way.

Washington was by now receiving a few reports through CIA channels about the participation of known extreme leftists among the pro-Bosch groups in downtown Santo Domingo early in the morning; these reports, as well as previous exchanges with the embassy, bore on the State Department's first formal instruction to Chargé Connett. In a cable drafted and sent at mid-morning by Deputy Assistant Secretary Sayre, apparently after consultations by Sayre with Undersecretary Mann and perhaps by the latter with the president, the department told Connett that it assumed he was in contact with leaders of the Dominican Armed Forces, and that he was urging them to unite to form some type of provisional government which could restore order and prevent a possible Communist takeover. Underlying its longstanding preoccupation, the department expressed its concern about the reports of extreme leftist participation in the pro-Bosch movement. The department also specifically invited Connett to report immediately any change in the situation which might put American lives in jeopardy.

The basic approach of the U.S. government, which ultimately led to armed intervention on Wednesday afternoon, was thus already set in this Sunday morning message. Concern about a possible Communist takeover, anxiety about American lives, and support for the formation of a military junta were the guidelines; no active involvement to promote compromise among the contending Dominican factions was authorized.

What no one in Washington realized, as these instructions were being drafted, was that the situation in Santo Domingo was already being transformed, because of quick action by Bosch's supporters and virtual inaction by his opponents. As would happen several times during the next few days, events in Santo Domingo moved so quickly that Washington's position was outdated before it could be applied.

During the first hours of Sunday, April 25, most of the participants in the Dominican crisis moved cautiously. Reid Cabral was hesitant, unable to sustain himself but unenthusiastic about turning power over to General Montés Guerrero. General Wessin, General De Los Santos, and Commodore Rivera were standing by, unwilling to help Reid but unsure what the alternatives would be. Reformista leaders were contacting various friends in the military to urge agreement on a junta, but the pro-Reformista officers had not made this coup, were not sure who had, and were waiting to see what would transpire. MPD partisans were wary, suspecting that the coup might be a U.S.-engineered ploy. The American embassy, too, was waiting, unwilling to try to rescue Reid in such dire circumstances but not anxious to become involved in promoting any specific alternatives. (It should be added, though, that the American intelligence officers began from the outset of the crisis to file a stream of reports on what Dominican Communists were doing, and that the embassy's defense attachés stepped up their contacts with Dominican military officers and began early to explore the possibility of a military junta arrangement.)

The only forces acting decisively were the pro-Bosch plotters and some of the extreme leftists supporting Bosch's return. Already on Saturday night, as has been noted earlier, supporters of the pro-Bosch cadre—including soldiers from the two Army camps and ex-soldiers connected with the plot (who obtained arms at the 27th of February camp)—had taken up positions within the city. On Sunday morning, PRD activists began to mobilize public opinion. While Reid Cabral was still in the Palace looking for support, pro-Bosch forces took over Radio Santo Domingo again, declared that Reid Cabral had fallen, and called on the public to gather at the National Palace. Thousands of residents of downtown Santo Domingo began to swarm around the Palace, cheering for Bosch. Thousands more heeded a broadcast appeal to gather at the Duarte Bridge to prevent any attempt by General Wessin's forces to enter the city from San Isidro.

A few minutes later, while General Montás was maneuvering to establish a junta and as representatives sent by Generals Wessin and De Los Santos were arriving at the Palace ready to negotiate, the pro-Bosch plotters acted decisively. A commission of officers led by Colonel Caamaño Deñó, Lieutenant Colonel Gutiérrez, and Lieutenant Colonel Vinicio Fernández Pérez entered the Palace, arrested Reid and Cáceres, and affirmed their intent to restore Bosch to the presidency. Taking custody of Reid and his aides, Colonel Caamaño declared, as reported by both Santo Domingo morning newspapers the next day: "Our fundamental purpose is only and exclusively to replace what was taken from the people on September 25, 1963; that is, the return to the Presidency of the Republic of Professor Juan Bosch . . . The return of Bosch will be effected as soon as possible, as soon as order is re-established."[8]

Radio Santo Domingo announced before noon that Dr. Molina Ureña, the highest-ranking member of the 1963 Bosch government then on Dominican soil, would be sworn in as "Provisional Constitutional President," pending Bosch's imminent return. Minutes later, the radio broadcast a statement by the Army, Air Force, and National Police commanders of the country's northern region, based at Santiago, who declared their decision to "support the popular call, aligning themselves with the military movement headed in Santo Domingo."[9] Swept away by and in turn contributing to a mood of exuberant enthusiasm, Radio Santo Domingo announcers told excitedly of Bosch's return and called on specific individuals to come to the Palace to participate in the work of state. The CIA reported that Bosch and Molina Ureña had just talked by telephone, that Bosch had told Molina he would return immediately, and that meanwhile Molina should be sworn in as provisional executive. Bosch, in San Juan, began to pack his suitcase.[10]

In Santo Domingo, Bosch's supporters felt victory near. Pro-Bosch leaders—the cadres of conspirators, military and civilian; many others who had been plotting to establish a junta to hold elections but could support the PRD's immediate return; and some (including various Communists) who had participated in neither conspiracy—began attempting to gather up the reins of power in the National Palace. An embassy political officer who talked with PRD leaders found them joyous and extremely confident; he reported they had indicated their hope that the United States would quickly extend economic assistance to the reinstalled Bosch government. A plane was reportedly being readied to fly a PRD commission over to San Juan to escort Bosch back.

In the embassy, Chargé Connett called the Operations Center to report that the pro-Bosch movement now definitely controlled the Palace and Radio Santo Domingo and that the anti-Bosch military groups were confused and divided. According to State Department records, Connett at this time recommended that the U.S. not try to prevent Bosch's return.[11]

III

The apparent takeover by pro-Bosch supporters in Santo Domingo now activated some of the elements which heretofore had been almost idle. Representatives of several moderate and rightist parties, encouraged by the embassy to express their views, became alarmed at the prospect of Bosch's imminent return and called upon U.S. officials to help establish an anti-

Communist interim regime. More important, many military opponents of Reid, who had favored his overthrow and assumed that a military junta would be established to succeed him, were shocked to hear of the rebels' determination to bring back Juan Bosch. The officers sent to the Palace by the service chiefs to discuss establishing a junta, for instance, learned only after they had arrived that the pro-Bosch group was determined not to establish a junta but rather to restore "constitutionality without elections" under Bosch, and that they were actually about to install Molina Ureña as Provisional President. Some officers left immediately, bitter about being misled. Others stayed, hoping to parley. Reformista representatives who arrived at the Palace to bargain found that some of their erstwhile supporters in the Armed Forces, impressed by the clamoring crowds around the Palace, were now convinced that public opinion demanded Bosch's return and that they could not oppose him. Reformista vice-president Lora sped to San Isidro to confer with Generals Wessin and De Los Santos and other military figures; other Reformista leaders appealed to the embassy for help.

Faced now with what they believed to be an immediate threat that Juan Bosch might actually return, General Wessin and General De Los Santos finally began to act. Their earlier appointed representatives having made no progress in talks at the Palace, the two generals told Molina Ureña and others by telephone that they demanded prompt agreement on a provisional junta. Discussions about forming a junta resumed; the Air Force and CEFA delegates, Colonel Pedro Benoit and Colonel Medrano Ubiera, apparently insisted on a junta in which they would participate together with Colonel Emilio Fernández Mota of the Army rebels. Soon four P-51's appeared in the air over the Palace to lend authority to the Air Force–CEFA demand. When the talks continued for half an hour more without result, General De Los Santos and his colleagues—fearing that any further delay would permit Molina Ureña to be sworn in and might facilitate Bosch's return—authorized the planes to strafe the National Palace and the 27th of February camp. The Navy soon contributed with several shellings of the Palace from the sea.

The strafing of the Palace, an escalation of violence unprecedented in Dominican history, gravely worsened the 1965 crisis.[12] The prolonged meetings in the Palace among various military and civilian figures now broke up in bitterness. Those who opposed Bosch's return left the Palace, several of them not knowing exactly where to turn.[13] Those who favored Bosch's return stayed, although many of the military officers who had cast their lot with the pro-Bosch movement began to feel uneasy as their Army and Air Force colleagues departed, leaving them to deal with a number of civilians they did not know or trust, including some known as extreme leftists.

In each group in the Palace on Sunday, particularly among the military officers, there were many who might have reached a compromise under more conducive circumstances. But now, literally under fire, they were forced apart. Colonel Benoit and his colleagues returned to San Isidro, while Colonel Fernández Mota and others from the pro-Bosch group swore Molina Ureña in as Provisional President. The lines of division widened.

How the decision to strafe the Palace was taken, and exactly what role, if any, was played by U.S. officials is not entirely clear. General Wessin himself has testified that all units of the Dominican Armed Forces except his own were ready on Sunday to accept the victory of the pro-Bosch movement. Wessin had led the 1963 coup, however, and he stood to lose a great deal from Bosch's return; he refused to capitulate. According to Wessin's own account, he finally sent two officers to General De Los Santos; the two officers then forced De Los Santos at gunpoint to order the planes to strafe the rebel positions.[14]

It is quite possible, of course, that General Wessin exaggerates the importance of his own role in this matter. Several other Dominican participants in the 1965 crisis, notably Juan Bosch himself, have claimed that it was a U.S. military attaché who advised (or "ordered," as it is usually put) the Dominican Air Force to strafe the rebels.[15] There does not appear to be any evidence to substantiate this charge, which is denied by American officials. It is even conceivable that U.S. officials did not know that the strafing would occur until it began. But the U.S.

government's own records do reveal that the embassy knew in advance that Generals Wessin and De Los Santos (and later Commodore Rivera Caminero) were determined to employ force if needed to prevent Bosch's return, and that U.S. officials sympathized with the resolve of these Dominican leaders. American officers may not have actually suggested the strafing, but it is likely that the general U.S. approval of their course encouraged Generals Wessin and De Los Santos to undertake that specific tactic at this particular juncture.

Longstanding U.S. government attitudes toward Bosch doubtless affected the decision to favor the resolve of anti-Bosch Dominican military leaders to use force if necessary to prevent Bosch's immediate return, but several other factors probably also contributed. First, the realization that General Wessin would fight in any case to prevent Bosch's return raised the spectre of almost certain civil war should Bosch actually attempt to return. Second, the embassy was concerned about the breakdown of order in some parts of Santo Domingo. Although National Police units had worked effectively the day before, now they were becoming inactive, probably because they did not wish to oppose rebel army units. There were also reports that crowds had attacked the headquarters of three political parties involved in the 1963 coup and had also sacked a number of stores and other enterprises.[16] Third, and perhaps most important, the embassy —especially its CIA component—was already becoming concerned about what it considered significant Communist participation in the revolt. Little was known about the junior officers in the pro-Bosch group which had imprisoned General Rivera Cuesta, but CIA informers reported Saturday night that PSP leaders had spoken of Captain Peña Taveras as a "friend of the party" and that Peña did have a number of extreme leftist friends and connections. Sunday morning CIA officers reported the presence in the Palace of a number of Dominican Communists, student leaders especially, participating in the discussions there. Other intelligence reports noted that various known Communists were obtaining and distributing arms, setting up paramilitary positions, manning sound trucks, and helping to direct crowds in the streets. Extreme leftists seemed to be trying to implement the previously proclaimed PSP objective of returning Bosch to the presidency "through mass actions." Some in the embassy, and several Dominicans who called embassy officials, were already warning that Communist activists could claim and exert strong influence should Bosch return under these circumstances.

When reporting to Washington at mid-afternoon that Generals De Los Santos and Wessin would cooperate to prevent Bosch's return, Connett therefore told the department that the country team had reluctantly agreed among themselves to accept the De Los Santos–Wessin plan as the only course of action having any real possibility of preventing Bosch's return and containing the growing disorders and mob violence. All members of the country team felt strongly, according to Connett, that it would be against U.S. interests for Bosch to return to the Dominican Republic and resume power at this time, especially in view of the extremist participation in the movement and the announced Communist advocacy of Bosch's return. Acknowledging that the Wessin–De Los Santos plan to oppose Bosch's return might cause bloodshed, Connett observed that he and his colleagues believed this risk should be taken. The embassy would take every opportunity to minimize bloodshed by encouraging unity among the Dominican Armed Forces.

Connett added that Wessin and De Los Santos, as well as Navy Chief Rivera Caminero, had each inquired what U.S. support they could expect if such support proved to be needed. Connett said that although the attachés had stressed to all three the strong U.S. feeling that everything possible should be done to prevent a Communist takeover in the country and to maintain public order, they had not encouraged the Dominican chiefs to expect U.S. military support, even a show of force, for the embassy felt that the now-unifying Dominican Armed Forces would prevail soon without such assistance. Specifically noting the possibility of utilizing the U.S. naval units already enroute to the vicinity of the Dominican Republic, however, Connett explicitly reserved his position on whether this question might have to be reconsidered later. But now a display of U.S. force would needlessly commit U.S. prestige at a late stage, when the favorable resolution of the crisis seemed probable anyway within twenty-four hours.

Early on April 25, U.S. officials had chosen not to try to sustain the Reid regime nor to support the proposed return of Bosch but rather to favor the establishment by Dominican military leaders of a provisional junta. It was assumed that the Dominican military officials could easily agree on a junta and that this formula would generally be accepted without a struggle, thereby quickly resolving the crisis caused by Reid's fall without directly involving the U.S. government. Rather than participate actively in forming a junta, U.S. officials stood apart, not wishing to act overtly or to commit American prestige to any possibly impermanent formula.

When Bosch supporters took over Radio Santo Domingo and the National Palace and indicated their serious intent to restore Bosch to the presidency at once, the situation changed, as anti-Bosch elements reacted to the possibility of Bosch's imminent return. Because partisans of Bosch and anti-Bosch Dominican military leaders failed to agree, the embassy felt itself forced to take a stand. Predisposed not to favor Bosch's return, concerned about leftist elements allied with the pro-Bosch movement, and still thinking that a military junta could be imposed easily, the embassy approved of the Dominican military's resolve to use force if necessary to prevent Bosch's return. No attempt was made by U.S. officials to interfere politically to the extent necessary to promote a possible compromise among the Dominican factions. Rather than involve itself deeply in the Dominican political crisis, the embassy simply chose sides, believing that no direct American participation in the struggle need thereby result.

Having chosen sides without expecting to participate, U.S. officials soon found themselves very deeply involved as the crisis escalated. In the next few days, American participation in the crisis was to go from encouraging the Dominican military, to advising them, to furnishing them communications equipment, then to landing five hundred Marines; finally to massive military intervention—American actions following almost ineluctably as the Dominican situation changed while the operating assumptions of U.S. policy remained the same.

The Air Force strafing on Sunday afternoon—added to and exacerbating the effects of the excited radio broadcasts, the appeals and activities of leftist extremists, and the distribution of arms to irregular forces—had consequences much more profound than were realized at first. It was obvious at once that the day's events had driven the opposed military factions farther apart, especially after some rebels reacted to the strafing by seizing members of a few of the pilots' families and displaying them on Radio Santo Domingo Television as hostages to prevent renewed air attacks. Public statements on Sunday evening by Bosch in Puerto Rico and by anti-Bosch military leaders in Santo Domingo revealed the extent of the division as well as the efforts of each side to consolidate its support in the Army and to win over waverers. Bosch, in a brief talk taped in San Juan and broadcast repeatedly Sunday night over Radio Santo Domingo, praised the rebel officers, declaring that they would be "known in history as soldiers of the people, and military men of liberty"; he promised to return "when and how the people demand, whenever the heroic military men who have launched this struggle say."[17] While Bosch was praising his Army supporters, anti-Bosch military leaders were literally bombarding them with leaflets urging them to abandon or take prisoner "your superiors who want to hand over the country to Moscow."[18] The split within the Dominican Armed Forces was fast widening.

What was not immediately apparent was that a change was already occurring in the nature of the crisis and in the scope of its participants. In the morning, the essential division had been between a minority of military officers favoring Bosch's return and a majority caught off guard but generally favoring the establishment of some sort of junta. A simple coup d'état was being attempted; the issue was who would take power and

The Decision to Intervene / 81

under what terms. There were relatively few participants in the struggle, and most of them were in the National Palace.

By nightfall, however, many of Santo Domingo's residents were entering the fray as a result of the day's events. Whatever the political, social, and psychological reasons, thousands of Dominicans—armed and unarmed, students and laborers, urban poor and middle class, and with varying motives and loyalties—now actively joined the pro-Bosch movement and showed themselves willing to fight against the Dominican Armed Forces. General Wessin, rather than the ousted Reid, quickly became the focal point of popular opposition. What had begun as a coup was rapidly turning into an incipient civil war.[19]

During Sunday afternoon, officials in Washington were paying increasing attention to the Dominican situation. Undersecretary Mann spent much of the day in the Operations Center, beginning to take on the key responsibility for directing the U.S. government's response to the crisis. Secretary Rusk stopped by the Center at mid-afternoon. The Secretary, like other top officials, knew little specifically about the Dominican Republic but had long thought of it as a potential "second Cuba"; his questions to those in the Operations Center reportedly focused on the strength of Communist elements trying to take over in Santo Domingo.

Ambassador Bennett, back from Georgia, arrived at the Operations Center at about 4:30 P.M. At the end of the afternoon, Defense Secretary Robert McNamara was also briefed. Pieces of specific intelligence about alleged Communist activities were discussed during the course of the day. Officials in Washington agreed that the efforts of Communist activists deserved careful watching, but they expected that the Dominican Armed Forces would soon establish a junta and preclude any chances for Communist gain.

Washington's relative calm about the Dominican crisis was based on reports from the embassy. As the political impasse deteriorated into civil-military strife on Sunday evening, the embassy did not sense the urgency of the crisis or the extent to which it was changing. Connett called the State Department at 8:45 P.M. to report that the shooting had died down, that the prospects for negotiating the establishment of a junta had improved, and that antirebel military leaders were drawing to gether after some indecision.

The embassy continued to depend upon the anti-Bosch leaders of the Dominican Armed Forces to establish a government, neglecting possible opportunities for exerting American influence to promote compromise. When Manuel Fernández Mármol and soon thereafter four leading PRD moderates came to the embassy that evening to ask that the U.S. try to prevent renewed air attacks, the embassy declined to do so.[20] The political officer with whom the PRD leaders spoke told them instead of the embassy's concern that a situation favorable to the Communists was being created by the failure to resolve the crisis. He strenuously urged the PRD leaders to persuade the rebel military leaders to negotiate in good faith and without preconditions with the "legitimate military hierarchy" (in the embassy officer's phrase), losing his temper in the process, according to the Dominicans present. No effort was made to discuss any possible political solution with these PRD leaders, at least one of whom concluded from the meeting that the U.S. government had decided not to allow the PRD to regain power and that further struggle was therefore useless.

The embassy's summary of the situation on Sunday night shows that the changed nature of the crisis was not yet fully perceived. The embassy restated the two options it had earlier outlined—accepting either Bosch's forcible return at the call of the PRD and extremists, or forcible action by strongly anti-Bosch military leaders to prevent Bosch's return and to establish a junta—and repeated its preference for the junta solution. Reiterating that it believed Bosch's return under the existing circumstances would be "most unfortunate," the embassy reported that it was "gratified" by signs that the Dominican military was stiffening and pulling itself together. General Wessin had informed U.S. officials that he now planned to have his forces cross the Duarte Bridge and enter the city early in the morning, and the embassy reported there were indications that the rebels were uncertain of their ability to keep Wessin's tanks out of the city. The embassy now thought General Wessin's move might resolve the crisis. It expressed the hope that no commitment of U.S. prestige would be necessary to prevent Bosch's return, in view of the exiled leader's obvious popularity and the fact that he had been the Dominican Republic's constitutional president.

During the evening, however, the ineffectiveness of the Dominican military establishment's efforts to resolve the crisis made itself apparent. Commodore Rivera Caminero of the Navy, now evidently convinced that the pro-Bosch movement would succeed, went to the Palace to put his forces at the disposition of the Molina Ureña regime. Although the U.S. naval attaché was soon able to persuade Rivera and his colleagues to reverse their position, the incident revealed the weakness of the anti-Bosch position; the embassy concluded that the chances for forming a military junta under pressure from San Isidro alone were now very slim. By Monday morning, April 26, the embassy reported that probably nothing short of major U.S. involvement could prevent Bosch's return.

By dawn on April 26, Generals Wessin and De Los Santos had already asked for U.S. troops. The embassy opposed this course, and told the Dominican generals not to expect U.S. forces to land, for it recognized that armed intervention under these circumstances would cast the U.S. government in the role of an interventionist power against a popular revolution of democratic elements overthrowing an unpopular, unconstitutional regime. Although the embassy believed that Communists were deeply involved in the rebel movement, it did not believe the U.S. could effectively argue, as a reason for armed intervention, that the pro-Bosch movement was Communist-controlled. But, Connett reported, there was a serious threat of a Communist takeover under these circumstances, and little time in which to act.

What the embassy sought, as "the only effective alternative we see," was authorization to undertake a strong diplomatic initiative designed to prevent the return of Bosch through the formation of a military junta pledged to hold elections in September. Connett now asked permission to approach Molina Ureña and his aides in order to make clear to them serious American concern about Communist influence in the rebel movement and about the state of public order, and to register the embassy's strong conviction that the quick establishment of a military junta to hold elections in September would be in the best interests of the Dominican Republic. Such an effort at direct embassy involvement to resolve the crisis might well have to be backed up later by a U.S. show of force, Connett noted, but a decision on whether to employ a show of force could be held in abeyance pending the results of the proposed talks.

Rather than approve the embassy's requests, officials in Washington instructed Connett to concentrate his efforts instead on obtaining a cease-fire, which could, it was hoped, be used to facilitate negotiations among Dominicans from which a provisional junta might emerge. It was in this connection that Washington instructed the embassy to begin the process of evacuating American citizens. The department told Connett to inform both sides in Santo Domingo that the U.S. government had received requests from American citizens wishing to be evacuated, and that the U.S. requested an immediate cease-fire to permit a safe and orderly evacuation. Officials in Washington did not want the embassy to employ direct pressures, not even the "strong diplomatic initiative" Connett had suggested, to promote the establishment of a junta, nor to participate directly in negotiations to form one, but merely to work for a cease-fire, without political preconditions.

It has been impossible to determine what different views were expressed on this point in Washington or to ascertain exactly why Washington rejected the embassy's request, but the general reluctance to become too involved again in the details of Dominican politics was probably most influential. Another factor, undoubtedly, was the desire to have Ambassador Bennett resume personal charge of the embassy before authorizing any possible diplomatic initiative. Bennett had met at noon on Monday with

President Johnson, who reportedly instructed him to return to the Dominican Republic as soon as possible and to work there for an immediate cease-fire and the establishment of a junta. The president, reinforcing the approach toward the Dominican Republic already built in at all levels of the U.S. government, is also said to have emphasized strongly the unacceptability of "another Cuba in this Hemisphere."[21] The president's instructions made absolutely clear his own primary concern, which inevitably shaped the U.S. government's approach in coming days. (It is not clear exactly how early in the crisis President Johnson's own personal concern on this score became a specific influence on the evolving crisis, but several sources suggest the president expressed this view to Undersecretary Mann on Sunday.) But the president reportedly was not yet very seriously disturbed about actually having to face the possibility of "another Cuba" in the Dominican Republic. There was as yet no crisis atmosphere in the White House; the president spent most of the day working on matters unrelated to the Dominican crisis.[22]

By the time on Monday that the embassy began pressing its efforts to promote a cease-fire, the Dominican situation made a fully effective cease-fire probably impossible of immediate achievement. On four separate occasions during the course of the day, embassy pressures caused the anti-Bosch military forces to halt their attacks, but each time they quickly resumed the fighting, as the rebel groups continued to resist. Rebel forces continued to distribute arms and to establish command posts, and attacks on policemen seemed to be increasing. More than thirty people were killed and about two hundred wounded as a result of Monday's fighting, according to Dominican press reports the next day.[23]

When the anti-Bosch forces opened up a radio station at about 11:30 A.M. (broadcasting as the "Voice of the Dominican Armed Forces"), a vigorous battle of the airwaves began between the competing stations, each increasingly strident.[24] The atmosphere was such that probably no one could have immediately stopped the violence; Molina Ureña and the others in the Palace simply could not control what was occurring in the streets, or even on the radio stations championing their cause.

But when Colonel Hernando Ramírez several times on Monday asked for a cease-fire and then was unable to produce Molina Ureña or other civilian negotiators or to stop various rebel tactics the anti-Bosch military leaders considered objectionable, both Dominican military leaders and U.S. attachés took this less as an indication of increasing disorder than as a possible reflection on Hernando's trustworthiness. They wondered whether Hernando and his colleagues were seeking these pauses mainly to regroup their own forces and they determined not to permit the rebels to gain strength in this fashion.

The attachés' suspicion that the rebels were asking for cease-fires in bad faith was only one aspect of the embassy's deepening distrust of the pro-Bosch group. The embassy had enjoyed little contact before April 24 with civilians in the PRD committed to Bosch's return, and little knowledge of, much less contact with, the pro-Bosch military officers. Aligned against the return of Bosch from the first hours of the crisis, embassy officers now found themselves increasingly cut off from the group in the Palace and willing, perhaps even eager, to believe the worst about it. Officials in Washington, too—having chosen to favor the anti-Bosch military forces partly out of fear that the pro-Bosch movement might have leftist connections—were asking the embassy to report any evidence of such ties, thus reinforcing the embassy's focus on the possibility that Communists might gain power. By Monday the emphasis on the role of Communists was coming to dominate the embassy's reporting, even in cases when the substance of the specific report was negative on this very point. Upon receiving information from a Dominican security officer that the Dominican Armed Forces had intercepted communications between the Palace and Castro Cuba, for instance, the embassy told Washington that its intelligence officers considered the source reliable and believed the Dominican report might be correct, even though it was conceded that U.S. officials had no information to confirm the report (and none was ever found). Responding to Washington's expressed interest, the embassy reacted to Molina Ureña's appointment of Alfredo Conde Pausas and Máximo Lovatón Pittaluga as Attorney General and Minister of Foreign Affairs respectively by reporting that Conde Pausas had two sons and two nephews in the PSP but was not known himself to be a party member and that Lovatón was not known to have Communist ties. Such appraisals neglected the general reputation of these political warhorses by concentrating on one trait they did not possess—known personal Communist connections. And CIA officers were sending to Washington a stream of reports on the activities of Dominican Communists; well over half the station's dispatches during the week reportedly dealt with what known Communists were doing.[25]

Increasingly distrustful of the movement they had rejected, U.S. officials were also disposed to believe and to report atrocity stories which turned out to have little or no foundation in fact, like the never-confirmed report sent to Washington on Monday evening that a policeman's head had been cut off and paraded through the streets on a pike. A self-reinforcing cycle of mutual distrust between the embassy and the pro-Bosch movement had already set in.

v

By Monday night both the embassy and U.S. officials in Washington realized that a cease-fire between the increasingly bitter Dominican factions would not easily be achieved and that the fighting, if not soon ended, might become even more violent. The U.S. government's concern mounted and precautionary steps were taken. The embassy intensified its efforts to implement procedures for evacuating American citizens from Santo Domingo, although the hour set for beginning the evacuation was postponed when a Peña Gómez radio announcement made some embassy officials think the rebels were about to give up. Before midnight, meanwhile, the Defense Department alerted the Caribbean Ready Amphibious Squadron (1,790 men) that it might be deployed in the Dominican Republic. The 82nd Airborne Division at Fort Bragg was unofficially warned at 10:00

P.M. and then, at midnight, formally alerted to ready one brigade (2,253 men) for possible action.[26] Related Tactical Air Units and a Marine Fighter Squadron at Roosevelt Roads were also notified.

By 4:00 A.M. on Tuesday, Major General Robert York, Commander of the 82nd Division, was briefing his subordinates (on the basis of a standing contingency plan) about the mission they might be required to perform: to secure the San Isidro Air Force Base, to take the highway leading from the base to the Ozama River, and then to establish positions on the Duarte Bridge leading to Santo Domingo. The 82nd Division encountered some minor problems in readying for action, owing to the fact that some updating of its plan had not yet been accomplished to reflect new tables of organization and consequent changes in troop lists. Some time was lost, therefore, in notifying support units, but the necessary corrections were quickly made. Within hours—long before it was called upon to act—the 82nd Division was ready to land at Santo Domingo.

Although Washington officials, realizing the depth of the Dominican crisis more fully, were now willing to authorize somewhat more active involvement by the embassy in attempting to resolve the crisis, embassy officers had become skeptical that negotiations could succeed. Neither Dominican faction seemed willing to talk except on its own terms, and anti-Bosch military leaders were increasingly confident that they could soon put down the revolt. In the first hours of Tuesday, April 27, Colonel Heywood informed Connett that Dominican Air Force and Navy leaders had decided to issue an early morning ultimatum to Molina Ureña's regime and then to strafe various parts of the city to compel agreement. After a series of air attacks on the Palace, the bridge area, and sections of downtown Santo Domingo, Air Force and CEFA troops and tanks would enter the city, according to the Dominican plan.

Apparently convinced that mere diplomatic pressures, even if actively exerted by the United States, would not now succeed in forcing negotiations, the embassy seems to have approved of the Dominican military leaders' proposal. The main embassy concern—expressed by a military attaché over an open radio line being monitored by pro-Bosch sympathizers—was that the projected military measures should not threaten the areas to be used for the planned evacuation of U.S. citizens nor interfere with the return of Ambassador Bennett, who had by now reached Ramey Air Force Base in Puerto Rico and was expected to fly over to Santo Domingo early in the morning.

The embassy's skepticism about the feasibility of negotiations without a prior demonstration of force by the anti-Bosch military may well have led it to miss several opportunities to promote a peaceful settlement of the Dominican crisis on Tuesday, April 27. In fact, the embassy's knowledge and apparent approval of the military plan to attack the city exacerbated the state of mutual suspicion already existing between pro-Bosch leaders and the embassy and thus made less likely a negotiated solution. Having been informed by rebel monitors of the attachés' radio contacts and discussions with Air Force and Navy officials, Colonel Hernando Ramírez called Connett at the embassy at about 5:00 A.M. Three times in the course of the call Hernando inquired whether the embassy knew of an alleged Air Force–Navy plan to attack and strafe the city, and each time Connett denied knowledge of any such plan. For Hernando and his colleagues, the embassy's obvious deceit and apparent complicity with the anti-Bosch leaders underscored their doubts about the good faith of the embassy's call for negotiations.

Within a few hours, in turn, the entry of a band of armed and rowdy rebels into the Hotel Embajador, where hundreds of Americans were gathered for evacuation, caused some embassy officials to doubt the sincerity of the pro-Bosch group's expressed commitment to guarantee American lives and property. Reports from the hotel were unclear but it appeared that rebel radio announcers had directed people to go to the hotel, and that some shooting had subsequently occurred there; embassy officials were indignant. Distrust between the embassy and the pro-Bosch movement deepened once more.[27]

Despite their growing distrust of the embassy, or perhaps

partly because of their now confirmed feeling that the embassy might back the planned Air Force attack and therefore assure both a rebel defeat and further bloodshed, Colonel Hernando Ramírez, Captain Peña Taveras, and several of their military colleagues went to the military attachés' section of the embassy on Tuesday morning to seek U.S. assistance in arranging negotiations. The embassy at once successfully exerted its influence to get the Air Force attack postponed, but no effective effort was made to use the time gained thereby actually to achieve negotiations. Because telephone communications were cut, the attachés did offer to use their radio facilities to communicate Hernando's desire to talk to Navy and Air Force leaders; soon an embassy political officer in the Palace put Molina Ureña in touch with the attachés as well. For two hours messages went back and forth about starting discussions, but Molina Ureña and the anti-Bosch military leaders deadlocked over the location of the proposed unconditional negotiations. Molina Ureña invited the military leaders to the National Palace; they countered by offering him safe conduct to board the Navy's yacht, the *Mella*. Apparently willing to compromise, Molina Ureña suggested the two sides meet at a neutral site, such as the Colombian embassy; but the military leaders refused. Throughout the exchange, the attachés faithfully communicated to each side the other's position, without exerting pressure on either side to accede to the other or even to accept a neutral site. A political officer urged Connett to end the impasse by inviting both sides to send representatives to the embassy's residence, but Connett declined the suggestion. Once again, possible opportunities to use American influence to resolve the crisis politically were missed.

Finally, Molina Ureña even offered to send Espaillat Nanita and Colonel Caamaño to the *Mella*. By this time, however, the anti-Bosch military leaders felt sure that they had the rebels on the run and should quickly press their advantage to resolve the situation by force. Anti-Bosch military leaders left a meeting with the U.S. naval attaché to begin again their planned attack upon the city.

The anti-Bosch military forces now seemed at last to be gaining the upper hand. In the western part of the city, General Montás Guerrero had finally decided to commit himself and his forces to action against the rebels; his units began moving toward Santo Domingo from San Cristóbal. To the east, General Wessin's tanks and armored personnel carriers, followed by an infantry column, were approaching the Duarte Bridge, where rebel resistance was due to be broken up by a concerted strafing. A dramatic shift in the situation appeared to be occurring, as the anti-Bosch forces seemed ready to prevail.

It was at this juncture both that the evacuation of U.S. citizens began and that Ambassador Bennett finally was able to return to the U.S. embassy, having been landed first at Santo Domingo's International Airport, then helicoptered to the *Boxer* and from there to Haina, west of Santo Domingo. When Ambassador Bennett reached the embassy, Captain Peña Taveras and some of his colleagues were back again, seeking the embassy's help in getting the strafing stopped and arranging negotiations. To this group and to PRD Secretary General Antonio Martínez Francisco, whom he called immediately, Bennett appealed for immediate cooperation to end what he regarded as "senseless slaughter." Bennett said he would talk in the same vein to leaders of the Dominican Armed Forces, but he emphasized to the pro-Bosch group that predominant force in the conflict was clearly on the other side and that they should capitulate.

While Bennett awaited the results of his first efforts to end the strife, he asked repeatedly that U.S. ships move in closer to shore, purportedly to make it clear to all who cared to look that U.S. carriers were not being used by the Dominican planes strafing the city, but also undoubtedly to make the U.S. presence more obvious.[28] Soon a call came in to the embassy from Martínez Francisco, who said that he was talking with Bosch by telephone and wished the embassy to send a representative over to speak directly with Bosch. Bosch has said subsequently that he wished at this time to offer to resign as "constitutional president" in favor of Molina Ureña, and it is entirely possible that he intended to make some such proposal to the U.S. embassy. But Bennett, believing the anti-Bosch forces close to victory anyway and wary of any involvement with Bosch, declined to send anyone, asking Martínez Francisco instead to convey to Bosch the embassy's view that Bosch could show his patriotism and responsibility by asking his supporters to put down their arms.

A fierce battle raged in Santo Domingo in the early afternoon. Following almost two hours of continuous strafing and machine-gunning of the city by seven to ten Air Force planes and an hour's bombardment from Navy ships, General Wessin's tanks and troops crossed the Duarte Bridge at about 2:00 P.M. By 4:00 P.M. they had advanced, against stiff resistance put up by rebel units from the Army and by armed civilians, up to the corner of Calle París and Calle José Martí, several blocks into the city from the bridgehead. Hundreds of people—some soldiers, mostly civilians—were killed or wounded in the heavy fighting around the bridge, the bloodiest single battle in Dominican history.

Their forces demoralized by the continued strafings and by Wessin's successful entrance into the city, rebel military leaders were now ready to negotiate on almost any terms. They returned to the embassy once more at mid-afternoon and met with the chief of the political section, who convinced them that Molina Ureña—still in the Palace—should be asked to join the discussion. Molina was sought in the Palace; he conceded that a compromise solution was absolutely necessary, and consented to go out to the embassy to seek help in arranging an end to the fighting. Accompanied by Colonel Hernando Ramírez, Colonel Caamaño Deñó (just that noon named Chief of Operations to replace the exhausted Hernando, who was soon to retire to a sickbed) and about fifteen others, Molina Ureña entered the embassy at about 4:00 P.M.

Details of the meeting which followed are remembered differently by various participants; some of the versions include elements of high drama. Some rebel participants claim Ambassador Bennett insulted them during this encounter; several charge that Bennett sought unjustly to tax the group with responsibility for activities—such as the incident at the Hotel Embajador and supposed atrocities—which they feel he exaggerated and for which they could not, in any case, fairly be blamed. Bennett himself recalls only having expressed his concern over such incidents and his belief that an end to the fighting was urgently needed. But it is clear even from Ambassador Bennett's own account that the ambassador declined Molina's request that Bennett accompany him, together with a representative of the Church and of the diplomatic corps, to begin negotiations with the anti-Bosch military leaders. Apparently convinced that the tide had turned and the revolt had already been put down, Ambassador Bennett let pass yet another possible chance for exerting U.S. influence to resolve the crisis.

The pro-Bosch group, their plea rejected at the embassy, left at about 5:00 P.M.; Ambassador Bennett observed that some of the group lingered, as if trying to avoid having to reenter the cruel world. Convinced that their movement had been crushed and that personal danger loomed, many gave up at this point. Some, including Molina Ureña, Espaillat Nanita, Martínez Francisco, Lovatón Pittaluga, and del Rosario, took asylum in the next few hours. Others who had not attended the embassy meeting but had learned of its outcome, like Antonio Guzmán and Salvador Jorge Blanco from Santiago, went back to their homes. Peña Gómez, whose radio announcement had started the week, now hid in the home of a friend and sought the assistance of a CIA officer, with whom he had previously been in contact, to arrange protection and safe conduct for himself. But the CIA officer, acting on instructions, declined to help, seeking instead to obtain testimony from Peña Gómez about the degree of Communist involvement on the rebel side. Relations between the embassy and the PRD leaders of the pro-Bosch movement were going from bad to worse as a result of such episodes, at the same time that the locus of power in the rebel movement itself appeared to the embassy to be moving, by default, to the left. With the retreat into hiding of many of the civilian non-

Communist rebels, the field of action was left largely to the military men—including Colonal Caamaño—who returned to the fray, and to the leftist extremists who kept up the struggle; the embassy knew much more about the latter group than about the former.

Bennett now conferred with Police Chief Hernán Despradel, who had been shaken by the events of the preceding days but felt somewhat buoyed by the apparent shift now occurring. Despradel predicted that the streets of Santo Domingo could be cleared of opposition that night. Having received confirmation that the forces under Wessin and Montás had each entered the city, Ambassador Bennett informed Washington that a mopping-up operation would probably soon be carried out; he acknowledged that some of it might be rough, but expected the anti-Bosch forces to prevail soon.

Washington's immediate concern at this point became to urge moderation on the presumably triumphant Dominican military leaders. Responding to Bennett's report of the situation, the State Department instructed him to take the earliest opportunity to urge the antirebel military leaders not to undertake reprisals or to commit atrocities.

The sense of crisis which had begun to gather in Washington now started to subside. A briefing paper prepared Tuesday afternoon by the State Department for the White House predicted that General Wessin would soon control Santo Domingo. At a news conference late Tuesday afternoon, President Johnson issued a formal statement deploring violence and disorder in the Dominican Republic, announcing the evacuation of those Americans who wished to leave, and expressing his hope that a peaceful settlement of internal problems would be found in Santo Domingo. But the president's mind was not primarily focused on the Dominican situation, nor were the interests of the press corps. Seven reporters asked questions about Vietnam, two queried the president about the India-Pakistan tensions, two asked about domestic affairs, and one elicited the president's views on disarmament—but not a single question concerned the Dominican Republic.[29]

Following his meeting with the press, President Johnson spent an apparently relaxed evening at a party with friends and high government colleagues who were bidding farewell to retiring CIA Director John McCone. The president and McCone, according to Charles Roberts's account, conferred briefly about the Dominican situation and agreed that "although the threat of 'another Castro' emerging . . . (there) would bear watching, U.S. intervention was not indicated."[30] Secretary Rusk, who attended the same party, recalls that the Dominican crisis seemed to have subsided by Tuesday evening; events in Vietnam were much more salient in his mind.

VI

The 1965 Dominican crisis might very well have ended with this result: many of the pro-Bosch forces in retreat and hiding, leftist extremists active but vulnerable, the Dominican Armed Forces reestablishing their authority, the U.S. embassy exerting its influence to prevent reprisals, and officials in Washington turning their attention back to other matters.

During the evening, however, the tide of events in Santo Domingo turned once more. General Montás's column entered Santo Domingo's outskirts on the west, but then failed to advance, probably because Montás was not sure which side was winning—communications were by now almost nonexistent—and partly because he did not trust General Wessin, who had helped oust him as Army Chief of Staff just two months before. To the east, on the Santo Domingo side of the Duarte Bridge over the Ozama, General Wessin's troops were pushed back from their farthest point of advance by the counterattack of rebel Army troops, led by Colonel Caamaño, Lieutenant Colonel Alvarez Holguín, Lieutenant Colonel Manuel R. Montes Arache, and others.[31] Reduced by defection and exhaustion, unused to opposition or even to action, and learning that their tanks were not very effective means to subdue a civilian population by now well-armed and aroused, Wessin's frightened troops were stopped. Wessin apparently ordered some of his tanks to withdraw back across the Ozama to San Isidro at nightfall, perhaps to protect them and allow his forces to regroup, or possibly because he still hoped to use his tank corps as a bargaining counter. Offshore, meanwhile, the U.S.S. *Boxer*—ready to depart for Puerto Rico with 294 evacuees aboard—was ordered to remain in the area just in case it might be needed.[32]

On Tuesday night and during the first hours after midnight, U.S. officials did not yet fully appreciate the extent of the Dominican Armed Forces' failure; it was thought that Wessin's forces would regroup during the night and reenter the city in the morning. The embassy's concern was increasingly focusing on the signs of Communist strength in the rebel movement. Ambassador Bennett reported Tuesday night that Radio Santo Domingo's broadcasts and telecasts had a "definite Castro flavor," and that known Communist groups, well-armed and organized, were moving rapidly to take advantage of the uncertain situation in downtown Santo Domingo. Given the evidence of increased extreme leftist activity, the ambassador was anxious on Tuesday night and early Wednesday to assure that nothing would interfere with the scheduled attempt by Dominican military units to reenter the city. Responding to a query from Washington, Bennett advised that no U.S. assistance should be offered to bring back from Puerto Rico the papal nuncio, Monseñor Emmanuele Clarizio, who sought transportation to Santo Domingo so that he could mediate and work to establish a cease-fire. In the early morning, having heard from General De Los Santos, Bennett moved to eliminate another possible obstacle to the Dominican military's attempt to control the city: the troubling lack of communications. He called Washington to urge that the U.S. immediately provide the Dominican forces with fifty walkie-talkie sets to facilitate communications during the mop-up maneuver.

The State Department's response to Ambassador Bennett's appeal for walkie-talkies illustrates the lag between events in Santo Domingo and Washington's perceptions of them; it also exemplifies the hesitant manner by which the U.S. government, rejecting overt actions at several junctures, was nevertheless drawn into massive military intervention. Although Bennett was by now saying that the essential fight that day would be mainly between Communists and non-Communists and that the latter needed the communications equipment, the department at first merely took note of the ambassador's request, pointing out to him that the United States had not interfered in the Dominican situation except verbally to promote unity and the restoration of order, and that the U.S. government wished to maintain this stance unless the outcome should actually be in doubt. Since the department at this time understood that the antirebel forces were expected to prevail, it at first declined to authorize delivery of the walkie-talkies.

Undersecretary Mann told Assistant Secretary Vaughn at about 11:00 A.M. that he had personally decided against sending in the requested equipment, although he added that it might be wise to send the walkie-talkies to the *Boxer* off the coast "just in case," but without letting the Dominicans know. Mann also approved, at this time, the return of the MAAG officers from Panama to Santo Domingo, but he emphasized that they were not to get involved in advising or helping the antirebel forces. If it looked as if there would be a Communist takeover, however, then "we would have to get into it," Mann pointed out.

Because it still seemed that the antirebel forces would prevail, Washington did not yet consider the Dominican situation critical, as Mann's decision on the walkie-talkies suggests. White House reporters were told during the morning that the president expected to leave Washington at about 2:00 P.M. on Thursday for a long weekend at the LBJ ranch.[33]

During the course of Wednesday, April 28, however, it became apparent in Santo Domingo that the capacity of the Dominican Armed Forces to restore order was very much in doubt. Late Tuesday night and in the early hours of Wednesday, Colonel Caamaño and others who had prevailed in the fighting at the Duarte Bridge—including Héctor Aristy, a civilian friend of Caamaño who was to play a leading role in the days and weeks following—had taken various steps to consolidate their hold on the city.[34] Caamaño went personally on Tuesday night to the offices of *Listín Diario* and telephoned the editor of *El Caribe* to emphasize to both newspapers that his forces controlled the city and that their morning editions should report this information.[35] Later that night, Caamaño, Aristy, and others took arms from the National Palace's arsenal and even some abandoned tanks from the Palace grounds and used these and other material to replenish their forces' supplies. On Wednesday morning, at about 9:00 A.M., Caamaño personally led a successful assault on an important police station next to the Palace of Justice in Ciudad Nueva, the heart of downtown Santo Domingo.

The antirebel forces, meanwhile, were unable to regain the momentum they had begun to build up the day before. Colonel Pedro Benoit, the CEFA representative in the Palace on Sunday, told two MAAG officials at San Isidro that the antirebel forces did not have enough personnel to maintain order in the city or to guarantee the lives and property of foreign nationals; Benoit appealed for U.S. assistance. The MAAG chief, reporting later to Ambassador Bennett, said the Dominican officers were discouraged, disorganized, and in disarray, and that their troops might not even be able to hold the bridgehead on the Santo Domingo side of the river, let alone advance into the city.

Both the embassy and officials in Washington thought one difficulty might be the lack of any coherent entity on the anti-Bosch side around which support could rally and to which rebel defectors could surrender; the embassy was instructed to urge the officers at San Isidro to establish a junta to resolve this problem. On Wednesday morning, however, General Imbert—never passive—informed the embassy that he and a group of men personally loyal to him had taken over the vacant National Palace, and that he now proposed to establish a five-man military junta, representing all the services, over which he would preside. The embassy immediately reported to Washington it was sympathetic to Imbert's plan. But soon came word over "Radio San Isidro," a new and more powerful radio station, that a junta under Colonel Benoit had already been named, and the Imbert proposal was hastily dropped.[36]

The establishment of the Benoit junta was not enough to

stem the tide, however. By noon, Ambassador Bennett felt the situation was becoming critical. He called Assistant Secretary Vaughn to ask him again for the walkie-talkies; Vaughn told the ambassador his request had been rejected in Washington. When Bennett protested that this was a great mistake, which might prove to be a turning point, Vaughn invited the ambassador to make his argument by cable. Bennett did so immediately, arguing that the communications equipment was the most serious lack of the Dominican Armed Forces in the existing situation. He stressed that denial of the requested equipment might actually cause the Dominican Armed Forces to lose the fight, both because the Dominican commanders needed better communications to organize their troops and because their morale would be further undermined by a negative U.S. response. Although he regretted that it was necessary to rely on a military solution for a political crisis, Bennett concluded, he believed the issue now was between "Castro-type elements" and their opponents. If the communications equipment were denied again, Bennett warned, the Dominican Armed Forces might fail and then he might be forced to ask for the landing of Marines to protect U.S. citizens "and possibly for other purposes." "Which," Bennett asked, "would Washington prefer?"

VII

Although the delivery of the walkie-talkies was eventually authorized—apparently by McGeorge Bundy and after at least one more telephone call on the subject from Bennett to Sayre—the equipment came too late to be effective. During the course of the afternoon it became increasingly clear that Dominican forces alone could not put down the revolt or restore order. Ambassador Bennett called Washington at about 2:00 P.M. to report that Police Chief Despradel, like Benoit, was saying he could no longer guarantee the lives of U.S. citizens in Santo Domingo. Heavy strafing runs were undertaken in the early afternoon, and Radio San Isidro kept proclaiming that the junta's final offensive—"Operation Clean-up"—was about to get under way. But Colonel Benoit, knowing better, telephoned the embassy at about 3:00 P.M. to ask that 1,200 U.S. Marines be landed "to help restore peace."

Ambassador Bennett's cabled report of Benoit's oral request for U.S. Marines observed that the junta's forces would certainly win if the situation were logical but he emphasized that the situation was not logical and that the outcome was still in doubt. Although he did not believe that landing U.S. forces was justified at this time, Ambassador Bennett suggested that Washington might wish to do some contingency planning in case troops were needed later. In the early afternoon, according to Tad Szulc's account, unarmed Marine "Pathfinders" from the *Boxer* landed at Haina to measure the beach there for possible amphibious landings.[37]

Upon receiving Bennett's cable in the White House at about 3:50 P.M., Bundy called Mann, who had not yet seen this dispatch. Mann said he would be opposed to sending in troops, or even just equipment, only to participate in a mopping-up operation, but that it would be an entirely different matter if the outcome were really in doubt. Bundy observed that the balance of force still appeared to be on the side of the junta, despite Benoit's request. Mann and Bundy agreed that they opposed the landing of Marines, but that the president should again be briefed about the Dominican situation. Bundy said he would do so at 4:15 P.M.

By this time on Wednesday afternoon, embassy and CIA reports were emphasizing not only that Colonel Caamaño's forces controlled the city and that General Wessin's troops had not moved in but also that, within the city, MPD and PSP activists were in high spirits and were moving fast to capitalize on the collapse of the military establishment. Having reported on the asylum of leading PRD civilians, and knowing little of the pro-Bosch military group still operating in the city, the embassy now focused even more attention on the activities of known Communists, who were seen as posing a threat to take over the rebel movement. Little was known about what was going on within the city, as the embassy admitted to Washington later in the day, but the worst was assumed.

At about 4:00 P.M., Colonel Benoit submitted to American

officials a formal written request (in English) for U.S. military support, the text of which the embassy immediately transmitted to Washington in its fourth "CRITIC" message of the week. This document emphasized that the "present revolutionary movement this junta represents is directed by Communists and is of authentic Communist stamp, as shown by the excesses committed against the population, mass assassinations, sacking of private property, and constant incitations to fight broadcast by Radio Havana." If the rebel movement were victorious, Benoit claimed, it would convert the Dominican Republic into "another Cuba." To prevent this from happening, Benoit asked the U.S. government to "lend us its unlimited and immediate military assistance."

Colonel Benoit's first written request, asking for U.S. military assistance to prevent "another Cuba" without even mentioning the need to protect American lives, was more than U.S. officials in Washington were yet willing to approve. This was reportedly conveyed to Ambassador Bennett at once.[38] By now convinced that the Dominican Armed Forces could not prevail without assistance, Ambassador Bennett sent another "CRITIC" message to Washington within an hour. This one said that the situation in Santo Domingo had deteriorated rapidly, and that the Police, far from being able to "mop up," were trying only to defend a few key installations. Bennett reported that the MAAG chief, just returned from San Isidro, said the officers there were dejected and emotional: several were weeping and General Belisario Peguero Guerrero—by now ensconced on the antirebel side was frantically urging retreat. Reiterating that Colonel Benoit had asked the MAAG chief for U.S. assistance to restore order, and referring to recent intelligence reports, Bennett reported the country team unanimously agreed that "now that we have a request from the military junta for assistance, (the) time has come to land the Marines." American lives, Bennett now added, were in danger. Marines could be used to establish a beachhead in the Hotel Embajador vicinity, where the evacuation center was established, and they could also take possession of the embassy grounds. "If Washington wished," Bennett suggested, they could be landed for the purpose of protecting the evacuation of American citizens; in any case, Bennett concluded, "I recommend immediate landing."

Almost immediately after filing this message, Ambassador Bennett asked the Commander of the Caribbean Ready Group—by now on five-minute alert—to send in helicopters to pick up a large group of evacuees at the Hotel Embajador and to augment the Marine Guard at the embassy by an armed platoon, steps which would bring Marines ashore immediately to reinforce the normal contingent.[39] As a result of this request, it appears that some U.S. troops were actually on their way in by helicopter when President Johnson at the White House received Bennett's "CRITIC" message calling for Marines immediately. The landing of additional American forces on Dominican soil had already begun, in effect, by the time President Johnson himself could consider whether the United States should intervene (although the president presumably could still have restricted these troops to an evacuation-related role at the hotel or to protection of the embassy building).

When the president and several of his key advisers—at the White House that afternoon reportedly to review the Vietnam situation—received Bennett's request just before 5:30 P.M., there was very little discussion before the request was authorized. President Johnson himself recalled a few days later that "on Wednesday afternoon, there was no longer any choice for the man who is your President."[40] Others present at the time have reported that "one or two spoke up and the general conclusion was that there was no real choice."[41]

After brief consultation with his aides present (including Rusk, Ball, McNamara, and Bundy) and a few quick telephone calls to other advisers (including Mann and reportedly including Senator Richard Russell of Georgia, Bennett's home state), President Johnson officially authorized the landing of five hundred Marines, with the proviso that they were not to fire unless fired upon.[42] Leaving his office for a previously scheduled meeting, the president instructed aides to call congressional leaders together for a briefing, to prepare a statement for him to announce the move to the nation and the world, and to notify Latin American ambassadors in Washington of the U.S. action.

By 6:00 P.M. on April 28, when President Johnson formally approved the landing of combat-ready U.S. Marines in Santo Domingo, unarmed Pathfinders, military police, and helicopter support units had landed at the polo field next to the Hotel Embajador and an armed platoon was already in the air. Captain James Dare, the Commander of the Caribbean Ready Group, was now told to land five hundred of the Marines aboard the *Boxer* if the ambassador so requested. After a three-minute conversation, according to Captain Dare's account, a helicopter landing operation by two rifle companies and the battalion headquarters was set in motion.[43]

Undersecretary Mann, meanwhile, was calling Ambassador Bennett from Washington to instruct him to obtain from Colonel Benoit a written statement for the record asking for U.S. military assistance to restore order and specifically mentioning the need to protect American lives.[44] By the time an embassy attaché could return from San Isidro with the requested statement, declaring that "American lives are in danger and conditions are of such disorder that it is impossible to provide adequate protection" and asking "temporary intervention to restore public order in this country," the Marines had been ashore for hours.

A new and complex phase of the Dominican crisis now began in Washington in which deciding what to say about events in Santo Domingo became almost as important as, and perhaps more controversial than, deciding what actions to take. From the moment the armed intervention was authorized, the question of whether and how to discuss the perceived Communist threat posed by the rebel movement in Santo Domingo was foremost. CIA Director William Raborn, sworn in Wednesday noon, reported to President Johnson before 7:00 P.M. that two of the prime leaders in the rebel forces were men with a long history of Communist associations; one, Manuel González y González, was a veteran of the Spanish Civil War. By 8:00 P.M. Raborn reportedly was telling congressional leaders about three Communist leaders and saying that the U.S. government was responding to a "Moscow-financed, Havana-directed plot to take over the Dominican Republic."[45] Accounts of the secret White House meeting differ, but Senators Russell Long and George Smathers later recalled that they were told "this was simply a matter of whether this country was going to stand aside and risk another Cuban-type Communist take-over" and that "the overwhelming consensus was that we wanted to be certain that the island of the Dominican Republic was not lost to Communists."[46]

When Dean Rusk, McGeorge Bundy, Richard Goodwin, and Bill Moyers sat down to draft a presidential announcement of the Marine landing, however, Bundy and Moyers reportedly argued that the president should not go beyond usable evidence about the Communist threat, and that he should confine his rationale for the use of force to the protection of American lives. When Rusk urged that the president's statement should express concern about the preservation of "free institutions" in the Dominican Republic, U.N. Ambassador Adlai Stevenson—just arrived from New York—is said to have joined Bundy, Goodwin, and Moyers in arguing, successfully, that not even such an elliptical reference to the supposed Communist threat should be made.[47]

When Ball, Mann, Vaughn, Sayre, Crockett, and Read conferred with Ambassador Bennett (via a secured telex system) about the proposed presidential announcement, therefore, the draft statement's emphasis was on the need to protect American lives; no mention was made of the fear of Communist takeover. Bennett endorsed the validity of the stated rationale, reporting —mistakenly, it turned out—that Americans being evacuated from the Hotel Embajador area had actually come under fire and that he had already authorized the Marines to shoot to protect them. But, Bennett recommended almost immediately, it *was* time for Washington to give serious thought to authorizing armed intervention which would "go beyond the mere protection of Americans and seek to establish order in this strife-ridden country." Arguing that all indications suggested that if the antirebel forces failed, then power would be assumed by groups "clearly identified with the Communist party," Bennett urged that "if the situation described comes to pass . . . we should intervene to prevent another Cuba from arising out of the present situation." Anticipating such a decision, Ambassador Bennett recommended that additional military units be dispatched to the area of the Dominican Republic, since the Caribbean Ready Group alone did not have sufficient forces to perform this kind of mission. Before 8:00 P.M., accordingly, the Second Brigade of the 82nd Airborne Division, consisting of two battalion combat teams plus supporting elements (2,276 men) was also alerted for possible deployment in the Dominican Republic; by 3:45 A.M. on Thursday, the entire 82nd Division had been alerted.

There are several indications that some U.S. officials, apparently including Secretary Rusk and Undersecretary Ball, wished to have additional troops sent in at this time, but that others—both in Santo Domingo and in Washington—still were hoping that the Dominican intervention could be limited to the Marine landing already authorized. During the night of April 28–29, Ambassador Bennett specifically rejected a U.S. Navy suggestion for an aerial show of force and declined to consider any additional troop landings until the morning. Bennett also turned down a request for permission to land at San Isidro from Vice Admiral K. S. Masterson—newly arrived to head the Caribbean Task Force—arguing that such a gesture would look like intervention and that no such decision had yet been taken, although Bennett noted he was "quite prepared to recommend we intervene" if a canvass of the situation later in the morning showed that it was continuing to deteriorate. Perhaps Bennett thought, as some in Washington apparently believed, that the mere presence of Marines might enable the antirebel forces to restore order in Santo Domingo because of their psychological and political impact in a country where American influence is very strongly felt.[48] Presumably hoping that the intervention could still be restricted, Washington officials instructed Bennett on Thursday morning that the Marines were to confine their activities to the established evacuation area around the Hotel Embajador and stressed that participation by U.S. troops in offensive action against anybody, including leftist extremists, could only be ordered by the president.

The process of massive military intervention had already been set in motion, however. In Washington, President Johnson and his key civilian advisers urged the relevant military officers to review the Dominican Republic contingency plan to assure that there would be enough troops in Santo Domingo to deal with any foreseeable eventuality. President Johnson, Secretary Rusk, Secretary McNamara, and other veterans of the Kennedy administration believed that a major American error at the Bay of Pigs and in Vietnam had been not to make sufficient force available at an early stage; they were determined not to make this mistake again.

Soon, according to former Marine Corps Commandant David Shoup, another factor began to contribute to expanding the intervention. Competition began between the Army and the Marines to test their respective mobility and to obtain overall command of the Dominican operation. Organizational procedures and intraservice rivalries increased the likelihood that the intervention would escalate rapidly.[49]

In Santo Domingo, meanwhile, events continued to unfold much as they had during the previous days. As Thursday began, Colonel Benoit informed the embassy that the junta's forces would again attempt to execute the previously announced mop-up operation. As before, the plan called first for Air Force strafing runs, then for Wessin's troops to enter Santo Domingo from the east, and Montás's forces to move in from the western outskirts of the city. The embassy realized that the junta's forces were by now tired and discouraged, but explicitly assumed that the rebels must also be weary and agreed that the junta's plan was worth another try. The junta's radio station was anxiously attempting to exploit the Marines' presence to boost their own morale and to intimidate opposition, and some still thought it possible that these efforts might help stem the rebel advance.

But the proposed mop-up operation never got off the ground. By Thursday morning, in fact, PSP leaders were confident that the junta's forces had been beaten. CIA sources reported that Manuel González was organizing a force in downtown Santo Domingo and was even talking about attacking the San Isidro base itself. Such an attack might not actually have been feasible, given the junta's monopoly of air power and the extensive open ground between Santo Domingo and San Isidro, but the failure of the junta's forces to enter the city Thursday morning was an obvious fact. Still plagued by defection, exhaustion, low morale, and poor communication, the antirebel forces could not regroup effectively. Another reason for their collapse, according to a political officer who returned to the embassy from San Isidro on Thursday morning, was the feeling on the part of some Dominican officers that they might now safely withdraw from the front line and leave it to U.S. forces to restore order. Earlier, American inaction had weakened the antirebel forces. Now, paradoxically, the result of American action was to weaken them still more.

As it became evident that the junta's troops would not enter the city, Ambassador Bennett obtained Washington's authorization to assign a few MAAG officers, finally returned from Panama, to help the San Isidro leaders develop new operational plans for attacking the rebel positions. But again the proposed U.S. action came too late to be effective. General Wessin's soldiers continued to desert, thus lowering the estimated strength of the junta forces to less than two thousand men, perhaps fewer than the number of armed rebels, and even these were scattered among four or five widely separated groups. An incident near the embassy in which a junta plane strafed a junta tank pointed up the lack of communication and coordination among the antirebel forces which remained. Reports were received at the embassy by noon that the Fortaleza Ozama, stronghold of the riot control police squad, might soon fall to a rebel attack in which MPD activists were said to be playing an important role. Rebel troops were also reportedly attacking the Army's transportation headquarters in the northern part of the city. Police stations throughout Santo Domingo were now in rebel hands and a couple of rebel tanks were seen heading west toward the Police barracks on the highway to Santiago.

There were also reports at this time, most of them grossly exaggerated it now appears, about alleged atrocities in Santo Domingo and about the degree of violence and disorder in the city. Colonel Caamaño was reported by the embassy to have gone berserk and to have personally executed Colonel Juan Calderón, Reid Cabral's bodyguard; in fact, Calderón had been superficially wounded by a stray shot with which Colonel Caamaño had no connection. A claim by a Dominican USIS employee that antirebel forces were being lined up against the wall and shot was urgently passed on to Washington. It turned out that the excited Dominican youth had not actually seen such an incident but had heard of it; no credible evidence ever appeared that such executions really took place in this period.[50]

The embassy by now had virtually no firsthand knowledge of what was happening in the downtown area except for the activities of known Communists, about which the CIA station continued to receive the reports of agents and infiltrators. Embassy officers knew almost nothing about the makeup of the rebel leadership after the withdrawal of several leading PRD civilians into asylum or hiding on Tuesday and Wednesday. The embassy first learned of the formation of the "Constitutionalist Military Command" under Colonel Caamaño, for instance, only when a British vice-consul gave an American official a copy of a mimeographed announcement his chauffeur had picked up. Embassy personnel knew very little about the seven signers of the communiqué other than Caamaño, all of them military officers or former officers. But given the longstanding American fear of a "Communist takeover" in Santo Domingo, what they thought they did know—the apparent disintegration of the pro-Bosch civilian group and the intensified activities of Dominican Communists—was enough to make them magnify every possibility of Communist influence. The embassy reported to Washington that information in the files suggested that at least two of the eight officers had extreme leftist connections, and noted that the available information might understate the extent of Communist participation in the rebel movement. And the CIA soon reported the presence with Caamaño of two Europeans who, the CIA suggested, might be Communist agents sent from abroad.[51]

While reports mounted showing that the junta's forces were ineffective, that known Communists were active and confident and that others who might be Communists were prominent in the rebel movement, that disorder in Santo Domingo was rife, and that the U.S. Marines and even the embassy had been fired upon, President Johnson conferred repeatedly with a number of his key foreign policy advisers. The president asked for further information on the role of Dominican Communists. By noon on Thursday, CIA Director Raborn was telling him that eight known Communists had been identified as prominent in the rebel leadership and FBI Director J. Edgar Hoover was reportedly reinforcing the president's concern about their potential strength. Defense Secretary McNamara and General Earl Wheeler, meanwhile, are said to have stressed that the *Boxer*'s Marine establishment was woefully inadequate to perform any mission against opposition; McNamara reportedly urged that the 82nd Division be authorized to deploy.[52]

Shortly after 2:00 P.M., after discussions about which it has been impossible to obtain detailed information, President Johnson ordered the immediate debarkation of all the Marines remaining aboard the *Boxer* (some five hundred men), apparently as part of a general authorization to the Defense Department to undertake all-out military intervention in Santo Domingo; subsequent exchanges between Washington and Santo Domingo appear to have formalized a decision taken already at this point. A few minutes later, for instance, Washington instructed Ambassador Bennett—then meeting in his office with the Commander of the Caribbean Ready Group, the Commanding Officer of the Marine Force aboard the Ready Group, and members of the embassy staff—to cable immediately his estimate of the situation and whether American military intervention was necessary. But Washington pointedly noted that "we cannot afford to permit the situation to deteriorate to the point where a Communist takeover occurs," leaving little doubt that the president was already disposed to authorize massive intervention. Ambassador Bennett soon confirmed that U.S. troops were needed, and by 3:00 P.M. the Joint Chiefs of Staff had directed that all remaining elements of the 6th Marine Expeditionary Unit aboard the Caribbean Ready Group (some 1,580 men and their equipment) be landed at once. By 3:14 P.M. the Third Brigade of the 82nd Airborne Division, the first Army unit alerted on Monday night, had been ordered to deploy in the Dominican Republic; it was to proceed to Ramey Air Force Base for staging before coming over for a drop landing near San Isidro the next morning.

All of this was formalized in a second communication late that afternoon between Rusk, Ball, McNamara, Wheeler, and Raborn in Washington and Bennett, Connett, the CIA Station Chief, and the Army and Navy attachés in Santo Domingo. While reaffirming their wish to avoid U.S. military action "as long as there is a reasonable chance orderly forces can prevail," the Washington officials made very clear their assessment that a rebel victory would "probably lead to a pro-Communist government" and that U.S. action would be needed to forestall this result. Responding to Washington's request that he "recommend whatever types of actions . . . are needed," Ambassador Bennett, in turn, passed the detailed answer on to "others more qualified," while stressing that "now that we are in this, we must do the full job as needed" and that "we should commit sufficient troops to do the job here rapidly and effectively."

While this communication proceeded, the remaining Marines with the Caribbean Ready Group were landing at Haina and the first elements of the 82nd Airborne were boarding 33 C-130 Hercules Aircraft at Pope Air Force Base, North Carolina. Before 8:00 P.M., the C-130's were airborne, headed for Ramey.

By 9:30 P.M., events had accelerated once more. Acting on a recommendation from Admiral Masterson, who had sent a number of his staff on to the San Isidro base, General Wheeler ordered the planes to proceed immediately to San Isidro.

Beginning shortly after 2:00 A.M. on Friday, April 30, and continuing through the early morning darkness, one American plane after another came in to land at the crowded and unlit San Isidro field. Besides the 33 C-130's carrying the troops, 111 planes loaded with equipment landed that morning.[53] For the next six days, an average of 243 flights landed every day at San Isidro, one every six minutes around the clock. Within ten days there were nearly 23,000 American troops on Dominican soil, almost half as many as were then serving in Vietnam.

4. Deploying the Troops

By dawn on Friday, April 30, the Dominican situation had become, from the standpoint of the United States, extremely critical.

In Santo Domingo, wearied U.S. officials—their nerves frayed from continuous sniper fire in the vicinity of the embassy itself —reported events in increasingly concerned terms and tone. Fighting continued, antirebel forces were reeling, and no established authority existed. A predawn conference in the ambassador's office was interrupted briefly when a captured Dominican Army tank, manned by rebels, made a foray along the street in front of the embassy.

An emergency atmosphere permeated Washington, where almost every top foreign policy official of the U.S. government, including President Johnson, was now devoting priority attention to the Dominican problem. Top American foreign policy advisers had not been continuously involved in handling the Dominican crisis during its first days, up until the reversals suffered by the antirebel forces and the embassy's urgent appeal for military intervention on Wednesday. The Marine landing was authorized on Wednesday afternoon; Wednesday evening was devoted mainly to informing congressional leaders, Latin

American ambassadors, and the American public of this action. It was not really until Thursday, after the president's decision to authorize massive military intervention, that a number of other potentially important steps to resolve the crisis could be undertaken. First, Ambassador Ellsworth Bunker, President of the Council of the Organization of American States for April, called the Council into session. Bunker encouraged OAS Secretary General José A. Mora to send an official appeal to the papal nuncio in Santo Domingo, urging him to convey to all parties the Organization's desire that hostilities cease at once and to report to the OAS Council on the overall situation and particularly on the prospects for a cease-fire. Second, consideration was begun in Washington about how U.S. troops should be used. U.S. officers in Santo Domingo were instructed to prepare a plan for sealing off the downtown area, by establishing a "cordon" around it, to contain the rebels and to provide time for the OAS or other parties to seek a solution to the crisis. Third, an informal communications channel was established between the White House and Juan Bosch, through the initiative of Chancellor Jaime Benítez of the University of Puerto Rico (a confidant of Bosch) and the receptivity of Benítez's good friend Abe Fortas, long one of President Johnson's closest advisers. Fourth, unofficial consultations were started with former President Rómulo Betancourt of Venezuela and former Governor Luis Muñoz Marín of Puerto Rico, both of whom happened to be in the United States when the Dominican crisis broke, and later with former President José Figueres of Costa Rica, whom Betancourt called and invited to Washington. Finally, just before midnight on Thursday, White House aide Bill Moyers called former ambassador John Martin in Connecticut and asked him to report to Washington for urgent consultations early on Friday morning. Martin, some Washington officials thought, might be able to facilitate communication with the rebels in Santo Domingo, who were embittered by Ambassador Bennett's stand and particularly by the U.S. intervention.

Each of these five initiatives was to produce significant results in the next days and weeks, but none promised any quick improvement. The OAS Council agreed in the first hours of Friday morning to call for a cease-fire and for the establishment of an "international neutral zone of refuge" (later called the "international security zone," or ISZ) to protect the various embassies in Santo Domingo. But the Council's discussions revealed deep differences within the membership on what to do next. There was no assurance that the OAS would be able to take any additional steps, even to secure compliance with its call for a cease-fire.

When the administration's principal foreign policy advisers met at the White House on Friday morning, the latest available information indicated that military opposition to the rebels was collapsing in Santo Domingo. Embassy reports suggested that the strategic Ozama Fortress at the eastern edge of the downtown area had either fallen into rebel hands or was about to, and it was presumed that the numerous arms stored there would soon be distributed to rebel sympathizers.

The Marines had already begun to move east from the Hotel Embajador polo grounds to establish the ISZ. Acting in accord with their contingency plan and with pencil-draft instructions from Admiral Masterson to General York, troops from the 82nd Airborne had secured the San Isidro Air Base and its environs and then moved west to take control of the eastern approach to the Duarte Bridge. The Airborne troops had no orders at this time to cross the bridge and move further west into Santo Domingo to link up with the Marines; it had been anticipated that junta forces would control the bridge and patrol the city.

As the Dominican Armed Forces continued to disintegrate, however, it was beginning to appear that U.S. troops would have to be ordered into the city to combat the rebels. American military officers in Santo Domingo and staff members of the Joint Chiefs of Staff in Washington began outlining plans to do so. The immediate question President Johnson and his advisers had to face Friday morning, John Martin recalls, was whether American troops should be sent into the capital city to shoot Dominicans.[1]

The president did not wish to authorize combat by American

forces but he could not rule out the possibility. His main feeling at this point, Martin reports, was that he did "not intend to sit here with my hands tied and let the Communists take that island. What can we do in Vietnam if we can't clean up the Dominican Republic? I know what the editorials will say," the president is said to have remarked, "but it would be a hell of a lot worse if we sit here and don't do anything and the Communists take that country."[2] But the president was also hoping to avoid a diplomatic disaster in Santo Domingo. He had already received a telegram from Venezuela's President Raúl Leoni angrily condemning the intervention and there were other indications that protest was building up throughout the hemisphere.

The president outlined his approach, therefore, in terms of two main immediate objectives: to prevent a Communist takeover of the Dominican Republic and to avoid having the United States caught alone in Santo Domingo, isolated from hemispheric opinion.

President Johnson entrusted Secretary of Defense McNamara and General Wheeler with the task of thwarting a possible Communist bid to take the Dominican Republic. Answering the president's query, they said that one or two divisions might be needed to take the Dominican Republic. Authorizing their use and whatever else was necessary to accomplish the aim of precluding a Communist takeover, the president ordered that the "best general in the Pentagon" be sent to Santo Domingo to take command of American forces there.[3]

Less than half an hour later, General Wheeler dispatched Lieutenant General Bruce Palmer, Jr., to take this assignment. Wheeler told Palmer orally: "Your announced mission is to save American lives. Your unstated mission is to prevent the Dominican Republic from going Communist. The President has stated that he will not allow another Cuba . . . You are to take all necessary measures . . . —to accomplish this mission." Specifically, Palmer was told he could count on as many troops as were needed and that the entire 18th Army (the 82nd and the 101st Army Airborne Divisions) was already at his disposal. At noon the Defense Department alerted two Marine Battalion

Landing Teams (2,854 men) aboard the U.S.S. *Okinawa*, supporting elements from the 4th Marine Expeditionary Brigade (2,050 men), and two additional Battalion Combat Teams plus supporting elements from the 82nd Airborne (3,302 men). Shortly after 2:00 P.M., the Third Brigade of the 82nd Airborne Division, comprising three more Battalion Combat Teams plus supporting elements (3,000 men), was also alerted for possible deployment, as was the entire 101st Airborne Division (12,891 men).

The president instructed Secretary of State Rusk and Undersecretary Ball to try to involve the OAS in resolving the crisis as quickly as possible, and to work to avoid any isolation of the United States from the Organization's members. He asked them whether the OAS could be persuaded to meet again right away; Rusk and Ball doubted this, since the Council had met until 3:00 A.M. that morning.[4] The president emphasized his intention to work through the OAS, his interest in securing Latin American understanding of and support for the military intervention, and his receptivity to constructive Latin American suggestions about how to proceed. Former Alliance Coordinator Teodoro Moscoso, once the U.S. ambassador in Venezuela, was to be flown to Caracas in a White House jet to confer with Leoni, to reassure him about U.S. intentions, and to seek his support for the establishment of some kind of OAS Special Committee to work on resolving the crisis. Consideration was given to sending Ambassador Ralph Dungan from Chile to San José to brief Costa Rican leaders and ask their advice. Former White House adviser Arthur Schlesinger, Jr. was also asked to help, and preparations were begun to send Ambassador Averell Harriman to key Latin American capitals. Undersecretary Mann was encouraged to follow up his contacts with Betancourt and his colleagues.

The president also ordered Martin to go to the Dominican Republic at once "to help Ambassador Bennett, to open up contact with the rebels, to help the OAS and the Papal Nuncio to get a ceasefire, and to find out what the facts were and report to the President."[5] Martin left immediately via Andrews Air

Force Base, taking with him Harry Shlaudeman, the State Department's Dominican Republic desk officer.

The embassy in Santo Domingo was instructed, meanwhile, to assist in the efforts under way to establish a cease-fire and set up the "international security zone," and to encourage the junta forces under Colonel Benoit to cooperate in doing so. Washington pointed out that establishment of the ISZ would considerably reduce the perimeter the junta's forces would have to defend and would allow them to concentrate on reasserting control of the downtown area; the embassy was urged to make this clear to junta leaders. It was emphasized that the Benoit junta was the only existing organized Dominican force friendly to the United States and as such must be preserved as the basis for an eventual government. The embassy was asked to impress upon the Benoit junta the need to avoid rash military actions which might either jeopardize its existence or force direct American participation in combat operations to rescue it. Washington officials, concerned that the Benoit junta or even the embassy might mistakenly be expecting American troops to attack the rebels directly, informed Ambassador Bennett that no such plan had been authorized. On the contrary, the president had ordered that U.S. troops use no more force than was necessary; Undersecretary Ball stressed in a telephone conversation with Bennett that no attack on the rebel stronghold was contemplated. The immediate objectives of the U.S. forces were to secure their positions at San Isidro and at the Hotel Embajador, to set up the ISZ, and to take over the strategic Duarte Bridge. Then, it was hoped, junta forces could be used to patrol the area between the ISZ and the Duarte Bridge, forming a defensive line around the main rebel-held portion of the city. The junta's forces would thus be able to rest, regroup, and then establish their authority over the rest of the city and the countryside. The embassy was told that Admiral Masterson was being instructed to send the best qualified officer on his staff to the Benoit junta's headquarters to improve their morale, act as an adviser on military tactics, and arrange for whatever supplies and equipment the junta might require, including the establishment of adequate communications facilities between the headquarters of the junta and the U.S. Task Force.

I

As John Martin flew to Santo Domingo on Friday afternoon, he saw the Dominican situation in terms of four major dangers to be avoided: "a Communist takeover, a full-scale U.S. military occupation, an entrenched Dominican dictator supported by the U.S., or a U.S. 'Hungary'—a frontal assault on the 'rebel' stronghold in Ciudad Nueva, with U.S. troops slaughtering thousands of Dominicans, including innocents." Personally unconvinced by the information he had received in Washington that the Communists had actually seized control of the rebel movement and assured by the president that he should freely report his own findings on the matter, Martin assigned high personal priority to ascertaining "the facts" and transmitting them to Washington. From the tenor of the White House meeting, Martin judged that he had "at least twenty-four hours, possibly the weekend, but no more, to find out what the facts were and to influence our policy."[6]

Even as Martin and Shlaudeman were in the air heading for Santo Domingo, the situation there continued to deteriorate. The hope remaining earlier that morning that the junta's forces might still regroup and revitalize themselves seemed to be fading. Shortly after noon, U.S. attachés and other military personnel conferred with Colonel Benoit at San Isidro about the junta's plans. Benoit handed the Air Force attaché a letter expressing gratitude for American assistance as well as his confidence that "the presence of units of your military forces will be sufficient and that there will be no necessity for them to take an active role in our struggle." Benoit told the American officers orally that he believed American troops would not have to shoot and he asked that the United States not order its forces into combat unless he requested this. General Montás Guerrero and other military chieftains argued forcefully, however, that American help was needed immediately, and the U.S. officers present tended to agree. After some discussion, it was agreed that the junta's forces would make one final effort to retake the city unaided, but that they would call for American assistance if necessary. Benoit's letter, the content of which had already been transmitted to Washington, was now belatedly withdrawn.

The junta's forces proved incapable of advancing during the course of the day. Paratroopers from the 82nd Airborne—who had met little resistance in securing the eastern approaches to the Duarte Bridge—now were ordered to cross the bridge and to establish control of its western approach and of the nearby electric power plant. Within three hours, after putting down some opposition, the American troops had cleared a semicircle with a six-block radius on the west bank of the Ozama River and had taken over the power plant. Anticipating that further action might be required, the Airborne commander told the Defense Department he would need more troops to push further into the city to link with the Marines.

No sooner had the U.S. forces established their positions at the western bridgehead than the junta's units, thus relieved, crossed the bridge and returned to San Isidro rather than take up their assigned patrol mission along Avenida García–Avenida San Martín.[7] Now there were no friendly forces between the just-established bridgehead and the Marines several miles to the west, and the latter were encountering resistance in their planned attempt to move northeast toward Avenida San Martín. Two Marines having been killed and eight wounded within minutes, a decision was made on the spot to halt for the day and to wait for dawn before moving on. The Marine commander, too, believed more U.S. troops were needed to accomplish the linkup.

The prospect that American forces would soon have to be engaged directly in bloody fighting to contain the rebels caused Washington officials, especially President Johnson personally, to assign urgent priority to obtaining an immediate cease-fire. Learning from OAS Secretary General Mora that the papal nuncio had said by telephone that he had just secured preliminary agreement on a cease-fire proposal from rebel and junta representatives and from Juan Bosch in San Juan, the president ordered his subordinates to follow up the report and get a cease-fire adopted. The State Department immediately instructed the embassy first to reassure junta leaders that the United States would maintain unaltered its determination to prevent a Communist takeover, and then to assist the nuncio in securing a formal cease-fire agreement. The department took note of the embassy's skepticism (already reported to Washington) about the nuncio's efforts and about the usefulness of a cease-fire at a moment when the rebels controlled most of downtown Santo Domingo but said that Washington now considered a cease-fire essential. Complaints from General Robert York, the field commander of the Airborne troops (until General Palmer's arrival) that compliance with a cease-fire would hinder the capacity of U.S. forces to prevent a "second Cuba" were similarly rejected; the Defense Department instructed York to cooperate in establishing the proposed accord.

When the nuncio arrived at the American embassy early Friday afternoon to discuss with Ambassador Bennett how to implement the preliminary agreement—which was to have become effective at 11:45 that morning—the embassy itself was under fire and rebel troops downtown were passing out more arms from the Ozama Fortress, which had finally fallen. The nuncio tried unsuccessfully to halt the shooting and rebel representatives admitted to him they could not control the acts of the group firing at the embassy. When shooting broke out again, the nuncio and Ambassador Bennett were forced to withdraw to the ambassador's bath to continue their talk.

Embassy officers felt that the futility of an immediate cease-fire order under the circumstances was obvious, and a draft cable was prepared which noted that "the situation is not so much one calling for a ceasefire as for the imposition of law and order." Ambassador Bennett told Undersecretary Mann by telephone that he doubted a cease-fire could control the rebels, whom he now described as "bandits." But Washington officials insisted, specific instructions to support the nuncio's efforts were sent, and the proposed comment was struck from the embassy's cable. Ambassador Bennett was told to provide the nuncio with a helicopter and to facilitate his trips to San Isidro and back. Both Ambassador Bennett and Admiral Masterson were enjoined to bring their influence to bear directly on General Wessin and to secure his cooperation and that of the other military chiefs in obtaining the cease-fire.

When Martin and Shlaudeman reached San Isidro late in the afternoon, they found there various American officials, including Ambassador Bennett and General York, meeting with the papal nuncio and with junta officers and rebel representatives. The talks had gone on for some time and seemed, or so Martin thought, to be in danger of breaking up without agreement; Martin heard a heated exchange as he joined the group. When Martin added his efforts to those of the others who had sought to persuade General Wessin to sign an agreement ratifying the nuncio's earlier cease-fire accord, Wessin agreed to do so, however. Wessin signed first; he was joined then by De Los Santos, the three members of the Benoit junta and several other anti-rebel officers; by Fausto Caamaño, Jr. (a brother of the rebel chief) and Héctor Conde on behalf of the pro-Bosch movement, the papal nuncio, the head of the Dominican Red Cross, and by Ambassador Bennett and, apparently, General York.[8]

Although the remarks exchanged at the San Isidro meeting indicated the bitter hatred that had developed between the two factions, each side accusing the other of crimes and atrocities, both sides proved willing to accede to the internationally supported call for a halt in the fighting. Within minutes, the agreed cease-fire text—which guaranteed the personal safety of individuals on both sides, regardless of ideology, and called on an OAS Commission to arbitrate the differences between the groups —was being transmitted by Radio San Isidro. Now it remained to be seen whether the cease-fire would be effective.

Leaving San Isidro, Martin and Shlaudeman turned next to the task of fact-finding and opening up contact with the rebels. Martin went first to talk with General Imbert in his home, while Shlaudeman visited Molina Ureña in the Colombian embassy. Each learned quickly that the gaps between the Dominican factions, and between the rebels and the U.S. government, were very wide.

The opening of communications between the U.S. and the rebel leadership was facilitated, however, by a development emanating from the contacts between the White House and Bosch through the Benítez-Fortas link. Washington instructed Martin to telephone Benítez in San Juan as soon as possible; soon Martin was able to speak with Benítez and then with Bosch himself.

Bosch assured Martin that he had personally instructed Colonel Caamaño to grant him an appointment on Saturday morning and that he had told Caamaño to cooperate fully with Martin. Both Bosch and Benítez complained, however, that American troops were advancing into the city, and each voiced the suspicion that General Wessin's forces might be planning to follow the U.S. forces in. Martin denied the charge but promised to check on the disposition of U.S. forces.

II

By Saturday morning, May 1, differences in perspective and priority about how the troops should be deployed were becoming apparent among relevant officials and agencies of the U.S. government.

U.S. military officers on the spot, concerned by the attacks upon their troops and about the tactical untenability of their unlinked positions on either side of the strife-torn city, were asking now for more troops, more helicopters, permission to advance to join their forces, and even authorization to go into the city in order to put down the rebel movement. General Palmer, who arrived at San Isidro just after Friday midnight, was told by General York of the cease-fire U.S. officials had signed; sizing up the situation, Palmer told York that the situation was most dangerous and that he did not recognize any cease-fire at that time.

What some U.S. military officers wished to do was exactly what presidential envoy Martin sought to prevent. Increasingly preoccupied by the thought, in his phrase, of a "U.S. 'Hungary,' " Martin felt his most immediate task was to assure that American forces would not be sent into the city to crush the revolt. On the spot and by telephone conversations with the White

House, Martin worked to make firm the already agreed cease-fire and to assure that U.S. troops would be bound by it.

Ambassador Bennett, meanwhile, was reiterating his objections to U.S. support for the cease-fire, which he reported was being observed by the junta but not by the rebels. The ambassador backed the U.S. military's requests for more troops and helicopters, urged that the U.S. forces be given permission to link up, and asked that they be authorized to act as necessary to contain the rebels. Concerned primarily with preventing a Communist takeover in Santo Domingo, Bennett supported his pleas with increasingly alarming reports of rumored rebel acts and intentions; he repeatedly stressed the "Castro-like" flavor of various aspects of the rebel movement, particularly the radio broadcasts.

Washington's immediate response to all this was to approve sending more troops—additional Marines and Airborne troops were directed to deploy Saturday morning—but to limit their use and to press for observance of the cease-fire. Washington officials, concerned not only with the risk of a "second Cuba" in the Dominican Republic but with the U.S. position elsewhere in the hemisphere and the world, were now concentrating much of their attention on the diplomatic front, particularly in the Organization of American States. The OAS was forming a Special Committee composed of five Latin American ambassadors who were to proceed immediately to Santo Domingo, and the U.S. government was eager to facilitate their speedy departure. Ambassador Bennett was told of the importance of working with the OAS; he was also asked whether Latin American ambassadors in Santo Domingo could be persuaded to sign the cease-fire document.

Behind the scenes, moreover, the administration was actively considering a suggestion that Betancourt and Figueres become involved in resolving the crisis, perhaps through an OAS trusteeship arrangement. It was clear that such a possibility—attractive because of the influence these leaders were thought to have with Latin American liberals—could only materialize if the U.S. government's conduct in Santo Domingo did not further alienate

Betancourt and Figueres and if scope were preserved for possible OAS action.

Priority was accorded, therefore, to making sure that the embassy and the U.S. forces in Santo Domingo would adopt a more nearly neutral stance. The ambassador was implicitly rebuked for the encouraging comments he had made to junta leaders over an open radio line. Strongly worded instructions were transmitted ordering the embassy to resist any attempt by the junta to transfer its headquarters from San Isidro to the National Congress area (behind the U.S. lines at the western end of Santo Domingo) on the grounds that such a move would identify the United States too closely with the junta. Instructions to avoid overidentification with the junta's forces were sent from Washington to U.S. military commanders in Santo Domingo. An attempt was now under way to make the actions being taken by the United States in Santo Domingo conform with the announced objective of the intervention and with its international legal and political rationale.

At about noon on Saturday, May 1, Martin and Shlaudeman —accompanied by the papal nuncio—had their first meeting with the rebel leadership, including Colonel Caamaño, Héctor Aristy, and others. Martin's first impressions were significant, for they confirmed and deepened American concern about dangers posed by the rebel movement. Reporting to Washington, Martin stressed particularly his feeling that Aristy, whom he recalled from his earlier stay in Santo Domingo as a slick and untrustworthy playboy type, seemed surprisingly well-informed on military dispositions and problems. Martin suspected that Aristy might be a "deep-cover" Communist agent; he urged Washington to investigate Aristy's entire background, suggesting specifically the possibility that Aristy might have received special training behind the Iron Curtain for his current role. Caamaño, whom Martin had not known before this meeting, impressed him as extremely dangerous—intelligent, commanding, cool, by no means crazy (as Imbert had described him). Indeed, Martin reported, Caamaño seemed to him to be the only

Dominican he had ever met who was capable of becoming "his country's Castro."

The main substantive point discussed at the meeting was Caamaño's vehement insistence that U.S. troops adhere to the April 30 cease-fire and maintain the positions they held then without further advance. Martin and Caamaño sat down to study a road map Martin had brought with him on which the "international zone" had been drawn, incorrectly it turned out; the map showed a northern boundary of the zone different from the one U.S. forces intended to patrol and also inadvertently left outside the zone the International Fair grounds, where the congress and other main Dominican government buildings are located. After considerable discussion, both men agreed that U.S. forces would adhere to their position on the west side of the city as marked on Martin's map, with the exception of a two-block expansion of the zone near the U.S. embassy, to which Caamaño agreed.

Their discussion of the situation in the eastern part of the city —near the Duarte Bridge and the electric plant, where Airborne troops had paused—was apparently less conclusive. Caamaño claimed that his forces controlled the electric plant, where shooting had been particularly heavy, but he complained that several of his men had been killed that morning, perhaps by U.S. forces, when they went to the plant to investigate possible repairs. He also charged that the Marines near the embassy were providing advance cover beyond the line for the police, who were firing at the rebels from National Police Headquarters near the embassy. Martin and Shlaudeman were unsure about the exact position of the Airborne troops and about the situation near the embassy; they insisted that U.S. forces were neutral, but indicated they could not guarantee exactly where they might be at the time.[9] The meeting ended dramatically, with Martin continuing to emphasize to Caamaño the importance of a cease-fire, while Aristy told cheering throngs outside the building that Martin would help them achieve constitutionality and democracy.[10]

The hours following this meeting were filled with intense

communications about the disposition of U.S. forces. At about the same time that Martin was leaving Caamaño, Marine and Army patrols were meeting in front of the Open Air Radio Theater on Avenida San Martín, just one block south of Radio Santo Domingo's studios; they began to patrol the area jointly.[11] Learning of this move, Caamaño called Martin to protest, and Martin offered to check. Peña Gómez called Shlaudeman, who also promised to investigate. Caamaño then telephoned Bosch in San Juan, who interrupted a "Face the Nation" interview being taped by CBS-TV to instruct Caamaño to tell his forces not to resist the American advance. Martin called the White House, which was asking for more information through military channels. Shlaudeman called the State Department, where officials were very confused about the position of both U.S. and rebel forces. Soon Fortas was talking by telephone with Bosch, who informed Fortas of the advice he had just given Caamaño; Fortas expressed his gratitude.

The immediate result of all this emergency communication was a top-level U.S. decision to halt the advance of U.S. forces and to order the patrols which had linked to return to their original positions, pending a decision on how the troops should be used. The ground rules for U.S. forces were now tightened as well. American troops were still to be allowed to fire and maneuver in self-defense, but it was made clear that they had to return to their original positions after each such operation and restrictions were placed on the arms that U.S. forces could use. Political decisions were being taken, General Palmer was later to reflect, "without taking into account important military considerations."

III

It took the better part of a day before the U.S. government could determine how American forces in Santo Domingo should be positioned.

It was very clear, General Palmer reported to Washington on Saturday afternoon, that the United States could not exploit its military power to stabilize the situation in Santo Domingo unless a ground linkup of U.S. forces were permitted, regardless of the politically motivated commitment not to move U.S. troops. If the cease-fire agreed to on April 30 and affirmed by Martin were to be literally followed and the movement of U.S. forces were consequently to be restricted, Palmer warned, there would be a grave risk of giving the Dominican Republic over to the rebels.

The preferred course, Palmer suggested, would be to allow U.S. forces to establish a "cordon" through the heart of downtown Santo Domingo, along Avenida Mella through Plaza Independencia and up Avenida Independencia. This "cordon," Palmer noted, would not only confine the rebels to downtown Santo Domingo but would also give U.S. forces control of the city's telecommunications facilities, its main post office, the major banks and other key downtown installations identified in the military's contingency plan.

Recognizing that to establish the suggested "cordon" U.S. forces would have to confront rebel troops directly, General Palmer proposed as a minimum alternative that his troops be permitted to establish a "cordon" along the route patrolled earlier in the day by Army and Marine units. Using this route would leave the rebels in control of key facilities and would enlarge their territory, but it would at least serve to contain the rebels in the city and would facilitate the protection and supplying of the ISZ. Without such a move by U.S. troops, Palmer pointed out, the ISZ—including the embassy—could be reached and supplied only by helicopter or by sea over the beach, for the docks were also in the rebel-held section of the city. As matters stood, General Palmer insisted, the position of U.S. forces was untenable; he requested authorization to establish a "cordon" over one route or the other.

Reporting to Washington late Saturday night on the basis of his first full day in Santo Domingo, John Martin strenuously opposed the continuing suggestion that American forces move into the downtown area. Now that U.S. troops were ashore, he suggested, a Communist military victory was precluded. The worst possibility still faced, he suggested, was that American troops might massacre Dominicans; to permit this to happen would be to play into the Communists' hands. The immediate need, Martin stressed, was to "gain some time . . . to maintain a ceasefire and hope that the people might come to their senses."[12] Martin conceded that a continued cease-fire would leave the rebels in control of much of the city. But now that the OAS had entered the picture, Martin emphasized, the United States could work for a nonmilitary solution of the Dominican crisis under the Organization's umbrella. In the meantime, a substitute for the obviously unpopular junta could be sought and other steps taken to improve the chances for resolving the crisis peacefully.

Ambassador Bennett, now aware of the priority President Johnson and other Washington officials were according to the cease-fire and to cooperation with the OAS, soon recorded his recognition that "highest U.S. policy interests" made it necessary to test the cease-fire; he agreed that his major concern— that "Castro Communists" might take over—could be discarded as long as substantial U.S. forces were ashore. Bennett concurred with Martin that the next phase could best be used to buy time and that priority should be accorded to assisting the junta to operate as an effective government. Eventual disarmament of the rebels might still require direct U.S. military action, he felt, but emphasis could be placed for the present on establishing the junta's authority outside the rebel stronghold.

The entire night passed without General Palmer's receiving word from Washington in response to his proposal. What apparently happened, later investigation suggested, was that a key message from General Wheeler to General Palmer on this point was lost.[13]

Referring to General Palmer's query, General Wheeler early in the evening sent messages to Palmer and to Admiral Masterson, asking each to estimate the forces and the time required, and the casualties likely to result, if U.S. forces were to establish a "cordon" along each of three different routes: the one Palmer preferred through downtown Santo Domingo, the one already scouted along Avenida San Martín, and a route farther out from the center of the city which would avoid the rebel strongpoint at the junction of Avenida San Martín and Avenida Puerto Rico. The message directed to General Palmer was sent, however, to Fort Bragg (Palmer's base in the United States), where it remained; it apparently never reached Palmer. Admiral Masterson, meanwhile, was advising Washington that to cut through the city might require twelve to fifteen battalions and twenty-four hours. Since only six battalions were then ashore, Masterson's estimate gave Washington officials reason to pause. A high-level meeting was called for Sunday morning to consider what instructions should be provided.

Details on the positions taken during this meeting are not available, but it is known that by early Sunday afternoon, May 2, the U.S. government's foreign policy-makers reached agreement on how U.S. forces should be positioned. Although it is unclear who proposed it—most likely someone from the White House staff—the key suggestion leading to a U.S. government decision at this time seems to have been that the stated purpose of linking up U.S. forces could be to secure a route from the ISZ to the airports, thus making it possible to present the repositioning of U.S. troops as consistent with their announced mission: to protect the evacuation of American and other foreign nationals. State Department officials, including a representative of the Legal Adviser's office who had been drafting a rationale for the intervention, reportedly were satisfied that this move could thus be explained, and Ambassador Bunker apparently agreed that it would probably be acceptable to members of the OAS.

Permission was given to the 82nd Airborne, therefore, to establish a Line of Communication (LOC)—the phrase "cordon" was explicitly dropped—essentially along the route its patrol had scouted the day before, detouring only slightly to avoid rebel strongpoints in order to minimize bloodshed. It was essential that an attempt be made to obtain prior approval of this move by the OAS Committee due to arrive in Santo Domingo that afternoon, Bennett and Palmer were told, for the U.S. would seek the Organization's aid in ratifying and enforcing the cease-fire, in administering relief measures, and in seeking a political solution to the crisis. But the Line of Communication would be established, Washington officials advised, regardless of the Committee's attitude.

The embassy in Santo Domingo arranged a meeting with the OAS Special Committee soon after its members arrived. After some discussion, the OAS representatives approved the U.S. plan and the embassy asked Washington to permit General Palmer to proceed. Washington soon did so, authorizing Palmer to implement the agreed plan on Monday, May 3. Just after Sunday midnight, three battalions of Airborne troops set out to establish the LOC; they had done so, with few casualties, by 1:30 A.M. An error led them to detour south rather than north at one point, thus losing the opportunity to take control of Radio Santo Domingo's main transmitter. But the LOC did seal off the main rebel force in downtown Santo Domingo (Ciudad Nueva) from the rest of the country, and it permitted U.S. forces to adopt a more nearly neutral stance in the days and weeks that followed. The most immediate dangers perceived by President Johnson, former Ambassador Martin, and others—to permit a Communist takeover or to undertake military actions that would have isolated the U.S. diplomatically by precluding the possibility of OAS participation in resolving the crisis—had been avoided. Attention could now be turned in Santo Domingo and in Washington toward devising a political solution for the crisis that would permit the eventual withdrawal of American forces. It would prove to be more difficult, however, to get the troops out than it had been to send them in.

5. *Explaining the Dominican Intervention*

Three fundamentally distinct approaches to explaining the Dominican episode may be identified in the available literature, although some individual authors incorporate aspects of more than one.[1]

What I would call the "official line" acclaims both the purposes and the results of the Dominican intervention.[2] It argues that the United States government consistently pursued and successfully achieved its stated objectives in the Dominican crisis: first, to protect American and other foreign nationals and to halt violence, later to prevent a Communist takeover and to restore constitutional processes to the Dominican people. The Dominican action is viewed as "an act of statesmanship and courage"; it is even regarded as "cooperation," not "intervention."[3]

What I would term the "radical view" condemns the aims and the effects of the Dominican intervention, which is seen as a classic example of the conservative (or counterrevolutionary) purpose of American foreign policy.[4] It argues that the United States treats the Dominican Republic as a client state, insisting that authorities there must always be approved by the U.S. government. Because Juan Bosch's movement was not acceptable to Washington, the United States landed its forces to thwart it and to assure that persons subservient to the U.S. would remain in power. The Dominican intervention, according to the radical interpretation, was "not an accident or aberration but a forceful example of what our Latin American policy has been for at least a decade."[5] Indeed, the radical view contends, the 1965 Dominican intervention was part of a coherent pattern of U.S. policy stretching back for decades and out to other areas of the world.[6]

What I would call the "liberal" view of American policy during the Dominican crisis assumes that fundamental U.S. aims were unobjectionable but criticizes the means chosen by American officials and laments their results.[7] The Dominican intervention is seen not as the consistent application of American purpose, but as a costly venture due to supposed errors by U.S. officials. Different opinions exist among liberal critics as to the main sources of the presumed blunders, but all agree that the Dominican intervention was "an individual deviation from the main track of policy."[8]

Each of these three approaches accounts differently for the events this study reviews.

The official line asserts that the U.S. government was uninvolved in the Dominican crisis during its first days. The United States, it is claimed, "refrained from 'supporting' the outgoing government or 'supporting' either of the two factions contending for power."[9] When the fighting in Santo Domingo intensified and public order disintegrated, however, it became necessary first to evacuate American citizens and then to land the Marines to protect them and to facilitate their evacuation.[10] After U.S. forces landed, it turned out that additional troops would be needed to protect the evacuees and the embassy itself. More Marines landed, therefore, early on Thursday afternoon. Only then did it become clear that Dominican Communists were trying to take advantage of the increasingly chaotic situation and that they might actually gain control of Santo Domingo unless their efforts were decisively countered.[11] Aiming to prevent a Communist takeover in the Dominican Republic and to stop bloodshed there, President Johnson ordered units of the 82nd Airborne Division to Santo Domingo.

The decision to intervene in the Dominican Republic occurred, then, in three distinct stages. First, five hundred Marines were landed to protect American citizens, then more Marines were required for the same purpose, and finally additional reinforcements were needed to forestall a possible Communist triumph.[12]

The intervention's humanitarian mission is evidenced, according to the official line, by the way American troops were deployed in the Dominican Republic. That U.S. forces were used to establish a Line of Communication to protect the evacuation route (and eventually the rebels), rather than in combat against the rebel forces, indicates the consistently neutral purpose of U.S. policy.

The radical view contends that the United States government was aiming from the outset of the crisis to keep Juan Bosch and his movement out of office. The radical view is asserted in many different forms, as various reasons are adduced for American opposition to Bosch, ranging from mechanistic assertions of the influence of commercial and financial interest to more subtle statements of ideological impulse and the psychopolitical demands of hegemony. But all agree that American policy consciously opposed Bosch and his party, and that "from the very start of the upheaval there was a concerted U.S. Government effort to checkmate the rebel movement by whatever means and at whatever cost," even by American military intervention, if necessary.[13]

According to radical critics, the U.S. chose first to entrust the Dominican Armed Forces with the task of defeating Bosch. When the local military establishment failed, the U.S. substituted its own force; "President Johnson ordered in the Marines . . . to do the job the Dominican military was unable to do."[14] The decisions to land five hundred Marines, then more Marines, and finally the 82nd Airborne were taken at moments when the victory of the pro-Bosch forces appeared imminent and it seemed that Bosch would soon return; each time the U.S. committed to action as many troops as were thought necessary to stop the pro-Bosch movement. That American actions were intended to stifle the revolution and to prevent Bosch's victory is further evidenced, radicals contend, by the use of American forces to encircle the rebel forces at a time when they might otherwise have taken control of all Santo Domingo and then of the rest of the Dominican Republic.

The liberal view attributes the Dominican intervention not to the U.S. government's supposed purpose but to individual blunders. That the U.S. government did not oppose Juan Bosch's movement as a matter of economic interest or ideological choice is shown, it is argued, by U.S. policy toward other non-Communist leftists in Latin America and by the postintervention negotiations the U.S. conducted with Bosch and his colleagues.[15] It is contended that the United States attempted throughout the crisis to remain neutral among the non-Communist Dominican factions, and that this is demonstrated by consistent U.S. support for the idea that free elections should determine the outcome of the crisis. The use of American troops to establish the Line of Communication, which eventually protected the rebels from attack, is offered as further evidence of the administration's neutral aim.

The intervention occurred, according to the liberal critique, not as a matter of established policy but because "Washington was stampeded into unfortunate decisions by a panicky, ill-informed embassy."[16] Poor information about what was happening in Santo Domingo, due to personal shortcomings of the embassy and CIA staffs; repeated (but presumably unrelated) failures by American officials to grasp various chances to resolve the crisis, especially the missed opportunities on Sunday, April 25, to deal with PRD representatives and Ambassador Bennett's refusal to mediate at the critical moment on Tuesday, April 27, when agreement might have been reached; frightened dispatches by tired men about the possibility that Americans might be massacred or that Communists might take power; excessive optimism about the likelihood that the Dominican Armed Forces would rally and take control; President Johnson's inexperience at foreign affairs, his supposed impetuousness, and his alleged preoccupation lest he be accused of weakness or irresolution for letting the Communists gain in the Caribbean while he was sending Americans to fight in Vietnam: all these and other individual errors and weaknesses are cited as the main explanations for American policy. Because they believe the Dominican intervention was due to "the unfortunate judgments of a few strategically placed individuals as well as the rapidity with which the crisis broke," liberals regard it as a special case.[17] Some liberal writers point out that Washington was predisposed to accept the embassy's reports and that questionable judgments were made by more than a few, but they tend to attribute the whole episode to the supposedly peculiar pathology of the Johnson administration; the Dominican intervention, it is argued, might not have occurred under a different administration.[18]

I

All three conventional explanations of the Dominican intervention appear, on close examination, to be inadequate.

The official line is probably the easiest to refute. The United States government was never neutral with respect to the Dominican power struggle. From the start, when the embassy and Washington agreed to favor the establishment of a provisional junta pledged to hold elections, American officials were taking sides in the Dominican conflict. Although U.S. officials may have made this particular choice partly because they thought it would involve the least direct American participation in the political crisis and because of their assessment of the balance of forces involved, their decision was undoubtedly due in part to the personal disdain and distrust felt within the U.S. government toward Juan Bosch.

Whatever the predominant motive of American support for the junta formula, this choice had the immediate effects of encouraging the anti-Bosch faction of the Dominican military establishment to employ force to block Bosch's return and also discouraging moderates among Bosch's followers about the possibility of a compromise solution. Even if American officials did not expect the United States to be directly involved in the crisis, it was clear to Dominicans that the U.S. did not wish to see Bosch's immediate return.

Having favored the establishment of a junta and encouraged the anti-Bosch faction from the beginning, the U.S. government first prepared to evacuate American citizens at least in part for political reasons, as a means of obtaining agreement among the Dominican factions for a cease-fire, which was thought likely to facilitate negotiations to form a junta. When it appeared on Monday evening, April 26, that Peña Gómez and other followers of Bosch were disheartened and might soon give in, the planned evacuation was postponed a few hours in the belief it might not be needed.

By Wednesday, April 28, there were more valid reasons to fear for the safety of Americans in an increasingly violent city. But the perceived threat of a Communist takeover in Santo Domingo was already the primary concern of American officials in Santo Domingo, and of at least some in Washington, when the Marines were landed that afternoon. Intelligence messages from the field stressed the Communist danger, and these were reinforced by FBI reports in Washington. Ambassador Bennett suggested that the protection of American citizens could be given as the purpose of the Marine landings if Washington preferred, and President Johnson's announced rationale for the intervention confined itself to the need to protect American lives, but both men had expressed their determination to prevent a "second Cuba" and were acting primarily to preclude that possibility. It is conceivable that some Washington officials had not focused on the supposed Communist danger in Santo Domingo by Wednesday. It is even plausible, although probably impossible to prove, that the president initially put the issue to some members of Congress and perhaps even to some of his advisers in terms of protecting American lives in order to assure a consensus on the need to intervene, while reserving to himself and other aides his own concern about a "second Cuba." But the need to prevent a possible Communist takeover was emphasized from the start of the crisis by intelligence officials, was made clear from the outset to American military personnel alerted for duty in Santo Domingo, and was understood by at least some of the Congressmen briefed at the White House on Wednesday evening.

By Thursday afternoon, when President Johnson ordered the landing of all the remaining Marines in the Caribbean Ready Group and also of units from the 82nd Airborne Division, the president's anxiousness to avoid a "second Cuba" was evident to all within the administration working on the Dominican problem, although it was not yet being discussed candidly by all officials. The president "bridled and switched the subject" when newsmen asked him on Thursday whether fear of a possible Communist takeover had influenced his decision to send the Marines.[19] Even as the first Airborne troops were landing early on Friday morning, Secretary Rusk called journalists in to urge them not to emphasize the "ideological aspects of this thing." Later that day, Rusk reportedly assured the Senate Foreign Relations Committee that the overriding reason for the intervention was to save lives; he omitted mentioning the administration's fears about a Communist takeover.[20]

But others in the administration were more forthright. In Santo Domingo late Thursday night, Ambassador Bennett briefed journalists who had just arrived and stressed the danger of a Communist takeover, reportedly emphasizing that the Communists had "worked with Bosch's PRD for months" and were "prepared well in advance of Reid's overthrow."[21] Pressed by the correspondents for evidence of the Communist role, Bennett passed around a typewritten list—supplied at his request by the CIA Station Chief—of alleged Communists said to be active in the revolt.[22] In Chicago, at about noon on Friday, Vice Admiral John McCain, Jr.—Commander of Atlantic Fleet Amphibious Forces—told a luncheon group that American troops were in Santo Domingo "to see that Castro and Cuban Communists do not get in."[23]

Still the White House itself did not even hint publicly that the intervention was intended to frustrate supposed Communist designs until Friday evening, when the president referred somewhat elliptically to "signs that people trained outside the

Dominican Republic are seeking to gain control."[24] But the administration's continuing reticence indicated uncertainty and even division within the administration about how to explain and justify the military intervention, not disagreement as to why it had been undertaken. Even before the outset of the crisis, and increasingly each day once it began, American officials at all levels had been concerned about the possibility of a Communist takeover in Santo Domingo. By the time the Marines were sent in, fear of a "second Cuba" preoccupied those reporting from Santo Domingo and shaped the decisions of the president and his advisers. Possibly some of President Johnson's aides did not understand fully the context of the initial authorization to land the Marines, and certainly some urged the president not to go beyond his usable evidence about the danger of a "second Cuba" in discussing the intervention even after they appreciated the president's viewpoint, but none disputed his decision to counteract the presumed Communist threat.

The administration's public discussion of the Dominican crisis at the time, as well as subsequent "official line" reconstructions of the three supposed stages of the decision to intervene—each with a distinct purpose and only the last for political reasons—do not conform accurately to the record. Nor does the official version of the establishment of the Line of Communication faithfully reflect the real origins of this move. Although the LOC was publicly presented simply as a means of protecting the evacuation route and therefore as neutral in aim, those who proposed the linkup of American troops intended this measure primarily in order to contain rebel forces. It is clear, indeed, that the deployment of American forces along the LOC did not reflect the wish of the Army, which sought to continue on into the city, but rather represented a compromise among conflicting views within the U.S. government.

The official line is obviously wrong. The radical view—that the United States sent its forces into Santo Domingo to stifle Juan Bosch's movement because of its revolutionary program—also seems inaccurate, but it cannot be so conclusively rebutted without a sure means of showing exactly what individuals have in mind. It can be shown, however, that the radical view is not demonstrated by the available evidence, that it is not necessary to explain any American action in the Dominican crisis, and that it does not account satisfactorily for some. Perhaps only the insistent and utter lack of candor by official spokesmen has made the radical view so credible.

It is true that from the start of the crisis American officials favored the establishment of a provisional junta to hold elections and did not even consider pressuring the Dominican military leaders to accept Bosch's immediate return. It is clear, too, that American officials in Santo Domingo and in Washington disliked Juan Bosch and frowned on his hopes to return to the Dominican presidency. It is by no means sure, however, that the American government's antipathy to Bosch owed mainly to his program or aims, as distinct from adverse judgments of his personal capacity and effectiveness. Nor is it certain just what effect American disdain for Bosch had on specific decisions taken during the 1965 crisis, particularly on the initial decision to favor the establishment by Dominican military leaders of a junta to hold national elections. Other reasons, difficult to separate from their attitudes toward Bosch, also inclined American officials toward the "junta plus elections" formula. American officials believed, probably correctly, that the attempt by a secret cadre to restore Bosch to power without new elections was opposed by most Dominican civilian and military leaders on April 24–25; by favoring the junta formula, the U.S. government felt it was taking a popular course. More important, the embassy, like Reid Cabral himself, at first underestimated the strength of the pro-Bosch movement within the Armed Forces. Even on Sunday morning, American officials believed that the movement was confined mainly to officers in two Army battalions and did not include representation from the other services. It was assumed, therefore, that the major factions in the Dominican Armed Forces would have little difficulty reaching agreement to establish a junta, thus resolving the crisis without American participation. Given their desire to remain as uninvolved in

Dominican politics as possible, it seems likely that American officials would have favored the establishment of a provisional junta even had their attitude toward Bosch been more favorable.

By Sunday noon, those Dominicans calling for Bosch's immediate return had taken over the National Palace. To gain actual control of the country, however, the pro-Bosch forces would still have had somehow to overcome the strident opposition of the most powerful sectors of the Dominican Armed Forces. Again, American officials might well have favored a provisional junta in this situation, even had their view of Bosch been more positive. Given the embassy's prior assessments that most Dominicans favored prompt national elections and that those insisting on an immediate "return to constitutionality without elections" were but a minority faction within the PRD, the junta formula seemed to be a generally acceptable solution, favored by the dominant military forces. Supporting the "junta plus elections" formula also seemed to permit the United States to influence the outcome of the Dominican power struggle without actively participating in it. A more difficult issue would have been faced had Juan Bosch attempted to fly back from San Juan to take charge of his movement, but he did not do so and there appears to be no evidence that American officials physically deterred his return at this or any other point.

The American decision to favor the junta formula was obviously influenced, or at least reinforced, by the negative view of Juan Bosch prevailing within the U.S. government, even if it is difficult to know exactly how or to what extent. There does not appear to be any evidence, however, to suggest that anyone in the U.S. government contemplated American military intervention, if necessary, to prevent Bosch's regaining office. On the contrary, there is every reason to believe that if American officials had regarded preventing Bosch's return as a very high priority objective, worth even landing the Marines to accomplish, the embassy would have been authorized early in the crisis to press forcefully for the establishment of a provisional junta. But no overt American participation in the crisis, not even verbal support for the idea of establishing a junta (which the embassy actually recommended), was authorized by Washington as long as American officials saw the issue simply as whether or not Juan Bosch would become president again.

By the time the military intervention occurred on Wednesday, April 28, the situation perceived by American officials had changed dramatically. The embassy did not call for the Marines to prevent a victory by those clearly aiming to restore Bosch, many of whom had already abandoned the struggle, but to interpose American forces in what had become a very unpredictable situation, thought by U.S. officials to be easily exploitable by Dominican Communists. When the decision was made within the U.S. government to oppose Bosch's return, there was no expectation that the United States would intervene militarily on this account, nor even a willingness to undertake overt actions far short of military intervention to stop Bosch from coming back. When the decisions were made to land the Marines and then to intervene massively, they were not made to prevent Bosch's own return but because American officials believed that a direct Communist takeover might otherwise result.

The struggle within the U.S. government over how to deploy the troops, the rejection of the U.S. military's recommendation that American troops be allowed to take over the city, and the long delay before even a linkup of U.S. forces was finally authorized further suggest the inadequacy of the radical view to account for American policy. What radical critics interpret as steps designed to defeat the pro-Bosch forces could also be viewed as measures to protect them and to facilitate political negotiations. To impute a single purpose to such actions, as if they were the result of a unified actor's will, is obviously misleading.

What accounts for American policy in the 1965 Dominican crisis, if not the purposes cited by official spokesmen or radical critics?

The liberal view suggests that the causes of the Dominican intervention were accidental, that the United States blundered into unexpected and unpredictable actions because of individual errors and because of circumstances peculiar to this case. Personalities and their interaction, and the impinging on persons of contingent events are seen by liberal writers as the keys for understanding and explaining the Dominican episode.

The liberal view seems to be substantiated in many ways by this detailed account, for accidents of personality and of timing clearly affected the development of the Dominican crisis and of American actions. Events might well have gone differently had Bosch been more daring or Caamaño less so, had Molina Ureña been more ambitious or Imbert less so, had Wessin been quicker to act or Peña Gómez less so, had the embassy staff in Santo Domingo been more assertive or Undersecretary Mann in Washington less so. Ambassador Bennett's personal abhorrence of disorder, Chargé Connett's uncertainty upon facing his first critical professional test, William Raborn's amateurish enthusiasm in his first days as CIA Director, Juan Bosch's posturing, Hector Aristy's cunning, Salvador Montás's scheming: all of these undoubtedly shaped the Dominican intervention. And the Dominican crisis might have evolved very differently had it taken place at some other time: had the ambassador and all other key staff members been at their posts when the crisis began; had the crisis not broken on a Saturday afternoon; had the Puerto Rican leaders who might otherwise have facilitated communication between Bosch and the U.S. government not been preoccupied that particular weekend with a funeral in San Juan; had there not been so much recent turnover of relevant personnel in Washington; and especially had this whole episode not occurred just a few weeks after the massive American buildup in South Vietnam had begun. It must be said, as well, that the kind of political crisis Santo Domingo experienced in 1965 would have produced a very different American response in some other place. The extraordinary involvement of the United States in Dominican politics, exemplified by the efforts of nearly every Dominican political group except the Communists to secure embassy backing on April 24 and 25, certainly skewed the outcome of the 1965 crisis.

With respect to each particular incident in the crisis, the

liberal focus on specific individuals and particular circumstances seems sensible and persuasive. More effective embassy and CIA officials undoubtedly could have informed the U.S. government better about the pro-Bosch conspiracy in the Dominican Armed Forces. Different political officers might well have seized various opportunities—including the PRD initiatives on Sunday and the ambassador's meeting with Molina Ureña and his colleagues on Tuesday—to resolve the crisis politically. More astute and better qualified officers—perhaps the absent MAAG contingent—might well have perceived more quickly that the Dominican Armed Forces would not pull together effectively, or might have helped them do so. Another president, especially one more comfortable in dealing with foreign affairs, would certainly have made his influence felt in different ways. Even the same president presumably might have acted differently earlier in his own administration, before the escalation of American commitment in Vietnam. And it is true that alternative actions at various critical points might have produced very different results: had Bosch returned promptly on Sunday instead of waiting; had the Air Force generals waited on Sunday instead of bombing; had Wessin's tanks crossed into the city on Tuesday instead of regrouping; had Caamaño, Montes Arache, and others joined PRD leaders in hiding and asylum on Wednesday instead of returning to the fight.

In trying to explain the Dominican intervention, it is tempting to highlight all these contingent factors and to resist the search for more fundamental causes. To do so is even somewhat comforting, for it allows us to regard the Dominican episode as a sort of freak, an isolated incident unlikely to be repeated in the future.

This level of analysis is not intellectually satisfying even as an explanation of a single case, however; it becomes all the less plausible when one considers what seems to be nearly parallel occurrences in other recent foreign policy crises. Although "mistakes" undoubtedly abound and the element of chance is always present, the repetition of similar errors and the recurrence of familiar patterns suggest that what was apparently "accidental" in the Dominican episode may have resulted from a more basic syndrome which makes such "accidents" predictable. One is compelled to seek more fundamental explanations, perhaps relevant to other cases.

II

The first step toward encountering more satisfactory explanations of the American actions which comprised the Dominican intervention is to abandon the constraints imposed by the "rational policy model" of foreign policy formation.

All available studies of the Dominican intervention, whether sympathetic to or critical of the landings of American forces, depend upon the assumptions of the rational policy model, which considers foreign policy occurrences the "purposive acts of national governments, conceived as unitary rational agents."[25] The model conceives of foreign policy as resulting from conscious, optimizing choice by a single actor ("the state"), picking among alternative ways to affect a foreign situation.

Like the Molière character who had unknowingly been speaking prose all along, writers on foreign affairs generally and on the Dominican crisis in particular have posed questions and framed answers based on the rational policy model, whether or not they have stated or even understood its assumptions. The approach implicit in every published work on the Dominican intervention has been to ask what purpose the U.S. government was pursuing and whether or not the actions taken actually advanced that purpose. It is assumed that purposes can be imputed from actions and their consequences, that policy is more or less unified and consistent, and that apparent inconsistencies can usually be attributed to accident or blunder.

Official spokesmen and radical critics both argue that the U.S. government consistently pursued and ultimately achieved its purpose in the Dominican crisis; they differ only about the nature and legitimacy of the supposed aim. Liberal critics also assume that the United States government generally makes foreign policy on the basis of rational choice in accord with established purpose. Faced with explaining a set of American actions at odds with their conception of the U.S. government's purpose—as was the case in the Dominican episode—liberals suggest that the United States did not consistently pursue its objective, for reasons they attempt to state. It is precisely their dependence on the rational policy model which causes liberal commentators to be puzzled by the seeming discontinuities of American actions in the Dominican crisis and which shapes their attempts to explain what are viewed as surprising acts. Since it is impossible to reconcile supposed purpose with observed occurrences, it is presumed that accident or blunder must account for the discrepancy.

This study lends further support to those writers who find the rational policy model inadequate and who seek new ways to explain foreign policy, understood as a term applied to impose unity upon various actions (or failures to act) of that collection of personalities, separate institutions, and overlapping bargaining processes we call "the state" in the international arena.[26]

The events this study reviews suggest that although such actions may sometimes derive from optimizing choice by responsible policy-level officials among a defined set of established alternatives, that is by no means always the case. Often they reflect not deliberate choice by officials at the top of the policy process, but spontaneous reactions by those close to the bottom of the foreign policy-making hierarchy: to go home because the crisis is believed over, to disbelieve the authenticity of possible overtures from the rebels, to refuse to offer the embassy as a site for negotiations, to lie to rebel inquirers on the telephone, to authorize the Marines to fire against reported opposition, or to order American troops to stop and hold for the night rather than to advance. Such actions usually result not from total choices among static alternatives—to land troops or not, for instance—but from a large number of partial choices in a dynamic stream of constantly changing possibilities: whether or not to press for the establishment of a junta or to work only for a cease-fire; whether or not to talk with Juan Bosch on the telephone; whether or not to provide walkie-talkies and then whether or not to reject a plea for them; whether or not to permit American forces to advance, then whether or not to require them to retreat. These actions are often aimed not to achieve a predetermined outcome but only to avoid another, or just to reduce uncertainty. They are likely to be designed merely to "satisfice," whether because of limits on resources or because of the strain for consensus among decisionmakers, as was the case both in authorizing more troops to be sent but restricting their movement and in permitting the LOC to be established.[27]

Foreign policy actions are often best understood as the outputs of established organizational procedures, which limit the range of effective choice to measures within the physical and administrative capacities of relevant government organizations and which make it possible for the government to do only what its components are prepared to accomplish.[28] The Dominican intervention occurred in part because the embassy was not prepared to provide much information, even basic biographical data, on the rebel military leaders while the CIA was ready to churn out numerous reports on what Dominican Communists were doing, and also because the State Department is not geared to anticipate an impending political crisis in the absence of action-forcing deadlines, like the elections scheduled in Santo Domingo for mid-1965, while the Defense Department is always prepared to land massive numbers of troops and equipment very quickly in a place like Santo Domingo.

Foreign policy occurrences also reflect the distinct perspectives of different government agencies—each with its own mission, priorities, recruitment and career structures, reward systems, information streams, and standard rules of procedure, and each somewhat able to impose its concepts on actions it is called upon to execute. That the CIA station reported early and often on the activities of Dominican Communists, that the attachés communicated repeatedly with their counterparts in the established Dominican Armed Forces even while the embassy's posture in the political crisis was supposed uninvolvement, that the embassy's political officers reported every possible sign of Communist influence but knew little about the rebel military or even about what was happening in the downtown area, that U.S. military officers began calling for more troops and equipment almost as soon as they arrived and wished to use them even as the White House was pressing for a cease-fire: all these actions followed naturally from the special role of each agency and all contributed to the sum total of American policy.

Foreign policy actions also register the differential access to and influence upon the policy-making process at various points by many individuals and institutions inside and outside the U.S. government, including personal advisers of the president or other key officials, foreign governments or other individual foreign leaders, international organizations, journalists, and the like. Foreign policy actions may be decisively shaped by the actions and recommendations of persons and groups outside the authorized and official policy-making structure. The deliberations and decisions on how to deploy American troops after they had landed were very much influenced, for instance, by the views—actual or anticipated—of Martin, Benítez, Fortas, the papal nuncio, Betancourt, Figueres, Muñoz Marín, the members of the OAS Special Committee, particular Latin American governments, and major U.S. newspapers.

Foreign policy may represent, as well, the outcome of bureaucratic politics, of simultaneous overlapping bargaining processes among policy-level officials in which the ultimate results are determined more by the power, vantage point, and skill of the respective participants, and even by the order in which they take part, than by the intrinsic merits of the positions they propose or defend.[29] The foreign policy-making process is political, not scientific, and personal judgments and preferences are often at its heart.[30] Individuals with different conceptions of personal, organizational, and national goals struggle to make their views prevail. By pulling and hauling in different directions, they often produce results different from what any of them intends, as was the case with the administration's public discussion of Communist participation in the Dominican revolt and also of the decision to establish the LOC.

Foreign policy actions are meant to affect not a clearly defined situation abroad, but rather a confusing set of events about which information is always incomplete and often inaccurate, and which looks different from moment to moment, or even simultaneously to different individuals and agencies.[31] The repeated cases in which State Department instructions were based on outdated reports of what was occurring in Santo Domingo, particularly with respect to the strength of the anti-rebel forces, suggest that decisions are often intended to influence situations that no longer exist by the time the decisions are actually taken. Key determinations may also be made without a consensus among those involved defining the basic elements of the situation with which they are dealing and sometimes even without any awareness that such a consensus is lacking.

Finally, foreign policy actions are inevitably affected, as well, by foul-ups and failures whether arising from carelessness, like the use of a misdrawn map; from mechanical flaws, like the misrouting of Wheeler's important message for Palmer; or from the human mistakes of individuals under stress, like the distraught reports of alleged atrocities.

Foreign policy actions, then, are shaped not so much by the purposes in terms of which they are usually discussed, but by perceptions and information, by the priorities and procedures of different actors in the policy-making process, by bargaining and politics, by external pressures and internal strains, by conflict resolution and consensus-building. Competition, compromise, coalition, and confusion combine in uncertain ways to produce the occurrences we term foreign policy.

What we call foreign policy is really a collage comprised of a great many specific actions, each undertaken separately although often related in many ways. Because "outcomes which would never have been chosen by an actor and would never have emerged from bargaining in a single game over the issue are fabricated piece by piece," analysis and explanation must begin by disaggregating "policy" and concentrating on particular occurrences.[32]

This study has made a start in that direction by focusing in some detail on a number of the decisions and actions which comprised the Dominican intervention of 1965. Much remains to be done, even on this single case, for the evidence now available does not permit confident statements about the perceptions and perspectives of many of the relevant actors; differences among presidential advisers in Washington are particularly hard to define, for instance, and evidence about the president's own views and actions is still fragmentary and uncertain.

What is clear from this account, however, is that the Dominican intervention was not the simple outcome of the U.S. government's single-minded pursuit of national objective. (One cannot even say without qualification that the Dominican intervention reflected a presidential choice to use military force, for the Dominican case exemplifies the fact that "the ultimate decision" may be largely determined by the time it reaches the president's desk.)[33] The Dominican intervention resulted, rather, from a complex of decisions and actions on lesser matters by various American officials up and down the line, none of whom seems to have expected or wished his decisions to lead to military intervention.

It remains to be asked, however, whether these many decisions and actions were mostly random and unpredictable, or whether they composed an identifiable pattern, largely attributable to more fundamental causes.

III

Systematic analysis of the materials in this study suggests that the series of actions which produced and comprised the massive American military intervention of 1965 should not be attributed mainly to individual incompetence, momentary fright, mere accidents of timing or personality, nor to a particular ambassador or president. Nor were these actions unconnected or capricious, however; they were, rather, the natural consequences of the attitudes and assumptions with which American officials generally had approached the Dominican Republic for some time and of the procedures by which they responded to events there in 1965. Far from being a puzzling aberration in recent American diplomacy, the Dominican intervention becomes quite comprehensible when the focus of inquiry shifts from purposes and personalities to premises and procedures.

Perhaps the single most striking fact about the Dominican intervention of 1965 is that it could occur without any (known) prior objection being raised within the U.S. government, despite the fact that the United States had for thirty years repeatedly foresworn unilateral armed intervention in Latin America. That American officials could so easily shed their inhibitions suggests that although the Dominican intervention violated important precepts of U.S. foreign policy, it also flowed naturally and consistently from other established premises, widely shared within the American foreign policy-making apparatus, at least in 1965.

Comprehensive analysis of the attitudes and assumptions with which American officials approached the Dominican crisis would begin at a very fundamental level. It would consider the impact of America's geography, history, and culture, of its political, economic, and social institutions, and even of its "national character" or "style" on the way the United States conducts foreign affairs.[34] It would examine the effect of America's continental expanse and its ocean-width distance from other centers of power on national feeling toward involvement abroad. It would assess the consequences of the origins and early history of the American nation in shaping a sense of this country's "manifest destiny and mission."[35] It would discuss the effects of America's abundant resources on this society and on its approach to others.[36] It would take up the significance for U.S. foreign policy of America's "liberal tradition" and of particular American values and ideals.[37] And it would analyze the specific manner in which this country's experience affects national assumptions about politics—the way, for instance, that Americans approach the problem of government-building by directing themselves primarily to the limitation of authority and the division of power rather than their creation and accumulation.[38]

A complete discussion of policy-makers' premises would also

include some consideration of basic general assumptions about inter-American affairs. It would note the continuing influence of the "western hemisphere idea" that "the peoples of this hemisphere stand in a special relationship with one another that sets them apart from the rest of the world."[39] And it would consider the degree to which Americans—perhaps ever since the time of James Monroe but at least since Herbert Hoover— have regarded Latin America, and especially the Caribbean, not only of special economic and security interest to the United States, but also of particular significance for domestic American politics. The effect on President Johnson and other American officials of their belief that the American people would not accept another setback in the Caribbean must have been very important.

A full analysis would deal not only with fundamental national attitudes but also with somewhat more specific premises about foreign policy shared by those whom Richard Barnet calls the "national security managers": the set of individuals responsible for administering American diplomacy since World War II. It would outline their "operational code," particularly their conceptions of America's national objectives and of the obstacles to their realization, their beliefs about the nature, causes, and effects of violence in international politics, and their ideas about the appropriate use of armed force as an instrument of policy.[40] And it would set out their ideas about the nature and objectives of Communism. It would stress, for instance, the perception U.S. government officials had in the early 1960's of a worldwide Communist challenge to American interests, from Berlin to Vietnam and at many spots—including Cuba and the Caribbean—in between.[41] That the U.S. government's response to the Dominican crisis was conducted by men who believed themselves engaged in an international struggle against Communism, and who had just committed themselves to an expanded war in Asia as a result, is obviously central to what occurred.

All these diverse sources as well as others—historical, cultural, organizational, and personal—undoubtedly shaped the general attitudes of American officials who dealt with the Dominican case, as they have affected the U.S. government's conduct of other foreign policy crises. Two key elements of the framework of assumptions and preconceptions with which American officials approached the Dominican events of 1965 may be attributed in part to the specific background of Dominican-American relations, however: the intense desire to preclude a Communist takeover in Santo Domingo and the somewhat contradictory aim to avoid involvement in Dominican politics.

Longstanding doctrine made American officials at all levels approach the Dominican Republic in 1965, as for decades before, as a potential enemy base from which foreign influence should be excluded, and to regard political changes there in terms of threat, not opportunity. More immediate experience, and the policy-makers' penchant for historical analogies, caused this general approach to be translated into a specific concern to avoid a "second Cuba" in the Dominican Republic and to preclude a "Communist takeover" there. International and domestic political considerations reinforced each other and sustained the U.S. government's determination not to allow a "second Cuba."

The U.S. government's preoccupation with avoiding a "second Cuba" had structured the way American officials looked at the Dominican Republic throughout the early 1960's, influencing what they noted and what they regarded as significant. Dominican politicians of various types were characteristically reported on with reference to their supposed place in the ideological spectrum, without recognition of the fragility of ideological and even personal commitments in contemporary Dominican politics. Dominican Communists were seen as potential agents of extracontinental power, not as weak and fragmented groups of dissidents. The Dominican Armed Forces, in turn, were conceived not primarily as rival bands of plunder but as an institution opposed to instability and to Communist advance. Dominican politics generally was not interpreted primarily in terms of praetorian disorder but more in terms of "Castro-Communist" attempts to gain power. What was asked about Dominican politics, time after time, was how a given set of circumstances would affect Communist strength. Organizational responses were predictable; about as many embassy officers were assigned to analyze and report on the activities of a few hundred known or suspected Communists as to follow all other Dominican political actors.

The distorting effect of this insistent focus on the "Castro-Communist" threat became most sharply evident during the 1965 crisis. From the very outset, both Washington officials and those in Santo Domingo keyed their questions and reports to the need to avoid a "second Cuba." Because American intelligence agencies were geared to produce lots of data on Communist activities but were unprepared to assess correctly the configurations of non-Communist Dominicans in this confused period, the picture they presented was bound to be unbalanced and wrong. Even accurate reports on Communist activities were very misleading because the setting was so imperfectly understood. The embassy knew too little about the pro-Bosch movement, especially within the Dominican Armed Forces, to understand its strength when the crisis broke or to appreciate its relative coherence during the week of April 24. Washington officials, in turn, reinforced the distorted embassy focus by asking repeatedly for more information and reports on Dominican Communists, rather than on the context in which they were operating.

Given the shared preoccupation of American officials with the "second Cuba" possibility, there was a tendency throughout the week (as previously) to err on the side of magnifying the Communist risk, by reporting on all the possible Communist connections of other Dominican actors in the crisis and by passing on to Washington all reports of presumed Communist plans and intentions, for instance. Because of their preoccupations, too, it is not surprising that American officials misperceived particular events—the rebels' exuberant radio appeals, their distribution of arms, their failure to observe several cease-fires, and the shooting of police—as part of a Communist pattern, nor is it incomprehensible that they believed and reported exaggerated and sometimes even virtually groundless stories about alleged atrocities. The supposed Cuban analogy influenced the embassy's perceptions and reporting at every turn; references to "Castroite radio appeals," "Castro tactics," and the like were common in the embassy's dispatches, and Colonel Caamaño was even tabbed "his country's Castro" although there was little objective basis for linking most of the rebels with Cuba or Caamaño with Fidel.[42]

That the Dominican Republic lacked an intensely dedicated, skillful, and attractive political leader like Castro; that no popularly based guerrilla movement existed there; that Dominican Communists were weak, fragmented, and totally lacking in rural support; that Dominican society was relatively unorganized and that power in Santo Domingo was nowhere centralized and susceptible to overnight seizure: all these facts were forgotten, or probably not known, by President Johnson and his aides as they considered what to do about the Dominican crisis. The power of preconception, reinforced by official rhetoric and bureaucratic repetition, to determine foreign policy perceptions and actions has rarely, if ever, been more conclusively demonstrated.

The second established American attitude which shaped the actions the U.S. government undertook during the Dominican crisis was the strong reluctance to interfere in the messy details of Dominican politics. In part this reluctance undoubtedly reflected a more general American desire to avoid overt intervention in foreign politics, but in the Dominican case this overall bias was sharply reinforced by the desire of American officials to avoid repeating what they perceived as excessive and counterproductive U.S. involvement in Dominican affairs during the early 1960's.

From the start of the 1965 crisis, when there emerged a relatively simple and probably reconcilable division between those Dominicans favoring Bosch's immediate return and those desiring elections, American officials let pass a number of possible opportunities to exert their influence directly, choosing instead to abstain from overt involvement. Established attitudes, not accidental circumstances or individual quirk, may be seen to account, for instance, for the Sunday morning decision that the embassy should favor the establishment of a junta but not directly pressure for it. Chargé Connett, Caribbean Country Director Crockett, Deputy Assistant Secretary Sayre, and Undersecretary Mann—those who consulted (perhaps with others) about the Dominican crisis early on Sunday morning—were acting on the basis of premises and appraisals widely shared within the U.S. government when they agreed that the embassy should encourage the anti-Bosch faction to establish a junta but should not itself become involved at all in arranging the details.

Given prior assumptions accepted within the U.S. government —the almost universal disdain for Bosch, the belief that the Dominican Armed Forces were basically united in opposing Bosch and that most politically active Dominicans preferred prompt elections to any other means of resolving the impasse, the fear that Dominican Communists could exploit any prolonged uncertainty, and the reluctance to become entangled again in Dominican politics—the Sunday morning decision was predictable. Had the U.S. government been enthusiastic about Bosch's prospective comeback, or even had the embassy merely believed that Bosch would speedily return and be accepted as president by the Dominican Armed Forces and the Dominican people, then there might have been no American disposition to favor the prompt establishment of an anti-Bosch military junta at this point. Alternatively, had the Dominican Republic not been viewed as a prime target of Communist subversion (or had the Cold War assumption about the need to limit "Communist advance" no longer been so powerful), the U.S. government might not have been very concerned about the possibility of prolonged struggle and uncertainty about who would govern Santo Domingo. But given the conflict, the supposed Communist threat, and the desire to avoid direct U.S. involvement, the U.S. government's decision to support an antirebel military junta without overt American pressure to set it up followed naturally.

From this Sunday decision on, American officials in Santo Domingo and especially in Washington repeatedly demonstrated their reluctance to participate in the Dominican crisis in relatively minor ways which might well have obviated the need later felt for military intervention. On Sunday morning, the embassy refused the PRD request to witness a transfer of power to them from Reid Cabral. On Sunday evening, the embassy declined to ask the Dominican Armed Forces to cease its strafing. On Sunday and often thereafter, American officials failed to exert direct pressures to promote the establishment of a junta or even to push actively for negotiations among the factions; on Monday, Washington specifically declined to authorize the embassy to do so. On Tuesday morning, embassy officials refused to provide a neutral site where talks could take place or even to try to convince the contending factions to settle on a meeting place. On Tuesday afternoon, Ambassador Bennett declined to mediate between the Dominican power-contenders and passed up a possible opportunity to negotiate directly with Juan Bosch. And on Wednesday, in an episode characteristic of the general process, Washington officials refused to supply walkie-talkies to the reeling anti-Bosch forces until it was too late for the equipment to make any difference. Each of these decisions, of course, was made for a variety of reasons, but they all shared as one element a conscious desire to minimize American involvement, a desire which contributed, paradoxically, to the perceived need for massive military intervention.

Two important procedural features also characterized the pattern of the U.S. government's response to the Dominican crisis and affected its evolution.

One, perhaps closely related to the desire to avoid overt involvement in Dominican politics, was the general tendency to "decide as little as possible" at each stage and to postpone difficult choices.[43] Before the crisis broke, American officials contributed to the deterioration of the Dominican situation by failing to face squarely the issue posed by Reid Cabral's unpopular attempt at *continuismo* and waiting instead for the deadline imposed by the elections schedule. When the April 24th coup occurred, American officials decided at first to help neither Reid nor the rebels and to favor the establishment of a military junta, but not to undertake any direct action to bring the junta into being. Then the embassy recommended that the U.S. government make clear its support for the junta formula but defer any decision as to whether a show of force might be employed to back up its position. Washington responded, characteristically, by ordering the embassy not to press directly for the formation of a junta, but only for a cease-fire which would facilitate negotiations. The next day, when the embassy called urgently for walkie-talkies, Washington declined to furnish the communication devices but made sure they would be available nearby. And so it went throughout these days, American officials reacting to the Dominican situation in limited ways, often too little and too late to affect as they wished a rapidly changing set of imperfectly understood circumstances, and with Washington officials —their approach largely affected by the desire to avoid further problems and involvements—tending to restrict the embassy's urge to act.

When overt military intervention began on Wednesday, however, this process changed remarkably, the U.S. government's involvement having been established. The determination of top officials to benefit from past experience as they understood it and therefore to use sufficient force early enough, reinforced by organizational procedures and rivalries, helped cause a very rapid expansion of the intervention's scope and scale. Until Wednesday afternoon, established attitudes and procedures combined to keep management of the U.S. government's response to events in Santo Domingo away from top officials and to limit American participation in the crisis. From the moment military intervention was authorized, however, other established attitudes and crisis procedures combined to put management of the crisis into the hands of the key decisionmakers and to escalate sharply the instruments available to achieve American objectives. Because general tendencies were reinforced in this case by President Johnson's personal style, the Dominican case provided an extreme example of this reversal. Attempts to keep the Dominican Republic "off the front burner" having failed, the

Dominican crisis took new shape after Wednesday as President Johnson began to tend the stove himself by becoming, in effect, his own desk officer.

Finally, the American response to the Dominican crisis reflected a tendency on the part of American officials to act on the basis of excessively optimistic appraisals and predictions, their analyses often having been influenced by their preferences. Until contrary evidence became overwhelming, American officials in Santo Domingo and in Washington generally exaggerated Reid Cabral's appeal and potential; this was undoubtedly related to their reluctance to conceive of a political comeback by Juan Bosch or Joaquín Balaguer, both of whom were disliked. Throughout these months, and even on the eve of the crisis, American intelligence officers discounted the possibility of a pro-Bosch military coup; reports specifically naming those who eventually pulled off the April 24th uprising were explicitly downgraded. When the crisis broke, embassy officers at first let themselves believe that Reid Cabral's television broadcast had been effective and that the coup was being put down. After Reid's collapse became obvious the next morning, the embassy continued to underestimate the strength of the pro-Bosch clique within the Dominican Armed Forces and to believe mistakenly that the antirebel faction would quickly assert control. Time and again over the next few days—at the moment of Ambassador Bennett's confrontation with rebel leaders in the embassy, for instance—American officials planned and acted on the assumption that the established Dominican Armed Forces were about to put down the revolt. Even as late as mid-afternoon on Wednesday, McGeorge Bundy and Thomas Mann agreed that Colonel Benoit's oral request for U.S. military intervention could be set aside because the balance of power was with the antirebel forces. By failing repeatedly to foresee the consequences of less than favorable developments, American officials allowed the Dominican situation to deteriorate until by late Wednesday afternoon President Johnson thought he had no alternative but to authorize the Marine landing. Because it had counted repeatedly on the desired to occur, the U.S. government felt itself forced to do the undesirable: to undertake unilateral military intervention in Latin America.

IV

Even a cursory examination of the available literature on U.S. foreign policy in other recent cases reveals striking similarities among the explanations of American conduct in very different situations, including the foregoing analysis of the Dominican intervention.

Townsend Hoopes's study of Vietnam, for instance, stresses the assumptions which skewed the reactions and perceptions of American officials and emphasizes the supposed individual traits of key decisionmakers: "President Johnson's own uncertainty and sense of insecurity in handling foreign policy," Dean Rusk's "knack for arguing by analogy," Walt Rostow's "compulsion for buttressing his own thoughts by a rapid culling of the evidence at hand, . . . (his mind being) an automatic mental filter which accepted only reinforcing data," and Robert Komer's "compulsive optimism."[44] In the Dominican case, Rostow and Komer were not involved at all and Rusk and Johnson played little role during the first crucial days, but exactly these assumptions and traits made themselves evident and produced a similar (if more limited and rapid) inadvertent escalation into military adventure.

Numerous analyses of the Bay of Pigs episode also highlight the effect of Cold War assumptions and the power of questionable analogies as well as the tendency to plan on the basis of over-optimistic projections and to filter out contradictory reports.[45] Richard Neustadt's analysis of Skybolt and Suez, John Steinbruner's analysis of the MLF case, and Jeffrey Race's essay on Vietnam, too, cite similar failures: the tendency of policymakers to rely on misleading analogies and on wishful thinking, to make judgments blurred by "the light of hope," in Neustadt's phrase, and to act on the "inference of impossibility," the psychological mechanism which "operates to prevent the necessity of taking an alternative into serious consideration."[46]

To establish what these brief comments suggest—that there

are persuasive general explanations for recent U.S. foreign policy failures—would go beyond the scope of this essay, which aims only to illuminate the Dominican case and thereby to facilitate systematic comparative analysis. Many more case studies, each of them identifying particular causes and even apparent "accidents," will be needed before inductive analysis permits confident general interpretations. But perhaps it is proper to suggest, at least, that the recurring patterns here identified seem to relate to the procedures of American foreign policy-making, more generally to the workings of large organizations, and even more fundamentally to the mental processes policy-makers employ.

It should not be surprising, for instance, that dubious analogies play such an important role in shaping the response of the American government (and presumably others) to international affairs. Foreign political realities are so complex—the Dominican Republic's "politics of chaos" being only one example —that simplifying concepts are needed. Policy-makers seize on evils they have experienced and wish to avoid in order to organize their information about events they do not have time to analyze from scratch. Subordinates do the same, at least in part to win the attention of those above them. Hence, unfamiliar problems are discussed in terms of the familiar. The more advanced thought policy-makers give to avoiding a possible situation—a "second Cuba," for example—the more likely they are to misperceive ambiguous events as resembling that situation.[47] The more intolerant they are of risk and ambiguity, moreover, the more likely they are to maintain their misperception even in the face of contradictory information.[48] Having identified a set of circumstances in terms of the dubious analogy, policy-makers act on the basis of the analogy until forced by failure to abandon it; by then, misperception may have adversely affected reality.

Conscious, forceful, and repeatedly critical questioning of the dubious analogy from within or from outside the bureaucracy might undermine its power, but such questioning rarely occurs before the costly results of accepting the faulty comparison have been experienced. On the contrary, the dubious analogy is preserved, given sanctity and power by public rhetoric, and reinforced in bureaucratic formulations up and down the line; it affects the questions asked, the evidence noticed, and the events recorded. By the time a crisis like that in Santo Domingo occurs, it is too late to escape the consequences; policy-makers are prisoners of their own and others' language and concepts.

The tendencies to decide as little as possible, to filter out contradictory information, and to accept optimistic appraisals are explainable at one level in psychological terms, but they are also organizational phenomena, related to the way bureaucracies generally function and reinforced by the particularly fragmented and incremental processes of American foreign policy-making. Within the extensive establishment the United States has by now amassed to handle foreign affairs, each official focuses on his small part of the puzzle, his vision distorted by the need to look for what he knows his superiors are most concerned about and constrained by the fact that other officials will have the responsibility for related aspects of the process. Each official knows that the task of completing the analysis and acting upon it will be someone else's; none seems to be responsible for questioning the premises of policy or for evaluating the adequacy of the questions he is being asked to answer. On the contrary, personal and organizational needs combine to suppress conflict and stifle doubt.[49] What dissent there is may be "domesticated," institutionalized in ineffective channels.[50]

Policy is made by piecemeal consideration of specific issues and choices, one at a time and in a limited context, by men who are not paid to question the premises of policy but only to act upon them. By accepting the established conceptual framework, even when it is inadequate, officials may make a series of individual decisions, each seemingly rational, which comprise a syndrome of miscalculation and produce undesired results. So it was in Santo Domingo in 1965.

Appendixes

Notes

Bibliography

Index

Appendix I. Alphabetical List of Persons Interviewed

Except for eleven persons—mostly officials of the Central Intelligence Agency and the Defense Intelligence Agency, some from the Department of State and the White House staff—all those I interviewed agreed to allow their names to be listed alphabetically in this Appendix.

I had at least one formal interview, and very often several, with each of the individuals listed. I have not included the names of countless others—including many Dominicans, members of the U.S. consulate in Santiago, journalists, and scholars —with whom I discussed these events informally.

For reference purposes, I have included a brief description of the position each person held at the time of the 1965 crisis or other information relevant in identifying the person's role or perspective. I have listed Dominican military officers as "constitutionalist" if they participated on the pro-Bosch side of the conflict. I have also identified the regime which accredited each Dominican holder of public office: the Bosch government (February–September 1963); the Triumvirate (September 1963 to April 25, 1965); the "Provisional Constitutional Government" (April 25–27, 1965); the "Military Junta of Government" (April 28–May 7, 1965); the "Constitutional Government" (May 4– September 1, 1965); the "Government of National Reconstruction" (May 7–September 1, 1965); the Provisional Government

(September 3, 1965–June 30, 1966); and the Balaguer government (July 1, 1966–).

Except where another name has been italicized, the last name listed is the governing name.

1. Ward Allen: Deputy U.S. Representative, Council of the Organization of American States.
2. Silvestre *Alba de Moya:* Minister of Agriculture, Provisional Government. President, Asociación de Hacendados y Agricultores.
3. Emilio Almonte: Minister of Public Works, "Constitutional Government."
4. Fernando *Alvarez* Bogaert: Minister of Agriculture, Balaguer government.
5. Alfonso Arenales: Political officer, U.S. embassy.
6. Héctor Aristy: Minister of the Presidency, "Constitutional Government."
7. Milagros Bosch de Bazanta: Niece of Juan Bosch, and his sometime secretary.
8. George Ball: Undersecretary of State.
9. Jaime Benítez: President, University of Puerto Rico.
10. W. Tapley Bennett, Jr.: U.S. ambassador to the Dominican Republic (1964–1966).
11. Pedro Benoit: Colonel, Dominican Army; President of the "Military Junta of Government."
12. José Armando Bermúdez: Prominent Santiago businessman.
13. Robert Berrelez: Associated Press correspondent.
14. Francisco Bobadilla: Captain (ret.), Dominican Army; a "constitutionalist" officer.
15. Juan Bosch: former President of the Dominican Republic.
16. Alvaro Alves da Silva Braga: General, Brazilian Army; Commander, Inter-American Peace Force (January 1966–September 1966).
17. Arthur Breisky: Political officer, U.S. embassy.
18. George Brown: Political officer, U.S. embassy.
19. McGeorge Bundy: Special Assistant to the President, National Security Affairs.
20. Ellsworth Bunker: U.S. ambassador, Council of the Organization of American States; member, Ad Hoc Commission (June 2, 1965–September 1966).

21. Francisco *Caamaño* Deñó: President, "Constitutional Government."
22. Ramón *Cáceres* Troncoso: Member of the Triumvirate.
23. Aníbal Campagna: President of the Senate, "Constitutional Government."
24. Pedro Manuel *Casals* Victoria: Presidential aide, "Constitutional Government."
25. John Cates, Jr.: Adviser on Latin American affairs, United States Mission to the United Nations.
26. Ramón de Clairemont Dueñas: Ambassador of El Salvador to the Council of the Organization of American States: member, Ad Hoc Commission (June 2, 1965–September 1966).
27. Emmanuele Clarizio: Papal Nuncio, Dominican Republic.
28. Barnard Collier: Correspondent, *New York Herald Tribune.*
29. Héctor Conde: Signed the cease-fire agreement of April 30, 1965, on behalf of the "constitutionalists."
30. William Connett, Jr.: Deputy Chief of Mission, U.S. embassy; Chargé d'Affaires from April 23 to April 27, 1965.
31. Lyle Coppman: Public Affairs officer; U.S. embassy.
32. John Crimmins: U.S. ambassador, Dominican Republic (1966–1969); member, Dominican Republic Task Force in Department of State (1965).
33. Luis *Crouch* Bogaert: Prominent Santiago businessman.
34. Jottin Cury: Foreign Minister, "Constitutional Government."
35. Guido d'Alessandro: Former President, Partido Revolucionario Social Cristiano.
36. Irving Davidson: Washington lobbyist who served as the communications channel between the U.S. government and Joaquín Balaguer during the 1965 crisis.
37. Arturo Despradel: Former Minister of Foreign Affairs; onetime Ambassador to the United States and Rector of University of Santo Domingo.
38. Bernard Diederich: Correspondent, *New York Times; Time.*
39. Enriquillo del Rosario: Dominican ambassador to the United States, Bosch government.
40. Theodore Draper: Author on foreign affairs.
41. Víctor Espaillat: Prominent Santiago businessman; a leading adviser of Balaguer.

42. Leopoldo *Espaillat* Nanita: Former President, Colegio Dominicano de Ingenieros; aide to Dr. José Rafael Molina Ureña; "Provisional Constitutional President."
43. Hunter Estep: Current Analysis Staff Chief, Office of Research and Analysis of American Republics, Department of State.
44. Julio Estrella: Chief editorial writer, *El Caribe;* author of *La revolución dominicana y la crisis de la OEA.*
45. Byron Fairchild: Historical office, Department of State.
46. Arletta Viuda *Fernández* Domínguez: Widow of Colonel Rafael Tomás Fernández Domínguez (Minister of Interior and Police, "Constitutional Government").
47. José Figueres: Former President of Costa Rica.
48. Thomas Fishburn: Lieutenant Colonel, U.S. Air Force; Air Attaché, U.S. embassy.
49. Benjamin Foreman: Chief legal adviser, Department of Defense.
50. L. Enrique Franco: Director, *La Información* (Santiago).
51. Manuel *García* Germán: Captain (ret.), Dominican Army; aide to the Chiefs of Staff, "Constitutional Government."
52. Héctor *García Godoy* Cáceres: President of the Dominican Republic, Provisional Government; Minister of Foreign Affairs, Bosch government.
53. Bonaparte Gautreaux: Presidential aide, "Constitutional Government."
54. Manuel *González* y González: Santo Domingo businessman reputed by U.S. officials to be a well-trained Communist agent and military strategist.
55. James Nelson Goodsell: Latin American correspondent, *Christian Science Monitor.*
56. Alejandro Grullón, President, Banco Popular Dominicano.
57. Julio Gutiérrez: Colonel, Nicaraguan Army; Chief of Staff Inter-American Peace Force.
58. S. Antonio Guzmán: Minister of Agriculture, Bosch government.
59. Howard Handleman: Correspondent, *U.S. News and World Report.*
60. Orlando *Haza* del Castillo: Secretary General, National Planning Board, Bosch government; aide to "Constitutional Government."
61. Homero *Hernández* Almanzar: Prominent lawyer; official

liaison between "Constitutional Government" and Organization of American States.
62. Fabio Herrera: Secretary of the Presidency, Triumvirate.
63. Rafael Herrera: Director, *Listín Diario*.
64. Ralph Heywood: Lieutenant Colonel, United States Marine Corps; Naval Attaché, U.S. embassy.
65. John Calvin Hill: Former U.S. Consul General and Chargé d'Affaires, Dominican Republic (1961–62).
66. Pat Holt: Staff consultant, Senate Foreign Relations Committee.
67. Antonio *Imbert* Barrera: Brigadier General, Dominican Armed Forces; President, "Government of National Reconstruction."
68. Emilio *Jiménez* Reyes: Deputy Chief of Staff, Dominican Navy.
69. James Johnston: Special Assistant to the Undersecretary of State for Economic Affairs.
70. Salvador *Jorge* Blanco: Attorney General, "Constitutional Government."
71. Luis *Julián* Pérez: prominent lawyer; adviser of Dr. Joaquín Balaguer.
72. William Lang: Deputy Assistant Secretary of Defense for International Security Affairs (Inter-American Affairs).
73. Alfred Laun: Public affairs trainee, U.S. Information Service.
74. Robert Linvill: Brigadier General, U.S. Army; Vice-Commander, Inter-American Peace Force (January–September 1966).
75. Andreas Lowenfeld: Deputy Legal Adviser, Department of State.
76. Alan McLean: Staff aide to U.S. Ambassador to the Council of the Organization of American States.
77. Malcolm McLean: Public Affairs officer, U.S. embassy.
78. Thomas Mann: Undersecretary of State for Economic Affairs.
79. John Bartlow Martin: Former United States ambassador to the Dominican Republic (1962–1964); Presidential envoy in May 1965.
80. Jacinto *Martínez* Aranha: General, Dominican Army; Chief of Staff, Dominican Army, "Government of National Reconstruction."

81. Paul Mayer: Colonel, Canadian Armed Forces; Assistant to the Military Adviser to the Secretary General, United Nations.
82. José Antonio Mayobre: Personal representative of the Secretary General, United Nations.
83. Leonard Meeker: Legal Adviser, Department of State.
84. Milton Messina: Dominican ambassador to the United States, Provisional Government.
85. Fidel *Méndez* Núñez: Minister of Finance and Minister without portfolio, Provisional Government.
86. Nicolás Mogen: Political adviser to Juan Bosch and others.
87. José Rafael *Molina* Ureña: President, "Provisional Constitutional Government"; former speaker, House of Representatives, Bosch government.
88. José Mora: Secretary General, Organization of American States.
89. Arturo *Morales-Carrión*: Former Deputy Assistant Secretary of State; member of the secretariat, Organization of American States.
90 Teodoro Moscoso: Former Coordinator of the Alliance for Progress. Sent to Venezuela as a presidential envoy during the 1965 crisis.
91. Luis *Muñoz* Marín: Former Governor, Commonwealth of Puerto Rico.
92. Bruce Palmer: Lieutenant General, United States Army; First Commander, Inter-American Peace Force; Vice-Commander, Inter-American Peace Force (May 1965–January 1966).
93. Tomás Pastoriza: Prominent Santiago businessman; brother-in-law and close adviser of Héctor García Godoy.
94. José Francisco *Peña* Gómez: Former Secretary General, Partido Revolucionario Dominicano.
95. Ilmar *Penna Marinho*: Ambassador of Brazil, Council of the Organization of American States; member, Ad Hoc Commission (June 2, 1965–September 1966).
96. Enrique *Pérez y Pérez*: General, Dominican Army; Minister of the Armed Forces, Provisional Government.
97. Federico Piantini: Captain, Dominican Army; a "constitutionalist" officer.
98. Santiago *Polanco* Abreu: Resident Commissioner, Commonwealth of Puerto Rico.

99. Hugo *Polanco* Brito: Bishop of Santiago.
100. David Quant: Acting Dominican Republic desk officer, International Security Affairs, Department of Defense.
101. Benjamin Read: Executive Secretary, Department of State.
102. Jack Ringler: Major, U.S. Marine Corps. Author of official U.S. Marine Corps history of the Dominican crisis.
103. Antonio Rosario: President, Partido Revolucionario Social Cristiano. Ambassador to the Organization of American States, "Constitutional Government."
104. Margaret Rhoades: Office of Research and Analysis for American Republics, Department of State.
105. Dean Rusk: Secretary of State.
106. Hewson Ryan: Deputy Director, U.S. Information Agency.
107. Robert Sayre, Jr.: Deputy Assistant Secretary of State (Inter-American Affairs).
108. Lorenzo Sención: Captain (ret.), Dominican Army; a "constitutionalist" officer.
109. Harry Shlaudeman: Chief, Dominican Republic Affairs, Department of State; Staff aide to John Martin, McGeorge Bundy, and Ellsworth Bunker.
110. Anthony Solomon: Assistant Secretary of State for Economic Affairs.
111. Ben Stephansky: Deputy U.S. Representative, Council of the Organization of American States.
112. Salvador Sturla: Minister of Public Works, Provisional Government.
113. Froilán Tavares: Former Dean of Law, University of Santo Domingo; adviser to the Ad Hoc Commission (1965).
114. Luis *Tejeda* González: Lieutenant Colonel, Dominican Air Force; a "constitutionalist" officer.
115. Enrique *Tejera* Paris: Venezuelan ambassador to the United States.
116. Hugo *Tolentino* Dipp: Professor, University of Santo Domingo; aide to "Constitutional Government"; reported by U.S. authorities in 1965 to be a Communist leader.
117. Cyrus Vance: Undersecretary of Defense.
118. Nicolás Vargas: Santiago business executive.
119. Benjamin Varon: Ambassador of Israel to Dominican Republic.
120. Jack Hood Vaughn: Assistant Secretary of State for Inter-American Affairs.

121. Bernardo Vega: Economic adviser to the Governor of the Central Bank of the Dominican Republic.
122. José Augusto Vega: Santiago lawyer; aide to "Constitutional Government."
123. Ramón *Vila* Piola: Minister of Industry and Commerce, Bosch government.
124. Sacha Volman: Director, International Institute of Labor Research (New York).
125. Joseph Weyrick: Colonel, U.S. Army; Army Attaché, U.S. embassy.
126. Jackson Wilson: Chief, Political section, U.S. embassy.
127. Gregory Wolfe: Director, Office of Research and Analysis for American Republics, Department of State.
128. Adam Yarmolinsky: Deputy Assistant Secretary of Defense. Head of U.S. Emergency Relief Mission to the Dominican Republic (May–June 1965).

Appendix II. A Guide to Public Sources for Study of the 1965 Dominican Crisis

A student of the 1965 Dominican crisis should begin by reviewing the official public record. Authoritative statements of U.S. policy may be found conveniently in the *Department of State Bulletin* and in the *Public Papers of the Presidents of the United States: Lyndon B. Johnson* (1965); the latter volume contains all of President Johnson's extensive remarks on the Dominican affair in speeches and press conferences. Some of the *Hearings* before the Internal Security Subcommittee of the U.S. Senate Committee on the Judiciary contain valuable information on the Dominican crisis, principally in the testimony of former Dominican General Elías Wessin y Wessin. The extensive hearings on the Dominican crisis held by the Senate Foreign Relations Committee in 1965 remain, unfortunately, unavailable to the public. Important details from the testimony were leaked, however, in newspaper articles which appeared in November 1965 by Max Frankel, David Kraslow, and Walter Pincus and in *Fulbright: the Dissenter* by Haynes Johnson and Bernard Gwertzman. Chairman J. William Fulbright's personal conclusions were expressed in his major address of September 15, 1965, on "The Situation in the Dominican Republic." Other important speeches in the Senate were delivered by Joseph Clark on September 16, 1965, and by Thomas Dodd on May 4, May 24, August 23, and September 16, 1965.

Various documents issued during and after the crisis by the Organization of American States are very useful, especially the Annual Reports of 1965 and 1966 of OAS Secretary General José A. Mora and Mora's final report "From Panama to Punta del Este" (1968), as well as his daily reports and radio messages filed from Santo Domingo in May 1965. Also important are the two reports issued by the Special Committee of the Tenth Meeting of Consultation of Ministers of Foreign Affairs and, for a later period, the various reports of the Ad Hoc Commission. A good deal about shifting circumstances in Santo Domingo, as well as about international politics in Washington, may be inferred from careful study of the minutes of OAS debates in Washington, both in plenary sessions and in the meetings of the General Commission. Several United Nations documents, particularly the reports of the Special Representative to the Secretary General and the Annual Reports of the Secretary General are also valuable. U.N. debate and actions on the Dominican crisis are recorded in the *Official Records* of the United Nations Security Council and are summarized in the *United Nations Chronicle*.

Another major source is the public record made by the two contending Dominican "governments" during the prolonged crisis. Each "government" published its own *Gaceta Oficial*, issued decrees, and released official statements on a wide variety of matters. The "Government of National Reconstruction" (GNR) regularly published a four-page bulletin called *Reconstrucción*, containing news reports, texts of speeches by GNR officials, and editorials reflecting the GNR viewpoint. The "Constitutional Government" used *La Nación* as a semi-official paper, although *Patria*—a second newspaper published in the "constitutionalist" zone—more accurately reflected the thinking of some factions in the "constitutional government." Each "government" also published a number of special bulletins and announcements. Other sources available to an enterprising researcher are the cables and official documents released by the two "governments," which are in the possession of individuals connected with the two sides.

Official statements on specific aspects of the crisis were released by a great number of organizations, including political parties, business groups, professional associations, labor unions, and Church officials. Of particular interest are the analysis published by the Partido Demócrata Cristiano in August 1965 and the self-criticism released by the Partido Comunista Dominicano (formerly the PSP) on August 16, 1965, as well as statements prepared by various business and commercial groups in Santo Domingo and in Santiago. Other important documents include the statement issued by the ORIT-affiliated CONATRAL and the strike calls issued by other labor groups, and the news-sheets and manifestos published before and after April 24 by the various political parties.

A related source is propaganda material: leaflets, flyers, and so forth; the efforts of the U.S. Information Service and of the U.S. military in this regard should not be overlooked. An interesting propaganda sheet put out by the "constitutionalists" under the direction of William Bailes, a U.S. citizen who aided their efforts, was titled "Dominican-American Common Sense: Exchange of Ideas."

Power Pack and *Dominican Crisis, 1965–1966*—two privately printed books prepared for members of the U.S. Armed Forces who served in the Dominican Republic—are worth consulting, both because of the many action photographs included and because of the information contained in the text; *Power Pack*, especially, conveys a sense of the tensions between American military officers and their civilian superiors.

Journalistic sources may be conveniently divided into Dominican and foreign accounts. The two leading Dominican papers, *Listín Diario* and *El Caribe*, carried good accounts, complete with vivid photographs, until they stopped publishing on April 28; the April 28 edition of *El Caribe*, prematurely announcing the defeat of the pro-Bosch movement, is somewhat of a collector's item. *La Información* of Santiago published daily until April 30, then every other day for two more weeks, but its coverage was undistinguished; most of its articles were standard UPI dispatches. Party newspapers were published before and during the crisis by the 14th of June movement (*El 1J4*), the Partido Socialista Popular (*El Popular*) and the Movimiento Popular Dominicano (*Libertad*), and a Social Christian publication called *Diálogo* began to appear during the summer.

Beginning in early May, a number of special newspapers began to publish. U.S. officials printed and distributed *La Voz de la Zona de Seguridad*, later called *La Voz de la OEA*, as part of the effort to legitimize U.S. activities by carrying them on under the mantle of the Organization of American States. On the "constitutionalist" side, both *La Nación* and *Patria* began to appear in May. *Patria,* the more leftist of the two, was probably the country's most widely circulated newspaper by the time the Provisional Government was installed in September. On the "Government of National Reconstruction's" side, apart from *Reconstrucción,* there also appeared by mid-May a right-wing daily, *La Hoja.*

Several other Dominican publications deserve particular mention. *Ahora!,* the country's most widely circulated weekly magazine, published just two issues after the crisis began. After resuming publication in September, *Ahora!* published interviews or articles by a number of participants in the 1965 crisis, including José Francisco Peña Gómez, Julio Cuello, and others. Of particular interest is a biographical sketch of the late Lieutenant Colonel Rafael Tomás Fernández Domínguez. *Unidad,* a publication released on a weekly basis early in 1966 by Héctor Aristy's "24th of April movement," also contains a number of interviews with leading "constitutionalist" figures as well as an incomplete listing of "constitutionalist" military personnel. *Pum!* and *Cachafú!,* weekly magazines of political cartoons, sometimes captured with striking poignance the significance of controversial events.

Although perhaps other writers have relied upon U.S. press accounts too exclusively for study of the Dominican crisis, they constitute an undoubtedly valuable source, for an unusual amount of information was published about this crisis, especially from April 29 to about June 15. Although there were several instances when lack of background information and the pressure to meet a deadline produced errors and even distortion, the overall success of American journalists at providing an independent evaluation of the Dominican crisis is clear. The best journalistic sources for study of the Dominican crisis are the *New York Times,* the *New York Herald Tribune,* the *Washington Post,* the *Christian Science Monitor,* the *Chicago Tribune,* the *Miami Herald,* the *Los Angeles Times,* and the *San Juan Star. Time, Newsweek,* and *U.S. News and World Report* kept reporters in Santo Domingo for many weeks. The reporting of Tad Szulc, Barnard Collier, Dan Kurzman, James Nelson

Goodsell, Robert Berrelez, Jules Dubois, and Howard Handelman is especially worth consulting, although not all that each of these reporters write was equally well-founded.

The 1965 Dominican crisis has already been the subject of almost twenty books and book-length reports published in the United States, the Dominican Republic, and elsewhere. The first book released—*Caribbean Crisis: Subversion Fails in the Dominican Republic* by Jay Mallin—was commissioned early in May 1965 by the U.S. government. A biased and unreliable account, its chief value is in expounding the perceptions and perspectives of, and some of the information then available to, some sectors of the U.S. government. *Dominican Action: Intervention or Cooperation?*, a special report published in 1966 by the Center for Strategic Studies at Georgetown University (and subsequently distributed in several languages by the U.S. Information Agency) is a more sophisticated attempt to present the Johnson administration's case; the report, prepared with the active cooperation of administration officials, contains much previously unpublished information based on classified sources but ignores or distorts some important points. A third account based on official sources is chapter 27 of John Bartlow Martin's memoir *Overtaken by Events*. Although incomplete and focused very largely on Martin's role as a presidential envoy from April 30 to May 17, 1965, the chapter presents a wealth of material on events in Santo Domingo as seen by Martin; the entire book, mostly about Martin's tenure as U.S. ambassador in the Dominican Republic in 1962–63, is essential background for any student of the 1965 crisis.

Dominican Diary by Tad Szulc, *Santo Domingo: Revolt of the Damned* by Dan Kurzman, and *Révolution de Saint Dominique* by Marcel Niedergang are all hurriedly written books by leading journalists who covered the crisis in Santo Domingo for the *New York Times,* the *Washington Post,* and *Le Monde* respectively. Each book reflects the author's preconceived approach to U.S. policy in Latin America and none is completely accurate, but each contains much information that might never have appeared but for the skepticism and investigative skill of these veteran reporters. Another source worth special mention in this connection is an unpublished manuscript, "Nothing but

Thunder," by Barnard L. Collier, then of the *New York Herald Tribune*, which contains important material on the failures of U.S. intelligence in the crisis, on the activities of U.S. military attachés, and on some of the negotiations conducted by U.S. officials.

Perhaps the most influential book published so far on the Dominican affair is Theodore Draper's *The Dominican Revolt: A Case Study in American Policy*, a compilation and revision of several articles by Draper that had previously appeared in *Commentary, New Leader*, and the *New Republic*. Draper's analysis is intelligent and superbly written and many of his criticisms of U.S. policy during the crisis are cogent and persuasive. The volume's usefulness is limited by Draper's almost exclusive reliance on public documents, newspaper accounts, and information supplied him by pro-Bosch sources, but no analyst of the Dominican crisis can fail to deal with the questions Draper raises in this important account.

Two recently published analyses by U.S. professors also deserve special mention. Jerome Slater's *Intervention and Negotiation: The United States and the Dominican Revolution* provides the only overall treatment available so far of the entire Dominican crisis, from the events of April 1965 through the 1966 election. Based on about eighty interviews and research in open and restricted sources conducted in 1967, this book includes significant new information, particularly on the various negotiations which followed the intervention. In contrast to my book, however, Slater's work concentrates more on judgments about the merits of American policy than on analysis of the internal process by which decisions were made. José Moreno's *Barrios in Arms: Revolution in Santo Domingo* (the published version of the author's Cornell Ph.D. dissertation) presents a number of insights, with a good deal of corroborating detail, as reported by a trained sociologist who used "participant-observer" techniques to gather material while serving as a Jesuit priest in downtown Santo Domingo during the crisis. Moreno's personal involvement and his openly expressed bias skew the political analysis in this work, but the extensive notes Moreno took on what he saw make this an invaluable source.

Three other books published in the United States are James Clark's *The Church and the Crisis in the Dominican Republic,*

John Carey, ed., *The Dominican Republic Crisis, 1965,* and the Institute for International Labor Research's *Dominican Republic: A Study in the New Imperialism.* Father Clark's book provides a firsthand account by a young American priest assigned to work in 1965 with the papal nuncio in Santo Domingo; besides its highly sympathetic account of the nuncio's role, the book contains an Appendix of useful documents, including various pastoral letters and papal messages related to the 1965 crisis. *The Dominican Republic Crisis, 1965* contains a working paper by A. J. Thomas and A. V. Thomas on international legal aspects of the crisis together with a panel discussion on this subject sponsored by the Association of the Bar of the City of New York. The Institute for International Labor Research's volume is a handy collection of articles critical of U.S. policy. Although most of the articles had previously been published elsewhere (including contributions by Juan Bosch, Theodore Draper, Robert Alexander, and Norman Thomas), two important articles by José Figueres and Luis Homero Lajara Burgos are nowhere else available in English.

Each of the five books by Dominican authors that have appeared so far is useful for a different perspective. The first to be published was *La revolución dominicana y la crisis de la OEA* by Julio C. Estrella, a leading Dominican publicist who was chief editorial writer for *El Caribe* when the 1965 outbreak began. Estrella's account provides some information on the background of the crisis as well as on some of the various attempts to form a Dominican government during the period from May to September 1965; the role of the Santiago business community is particularly emphasized. *La tragedia dominicana* by Danilo Brugal Alfau is primarily a defense of General Imbert's "Government of National Reconstruction," which Brugal served as director of public relations. Bitterly critical of the alleged betrayal of the GNR by the United States government and the OAS, the book weaves together a number of valuable documents and memoranda and the author's somewhat less helpful commentary. An analysis from the opposite end of the Dominican political spectrum is Franklin J. Franco's *República Dominicana: clases, crisis y comandos,* awarded first prize by Fidel Castro's Casa de las Américas in 1966. Franco, a recent graduate of and now professor at the Autonomous University of Santo

Domingo, attempts a sociological analysis of the Dominican Republic as the backdrop for his discussion of the 1965 crisis. Although far from satisfactory as social science, the book combines interesting insights and also includes the purported text of the minutes of the July 8, 1965, meeting of the "constitutional government" at which its decision to accept Héctor García Godoy as Provisional President was ratified. The two other Dominican books, *Paso a la libertad* by Daría Meléndez and *Guerra patria* by Ramón Ferreras, both contain some valuable information about the background of the April 24 uprising and about the first days of the crisis amidst pages of anecdotes. Ferreras, who organized and edited *Patria* during the crisis, also includes a number of interesting photographs in his clandestinely published work.

At least five books on the Dominican crisis by other Latin Americans have appeared so far. *A Guerra da America Latina* by Newton Carlos, *La intervención ilegal en Santo Domingo* by Isidro Odena, and *Aquí, Santo Domingo* by Gregorio Selser are accounts critical of the U.S. intervention by a Brazilian and two Argentines; Selser's volume is an edited collection of articles, of which the author's own contributions are the most interesting. Luis Conte Aguero's *Cuba en Santo Domingo* and Antonio Llanos Montes's *Santo Domingo: barricadas de odios* provide anti-Communist perspectives by Cuban refugees. Llano Montes, who served as public relations adviser and consultant on ideological matters to General Wessin y Wessin, includes a number of interesting details in his lively if not altogether reliable account; Conte's account focuses on his own role as an adviser to General Imbert.

A number of books devote a chapter to the 1965 Dominican crisis. Of these, probably the most important are those contained in three studies of President Johnson by well-known Washington correspondents: Philip Geyelin's *Lyndon B. Johnson and the World*, Charles Roberts's *LBJ's Inner Circle*, and *Lyndon B. Johnson: The Exercise of Power* by Rowland Evans and Robert Novak. All three draw on unusual access in and around the White House to present detailed and generally sympathetic accounts of the president's handling of the Dominican affair, and each presents bits of information unavailable elsewhere.

Richard Barnet's *Intervention and Revolution: America's Confrontation with Insurgent Movements Around the World,* Ronald Steel's *Pax Americana,* and Seyom Brown's *The Faces of Power: Constancy and Change in United States Foreign Policy from Truman to Johnson* all include intelligent analyses of the Dominican intervention as part of general appraisals of postwar U.S. diplomacy. William McGaffin and Erwin Knoll include some perceptive observations on relations between the Johnson administration and reporters covering the Dominican affair in *Anything But the Truth: The Credibility Gap—How the News Is Managed in Washington.* Richard Stebbins presents a concise and accurate summary of the events of the crisis and of U.S. actions, without analysis of the policy process which produced them, in the 1965 volume of the annual series on the *United States in World Affairs,* published by the Council on Foreign Relations.

The Bibliography lists a very considerable number of articles, reports, speeches, statements, interviews, published letters, and other commentaries on the 1965 Dominican crisis. Especially valuable as sources are those by participants, including Juan Bosch, Francisco Caamaño Deñó, Miguel Angel Hernando Ramírez, Pedro Bartolomé Benoit, Donald Reid Cabral, José Francisco Peña Gómez, Monseñor Hugo Polanco Brito, Leopoldo Espaillat Nanita, Angel Miolán, Pedro Manuel Casals Victoria, Antonio Rosario, Antonio Martínez Francisco, Cayetano Rodríguez del Prado, Julio Cuello, José Israel Cuello, Narciso Isa Conde, José Figueres, Rómulo Betancourt, Thomas Mann, W. Tapley Bennett, Jr., John Bartlow Martin, and others. An important subcategory of these first-person accounts is the number of publications on military aspects of the crisis by members of the U.S. Armed Forces, particularly those by General Bruce Palmer, General R. McC. Tompkins, Captain James Dare, Lieutenant Colonel Wallace Moulis and Major Richard Brown, and Major William Klein.

Other useful articles are those by academic specialists who have analyzed specific aspects of the 1965 crisis, of the Dominican political background, or of U.S. policy in the period immediately preceding 1965. Worth special attention are the various publications of Dona Baron, Lloyd Free, Jerome Slater,

Henry Wells, Howard Wiarda, and Larman Wilson; the Bibliography also lists five articles of my own. Several other commentaries on the 1965 crisis by nonparticipants are cited in the Notes to Chapter 5.

Of the many unpublished manuscripts I have seen, I would single out three for special mention. Herbert Tillema's "Dominican Republic, 1965," chapter 4 of his 1969 Harvard Ph.D. dissertation on "United States Military Intervention in the Era of Containment" is a detailed account based on public sources included in a valuable comparative analysis of situations between 1945 and 1967 which produced—or failed to produce—overt military intervention by the United States. Frederick Richman's "The Dominican Intervention: A Case Study in American Foreign Policy" makes use of attributed personal interviews and private correspondence to provide some additional details on the Dominican intervention. Bryant Wedge's "Communism and the Development of the Dominican Revolutionary Youth Movement: An Interpretative Analysis" includes some shrewd observations by a trained psychiatrist who interviewed a number of "rebel" youths in Santo Domingo in September 1965 in connection with a mission supported by the U.S. government.

Finally, the notes taken on the discussions of the "Seminar on United States Policies in the Dominican Republic" held at the Center for International Affairs, Harvard University, in 1966–67 provide a useful introduction to many of the questions raised by the 1965 Dominican crisis.

Notes

INTRODUCTION

1. The American-sponsored invasion of Cuba at the Bay of Pigs, an apparent exception, actually seemed to prove the rule of American nonintervention in Latin America. When the need for additional air cover forced President Kennedy to choose between overt American intervention and the failure of the invasion, Kennedy let the invasion collapse. See Arthur Schlesinger, Jr., *A Thousand Days: John F. Kennedy in the White House* (Boston, 1965), 255–261.

2. See James N. Goodsell, "Are Dominican Rebels Reds?" *Christian Science Monitor* (May 18, 1965), for a particularly devastating analysis of the list of supposed Communists.

3. James Reston, "Washington: The Impulsive Giant," *New York Times* (May 21, 1965).

4. Cartoon published in the *Houston Post* (March 29, 1966).

5. Russell Baker, "The Observer," *New York Times* (May 1965).

1. THE UNITED STATES AND THE DOMINICAN REPUBLIC TO 1965: BACKGROUND TO INTERVENTION

1. Charles C. Tansill, *The United States and Santo Domingo, 1798–1873: A Chapter in Caribbean Diplomacy* (Baltimore, Johns Hopkins, 1938), 130.

2. Ibid., 154.

3. Sumner Welles, *Naboth's Vineyard: The Dominican Republic, 1844–1924*, 2 vols. (New York, 1928), I, 395. In 1871 Dominican President Buenaventura Báez tried to reinterest Grant in annexation by alleging Prussian designs on Samaná; this was probably the first use of what was to become a standard ploy in Dominican-American relations. Ibid., I, 403.

4. William R. Tansill, "Diplomatic Relations between the United States and the Dominican Republic, 1874–1899" (Ph.D. dissertation, Georgetown University, 1952), 212 ff.

5. David C. MacMichael, "The United States and the Dominican Republic, 1871–1940: A Cycle in Caribbean Diplomacy," (Ph.D. dissertation, University of Oregon, 1964), 72.

6. Edgar C. Duin, "Dominican-American Diplomatic Relations, 1895–1907," (Ph.D. dissertation, Georgetown University, 1955), 112.

7. Earl R. Curry, "The United States and the Dominican Republic, 1924–1933: Dilemma in the Caribbean," (Ph.D. dissertation, University of Minnesota, 1965), Introduction.

8. Perhaps the best single account of the process by which the U.S. government was drawn more deeply into Dominican affairs and finally into military intervention may be found in relevant chapters of Dana G. Munro's *Intervention and Dollar Diplomacy in the Caribbean, 1900–1921* (Princeton, 1964). Other works I have used in analyzing this period, besides those previously noted, include: Wilfrid H. Callcott, *The Caribbean Policy of the United States, 1890–1920* (Baltimore, 1942); Melvin M. Knight, *The Americans in Santo Domingo* (New York, 1928); Max Henríquez Ureña, *Los Yanquis en Santo Domingo* (Madrid, 1929); Charles E. Chapman, "The United States and the Dominican Republic," *Hispanic American Historical Review* (February 1928), 84–91; J. Fred Rippy, "The Initiation of the Customs Receivership in the Dominican Republic," *Hispanic American Historical Review* (November 1937), 419–457; and Carl Kelsey, "The American Intervention in Haiti and the Dominican Republic," *Annals of the American Academy of Political and Social Science* (March 1922), 113–202.

9. There is as yet no good comprehensive analysis of the U.S. occupation in the Dominican Republic. Among the sources I have consulted, besides those already cited, are: "Inquiry into Occupation and Administration of Santo Domingo," *Hearings*

before a Select Committee of the United States Senate, 2 vols. (Washington, 1922); Military Government of the Dominican Republic, *Santo Domingo—Its Past and Its Present Condition* (Santo Domingo, 1920); Marvin Goldwert, *The Constabulary in the Dominican Republic and Nicaragua: Progeny and Legacy of United States Intervention* (Gainesville, Fla., 1962); Antonio Hoepelman and Juan A. Senior, eds., *Documentos históricos que se refieren a la implantación de un gobierno militar americano en la República Dominicana* (Santo Domingo, 1922); Enrique A. Henríquez, *Episodios imperalistas* (Ciudad Trujillo, 1958); Luis F. Mejía, *De Lilís a Trujillo* (Caracas, 1944); C. C. Baughman, "United States Occupation of the Dominican Republic," *United States Naval Institute Proceedings* (December 1925), 2306–2327; Rufus H. Lane, "Civil Government in Santo Domingo in the Early Days of the Military Occupation," *Marine Corps Gazette* (June 1922), 127–146; Robert C. Kilmartin, "Indoctrination in Santo Domingo," *Marine Corps Gazette* (December 1922), 377–486; and T. J. Saxon, Jr., "Diplomatic Spurs: Dominican Republic, 1916–1924," *Marine Corps Gazette* (November 1965), 40–41.

10. See Curry, "The United States and the Dominican Republic," and Joseph R. Juárez, "United States Withdrawal from Santo Domingo," *Hispanic American Historical Review* (May 1962), 152–190.

11. Curry, "The United States and the Dominican Republic," 258.

12. George P. Atkins and Larman C. Wilson, *The United States and Trujillo: A Policy Study of U.S. Relations with Latin American Dictatorships,* Rutgers, N.J.: Rutgers University Press, forthcoming.

13. See Atkins and Wilson, *The United States and Trujillo,* for a systematic review of Dominican-American relations during the Trujillo period. For further information, see Raymond H. Pulley, "The United States and the Trujillo Dictatorship, 1933–1940: The High Price of Caribbean Stability," *Caribbean Studies* (October 1965), 22–31; Theodore P. Wright, "The United States and Latin American Dictatorship: The Case of the Dominican Republic," *Journal of International Affairs* Vol. 14 (1960), 152–157; and Robert D. Crassweller, *Trujillo: Life and Times of a Caribbean Dictator* (New York, 1966), esp. 421–431.

14. See Jerome N. Slater, *The OAS and United States Foreign Policy* (Columbus, Ohio, 1967), 183–216.

15. Varying accounts of Trujillo's assassination which discuss alleged American involvement include Crassweller, *Trujillo: Life and Times*, 433–439; Arturo Espaillat, *Trujillo: The Last Caesar* (Chicago, 1963), 7–22; Selden Rodman, *Quisqueya: A History of the Dominican Republic* (Seattle, 1964), 152–158; Norman Gall, "How Trujillo Died," *New Republic* (April 13, 1963), 19–20; Sam Halper, "The Dominican Upheaval," *New Leader* (May 10, 1965), 3–4; and Rafael C. Hoepelman, "Las armas para ajusticiar a Trujillo fueron proporcionadas por Wimpy," *La Nación* (Santo Domingo, December 7, 1961), 4.

16. Slater, *The OAS and United States Foreign Policy*, 185.

17. *New York Times* (June 2–3, 1961); *New York News* (June 2, 1961). For further information, see Harold R. Lamp, "The United States Role in the Dominican Republic's Transition Toward Democracy: 1960–1961" (M.A. thesis, Georgetown University, 1964), 82–89.

18. *New York Times* (November 19, 20, 21, 1961); *Wall Street Journal* (November 20, 1961).

19. See Slater, *The OAS and United States Foreign Policy*, 198–200; John Bartlow Martin, *Overtaken by Events: The Dominican Crisis From the Fall of Trujillo to the Civil War* (New York, 1966), 82–83; Abraham F. Lowenthal, "Foreign Aid as a Political Instrument: The Case of the Dominican Republic," *Public Policy* (1965), 144–145; Thomas Wellington, "US Diplomacy and the Dominican Crisis," *SAIS Review* (Summer 1963), 25–30; and Howard J. Wiarda, "The Context of United States Policy Toward the Dominican Republic: Background to the Revolution of 1965," unpublished paper, Center for International Affairs, Harvard University (December 8, 1966), 18–20.

20. Lowenthal, "Foreign Aid as a Political Instrument"; Slater, *The OAS and United States Foreign Policy;* Wiarda, "The Context of United States Policy"; and Juan Bosch, *The Unfinished Experiment: Democracy in the Dominican Republic* (New York, 1965), 38–54. President Kennedy's statement of December 20 may be found in the *Department of State Bulletin* (January 22, 1962), 128.

21. Lowenthal, "Foreign Aid as a Political Instrument," 146.

22. See Martin, *Overtaken by Events*, 84–302; and Lowenthal, "Foreign Aid as a Political Instrument," 146–150.

23. See Henry Wells, "The OAS and the Dominican Elections," *Orbis* (Spring 1963), 150–163.

24. Martin, *Overtaken by Events*, 225–230; and Bosch, *The Unfinished Experiment*, 102–107.

25. Martin, *Overtaken by Events*, 292.

26. Ibid., 230.

27. Bosch moved immediately after his election to establish his independence, especially by denouncing a contract the Council of State had made with Standard Oil Company of New Jersey and by negotiating a $150 million line of credit with a European consortium. See Bosch, *The Unfinished Experiment*, 162–165; Martin, *Overtaken by Events*, 309, 324; and Lowenthal, "Foreign Aid as a Political Instrument," 154.

28. Bosch acknowledges that Ambassador Martin and AID Mission Director Newell Williams "displayed exemplary tact" and "always respected my national pride." See Bosch, *The Unfinished Experiment*, 164.

29. Slater, *The OAS and United States Foreign Policy*, 202.

30. Philip W. Bonsal, "Open Letter to an Author," *Foreign Service Journal* (February 1967), 40.

31. See Martin, *Overtaken by Events*, passim, esp. 323, 349, 418–420, 486–488, 499, 508–518, 562–565.

32. Abraham F. Lowenthal, "Limits of American Power: The Lesson of the Dominican Republic," *Harper's* (June 1964), 87–89, 94–95.

33. Martin, *Overtaken by Events*, 310–311, 348, 467, 471.

34. Lowenthal, "Foreign Aid as a Political Instrument," 155–157; Martin, *Overtaken by Events*, 309–310, 329, 457; and Bosch, *The Unfinished Experiment*, 167–178.

35. Lowenthal, "Foreign Aid as a Political Instrument," 156–158; Wiarda, "The Context of United States Policy," 24; Ruth Shereff, "How the CIA Makes Friends and Influences Countries," *Viet Report* (January–February 1967), 15–19, 26; Dan Kurzman, "Dominican Unions Are Still Feuding," *Washington Post* (June 13, 1966); and Sacha Volman, "Latin American Experiments in Political and Economic Training," unpublished report, Foreign Policy Studies Division, Brookings Institution (April 1964).

36. Martin, *Overtaken by Events*, 343–578.

37. Ibid., 568. According to his own account, Martin considered going to the Palace, where Bosch was meeting with the military leaders, even after the final meeting started, but he was dissuaded by members of his embassy staff. See 571–572.

38. See Lowenthal, "Limits of American Power," Donald A. Allen, "Santo Domingo: The Empty Showcase," *Reporter* (December 5, 1963), 28–36; Sam Halper, "US-Backed Reform Flops as Bosch Gets the Bounce," *Life* (October 18, 1963), 49–50; and Norman Gall, "Anatomy of a Coup: The Fall of Juan Bosch," *Nation* (October 26, 1963), 253–256.

39. Martin, *Overtaken by Events*, 574, 580–581.

40. Ibid., 589.

41. Ibid., 601–602; 605–606.

42. Ibid., 606–632.

43. For further biographical information on Bennett, see "Envoy on Firing Line: William Tapley Bennett, Jr.," *New York Times* (May 1, 1965).

44. For further information on U.S. government-financed political development activities through the International Development Foundation, see Shereff, "How the CIA Makes Friends," 19, 26. For published information on the secret poll taken for the U.S. government before the April crisis, see Walter Pincus, "Dominican Poll's Use in Setting Policy is Hit," *Washington Star* (November 21, 1965), and Martin, *Overtaken by Events*, 639.

45. For an analysis of the role of domestic American pressures in ending the 1916–1924 U.S. occupation of the Dominican Republic, see Juárez, "United States Withdrawal," 170 ff.

46. So brief an analysis is necessarily oversimplified, discounting the roles of personality and accident, the effects of organizational procedures and bureaucratic politics, and the influences of events elsewhere and of wider policies and trends.

47. To cite one recent study of U.S. policy in the Dominican Republic, for instance, "while Kennedy and Johnson used different mechanisms to dominate Dominican society . . . their objective remained the same . . . maintaining a safe place for investment with a high profit rate, developing a market for goods and services, [and] . . . securing a source of cheap raw materials and labor." See Fred Goff and Michael Locker, "The Violence of

Domination: U.S. Power and the Dominican Republic," in Irving Louis Horowitz, Josué de Castro, and John Gerassi, eds., *Latin American Radicalism: A Documentary Report on Left and Nationalist Movements* (New York, 1969), 249–291.

48. For a particularly colorful example, see *Report of James D. Phelan, Special Commissioner named by the Secretary of State . . . To Investigate Charges Against the United States Minister to the Dominican Republic* (dated May 9, 1915).

49. Some writers, including Goff and Locker, assert that business pressures have been successfully brought to bear on those in Washington who make general U.S. policy that affects the Dominican Republic. That possibility cannot be excluded, but I know of no substantial evidence that business pressures have significantly affected major U.S. decisions regarding Dominican politics in recent years. The evidence Goff and Locker present in order to suggest that U.S. sugar interests have dictated American policies toward the Dominican Republic (e.g., that Adolf Berle, Abe Fortas, and Ellsworth Bunker have been directors of large sugar corporations) does not appear to me to be persuasive. See Goff and Locker, "The Violence of Domination," especially 280–282.

50. See Munro, *Intervention and Dollar Diplomacy*, 535–538, and MacMichael, "The United States and the Dominican Republic," 302. Herbert Feis argues persuasively that the motivation for dollar diplomacy after World War I generally was political, and the main initiative for involvement of U.S. firms abroad often came from the U.S. government. See Herbert Feis, *Diplomacy of the Dollar: First Era, 1919–1932* (Hamden, Conn., 1965).

51. MacMichael, "The United States and the Dominican Republic," 51.

52. See Dexter Perkins, *Hands Off: A History of the Monroe Doctrine* (Boston, 1941). For general insights on the influence of axioms on U.S. foreign policy decisions, see Ernest R. May, "The Nature of Foreign Policy: The Calculated versus the Axiomatic," *Daedalus* (Fall 1962), 653–657.

53. Charles Tansill, "The United States and Santo Domingo," 129; William Tansill, "Diplomatic Relations between the United States and the Dominican Republic," 212–213.

54. Duin, "Dominican-American Diplomatic Relations," 112.

55. Ibid., 245.

56. MacMichael, "The United States and the Dominican Republic," 206.

57. Cf. William Kamman, *A Search for Stability: United States Diplomacy Toward Nicaragua, 1925–1933* (Notre Dame, Ind., 1968).

58. I am indebted to Howard Wiarda's previously cited unpublished paper, "The Context of United States Policy Toward the Dominican Republic," and to the discussion it provoked at the meeting of the Seminar on United States Policy in the Dominican Republic at Harvard's Center for International Affairs on December 8, 1966, for help in formulating some of the points raised in the rest of this chapter. I have also benefited from consulting an unpublished manuscript by William Everett Kane: "American Involvement in Latin American Civic Strife," draft paper for American Society for International Law (February 1967).

59. Munro, *Intervention and Dollar Diplomacy*, 99–111.

60. Ibid., 272–273; 275–309.

61. Lane, "Civil Government in Santo Domingo," 129. Similar naiveté was exemplified by the U.S. effort to establish a civil service system. Having concluded that "one of the fundamental causes of political unrest . . . had been the possession of public office by virtue of political association," U.S. bureaucrats set up a civil service and believed that consequently "the future would hold less reason for repetition of disorders." See Baughman, "United States Occupation," 2320.

62. See Goldwert, *The Constabulary in the Dominican Republic*, and Crassweller, *Trujillo: Life and Times*.

63. Some writers, Dominican and American, have suggested that the U.S. emphasis on administrative and legal reforms, including the complete revision of the country's real property system, was designed primarily to advance the interests of U.S. sugar companies. U.S. companies were undoubtedly interested in some of these reforms and certainly benefited from them. It seems likely to me, however, that the chief aim of these measures was to eliminate obstacles perceived by U.S. officials to be reducing the Dominican Republic's chances for economic prosperity and, consequently, political stability. For the contrary view, see Melvin Knight, *The Americans in Santo Domingo*, 40 ff.

64. See Bryce Wood, *The Making of the Good Neighbor Policy* (New York, 1961).

65. "The Acting Secretary of State to the Minister in the Dominican Republic," (March 19, 1930), *Foreign Relations of the United States* (1930), II, 718.

66. See Atkins and Wilson, *The United States and Trujillo,* and Raymond H. Pulley, "The United States and the Trujillo Dictatorship," 22–31.

67. Wood, *The Making of the Good Neighbor Policy.*

68. Although U.S. military assistance to the Dominican Republic during this period was avowedly intended to help the Dominican Republic contribute effectively to hemisphere defense (first against Nazi Germany and then against the Soviet Union), one unpublished study concludes that the military aid was granted "primarily to promote internal political stability." See Atkins and Wilson, *The United States and Trujillo.*

69. Roosevelt's supposed remark about Trujillo, perhaps apocryphal, has been quoted in a number of places, such as Robert F. Smith's *The United States and Cuba* (New York, Bookman Associates, 1960), 184. Other writers have reported Roosevelt's statement being made with reference to Chiang Kai-shek or Anastasio Somoza.

70. Slater, *The OAS and United States Foreign Policy,* 183–216.

71. See *Public Papers of the Presidents of the United States: John F. Kennedy* (1961), 174. President Kennedy again singled out the Dominican Republic for special attention in his 1962 State of the Union address. See *Public Papers* (1962), 12.

72. See Arthur M. Schlesinger, Jr., *A Thousand Days: John F. Kennedy in the White House* (Boston, 1965), 769–773; Martin, *Overtaken by Events,* 151, 164.

73. See De Lesseps Morrison, *Latin American Mission,* ed. Gerold Frank (New York, 1965), 113–114 ff.

74. See Schlesinger, *A Thousand Days,* 769.

75. See Slater, *The OAS and United States Foreign Policy,* 202–203.

76. See Martin, *Overtaken by Events,* passim (e.g., 331).

77. Ibid., 347–350; 509–510; 562.

78. Ibid., passim (e.g., 196, 459, 539).

79. Ibid., 453.

80. Ibid., 570.

81. The effects of President Kennedy's condemnation of the Dominican and Honduran coups and the actions taken by the U.S. government to dramatize its displeasure were tempered somewhat when an article by Assistant Secretary of State Edwin M. Martin, published in the *New York Herald Tribune*, seemed to accept such military overthrows as inevitable and sometimes even justified. In retrospect, it appears that the U.S. government's strong desire to strengthen the prospects for free elections in Venezuela, more than anything related to the Dominican Republic itself, may have motivated the president's strong public stand against the overthrow of Bosch. For further background, see Martin, *Overtaken by Events,* 602.

82. Martin's own comments on this point raise more questions than they answer. See Martin, *Overtaken by Events,* 570–574 and especially 722–725.

83. Martin, *Overtaken by Events,* 601.

84. Ibid., 604–607; 631–634.

85. Theodore Draper, *The Dominican Revolt: A Case Study in American Policy* (New York, 1968), 16.

2. THE ORIGINS OF THE 1965 DOMINICAN CRISIS: SETTING THE STAGE

1. Abraham F. Lowenthal, "The Dominican Republic: The Politics of Chaos," in Arpad von Lazar and Robert R. Kaufman, eds., *Reform and Revolution: Readings in Latin American Politics* (Boston, 1969), 34–58.

2. The 1963 coup, in turn, must be traced to its own immediate causes and to deeper divisions within Dominican society. For obviously partisan but nonetheless valuable analyses of the reasons for the 1963 coup, see Juan Bosch, *The Unfinished Experiment: Democracy in the Dominican Republic* (New York, 1965); Centro de Enseñanza de las Fuerzas Armadas, *Libro Blanco de las Fuerzas Armadas y de la Policía Nacional de la República Dominicana: Estudios y pruebas documentales de las causas del movimiento reivindicador del 15 de septiembre de 1963* (Santo Domingo, 1964); and John B. Martin, *Overtaken by Events: The Dominican Crisis from the Fall of Trujillo to the Civil War* (New York, 1966). For extensive discussion of the overthrow of Juan Bosch, see Hoon Mok Chung, "The 1963

Coup d'Etat in the Dominican Republic," mimeographed paper prepared for the Caribbean Project, Foreign Policy Research Institute, University of Pennsylvania (Philadelphia, 1966).

3. Colonel Fernández Domínguez was the son of General Ludovino Fernández, one of Trujillo's most ruthless henchmen. Educated for a professional military career, Fernández brought to his work a combination of his father's courage and ability and his own ambitions, which seem to have focused on a desire to cleanse the reputation of his family and of the whole Dominican Armed Forces.

4. No analysis of the 1965 Dominican crisis can ignore the impact of the personality of Juan Bosch, the Dominican writer and political leader who returned from twenty-five years' exile to win the presidency in the 1962 elections, only to be ousted from office after seven months. Oversimplifying necessarily, it may be said that Bosch's extraordinary capacity to assess the structure of a given situation far exceeds his capacity to affect events favorably. While proclaiming his dedication to the "unfinished experiment" of making constitutional democracy work in the Dominican Republic, Bosch seemed to lack the fundamental optimism and singleminded determination necessary to let the experiment proceed. Bosch's writings reveal that, as a political analyst, he has always doubted that Dominican society can sustain constitutional democracy. This skepticism about democratic institutions—and similar doubts about the United States, the middle class, and other possible allies—seems to have had the effect on Bosch's actions of self-fulfilling prophecy. At the time of the 1963 coup Bosch struggled little, if at all, to retain power, perhaps because he believed his overthrow to be inevitable. A similar approach may explain Bosch's conduct during the 1965 crisis and the 1966 election campaign and may account, in part, for his since-announced loss of faith in democratic forms and his appeal for "dictatorship with popular support."

5. Molina Ureña and Peña Gómez—each an intimate associate of Bosch and also of Sacha Volman, Bosch's former colleague at the Institute for Political Education in Costa Rica and one of Bosch's closest confidants—became from the start the leading civilian activists in the attempt to restore constitutional government. Molina Ureña, a lawyer, developed support for

Bosch among other professionals. Peña Gómez, a young orator with a compelling style and commanding presence, was the party leader most influential with youth, with enlisted men in the Armed Forces, and with the urban poor, many of whom listened to his daily PRD radio program. Peña's vital role in Bosch's own conception may be inferred from the fact that Bosch dedicated *The Unfinished Experiment* "to José Francisco Peña Gómez, and in him to the youth of the country."

6. *New York Times* (October 19, 1963).

7. Supporters of former presidents Balaguer and Bosch, as well as military officers ousted by the Council of State in 1962, shared an intense dislike of the "cívicos," the Dominican political grouping which had gained power by exiling the Trujillos in 1961 and Balaguer early in 1962, had lost out to Bosch late in 1962, and was now regaining its position in 1963. Friendly relations between Bosch and Balaguer, and among many of their followers, date back to the 1961–62 period.

8. Already in July 1963—at the time of a major confrontation with key military officers—Bosch had spoken of "military forces ready to defend the Constitution at any cost," who would allow a coup less chance to last than a "cockroach in a chicken house"; Colonel Fernández's group was presumably what Bosch had in mind. See Martin, *Overtaken by Events*, 489–90, 644.

10. See Chapter 1, 29–30.

10. Five of the six parties had together polled less than 6 percent of the vote in 1962, but the sixth was the major opposition party, the UCN. For complete returns of the 1962 election, together with very useful background information on some of the personalities and issues of recent Dominican politics, see Howard J. Wiarda, ed., *Dominican Republic Election Factbook: June 1, 1966*, published in 1966 by the Institute for Comparative Study of Political Systems (ICOPS), Washington, D.C.

11. Reid, the son of a Scottish bank executive who married into one of the Dominican Republic's most politically-minded first families, was a young businessman with some political interests and experience. In 1960 and 1961 he lived in Washington and served as a contact between the anti-Trujillo groups and the United States government. In 1962 he served as Second Vice-President of the seven-man Council of State and impressed Ambassador Martin as capable, eager, and usually sensible, if

strong-willed. See Martin, *Overtaken by Events,* passim, especially 11–12.

12. The world market sugar price had fallen to less than 2.5 cents by early 1965, and the Dominican Republic had been unable to win any significant increase in its quota for sales at the preferential U.S. price. Prices for all four types of Dominican coffee were also falling in 1965, and the price for Dominican cacao plunged from 19.61 cents on January 1, 1965, to 12.22 cents—its lowest point—on April 22. See *Informe del Banco Central de la República Dominicana* (November 12, 1965), 11–13.

13. See "Informan sobre situación balanza comercial R.D." *Listín Diario* (December 29, 1964).

14. See, for instance, reports in *El Caribe* and *Listín Diario* on January 26, February 3, 7, and 9 about the government's failure to pay university personnel, workers at the National Potable Water Institute, public works employees, and even the legally required monthly subsidy to hospitals.

15. See *Listín Diario* (January 9, 1965), which estimated unemployment at 31.05 percent of the work force.

16. See, for instance, the lead editorial in *La Información* on April 9, 1965.

17. *Listín Diario* (March 3, 4, 5, 1965).

18. Except for a few committed to Marxism, Christian democracy, or other (mainly imported) approaches, most Dominican politicians should not be classified primarily by ideology, for their political activities indicate easy switches all along the ideological spectrum. See Lowenthal, "Politics of Chaos," 44–46. Cf. James Payne, *Political Conflict in Colombia* (New Haven, 1968), esp. 155–158.

19. See *Listín Diario* (January 18, 25, 1965; March 1, 3, 1965).

20. On April 14, 1965, for instance, Lora declared that elections were "the only solution adequate to the crisis which maintains the country at the abyss of a civil war of incalculable proportions." See *Listín Diario* (April 15, 1965).

21. One of Bosch's chief lieutenants, Manuel Fernández Mármol, put the argument simply in a newspaper article published in March: "Why should there be elections if the people already voted?" See *Listín Diario* (March 1965).

22. See, for instance, "Sobre elecciones," an article by PRD leader Máximo Lovatón Pittaluga published in *Listín Diario* on March 11, 1965. Lovatón noted that "the PRD, because of its ideological principles, cannot be intransigently opposed to an electoral solution, but it will maintain its thesis against elections as long as there are not conditions for truly impartial elections."

23. *Listín Diario* (January 3, 1965).

24. Colonel Caamaño, like Colonel Fernández Domínguez, is the son of a key Trujillo henchman, General Fausto Caamaño. Colonel Caamaño's relations with the pro-Bosch cadre of conspirators within the Armed Forces is not entirely clear. He had participated in the controversial Palma Sola massacre, vigorously condemned by Bosch, and had joined other officers in opposing President Bosch in 1963. It is known that, whatever his motivations, Caamaño did join another disaffected police officer in January 1965 in protesting the corrupt activities of Police Chief Belisario Peguero Guerrero. Dismissed from the National Police and transferred to the Air Force as a result of the ensuing struggle (which also saw the forced retirement of General Peguero), Caamaño appears to have harbored his own personal resentments at the treatment he received from the Reid regime but not to have been linked very closely with Hernando and others working directly with Juan Bosch. When the crisis broke on April 24, Caamaño joined the pro-Bosch faction at once, and remained active in the rebel leadership thereafter except for a few hours on Sunday evening, April 25, when he apparently took asylum in belief that his cause had been defeated. The rapidity with which Caamaño became the acknowledged leader of the rebel forces, and his as-yet unclarified disappearance in November 1967, pose intriguing questions for the eventual historian of the Dominican crisis.

25. General Wessin—promoted from Colonel the day after he engineered Juan Bosch's overthrow—commanded the autonomous Armed Forces Training Center (CEFA), a privileged unit established by Trujillo as a counterweight to the Army and the Air Force and endowed with its own planes and tanks. A skilled politician in mufti operating from his position of strength at the San Isidro Air Base just east of Santo Domingo, Wessin periodically lent his support to Reid to make possible the ouster of other strong military figures. Each time Wessin used his

forces as a counter, without having to commit them to action. His apparent attempt to use this ploy again in the first days of the crisis was to leave Wessin without effective power when others acted.

26. Employing a tactic familiar in Dominican political history, Reid used the foreign press to float trial balloons for his possible candidacy. On December 14, 1964, *El Caribe* republished an interview Reid had granted with O. Castillo of American Literary Agency in which Reid declared: "If a good number of citizens proposed me to be a candidate . . . I would accept." From then on Reid hinted several times that he would either run himself or postpone the elections, and he encouraged his intimates to prepare campaign materials. See *Time* (March 23, 1965), various Associated Press dispatches by Louis Uchitelle in March and April 1965, and Al Burt's report in the *Miami Herald* of April 17, 1965 (mentioned in *El Caribe* the next day) for some examples.

27. Some information on this poll was presented in executive session to the Senate Foreign Relations Committee and later leaked to the press. See Walter Pincus, "Dominican Poll's Use in Setting Policy Is Hit," *Washington Star* (November 21, 1965).

28. The embassy's earlier hedge on its support for elections laid the groundwork for such a position.

29. Never officially aligned with the PRD but established for Bosch by his close associates, the group successfully encouraged various professional associations to attack the regime and organized a highly successful campaign to obtain the signatures of over 2,000 professionals for a major statement (published February 27, 1965) criticizing the Reid regime and calling for a return to constitutional government. Following up on this successful venture, the group began to set up a new organization—the Fuerza Dominicana de Profesionales (Dominican Professionals' Force)—with the avowed objective of "struggling for the return to the constitutional order." Bosch personally approved the draft manifesto proclaiming the new organization at a mid-April meeting with Molina Ureña and Espaillat Nanita in San Juan, and plans were made to publish the document later in the month.

30. Very similar arguments were presented by Bosch's colleague Sacha Volman in a pamphlet which was circulating in

the Dominican Republic by April 1965. Volman argued that the process of Latin American development "could be truncated, and probably will be, by young military officers allied with elements of the middle class." Like Bosch, Volman emphasized the "revolutionary vision" which could split the Armed Forces as an essential key to political change. See Sacha Volman, "Quién impondrá la democracia?" *Panoramas* (July–August 1965), 39–84.

31. See *Listín Diario* (January 29, 1965) for an article on Bosch's book noting that it had at once become a "best-seller." See also Sacha Volman, "Significance of Sale of Juan Bosch Book in the Dominican Republic," undated memorandum circulated by Volman in February or March 1965.

32. The information contained in the next several paragraphs is based mainly on personal interviews, but I have also drawn on several personal letters written to Theodore Draper by various participants, including Lieutenant Colonel Miguel Angel Hernando Ramírez. I am very grateful to Mr. Draper for allowing me to use this valuable source material.

33. For a discussion of the motivations of different types of "rebels" in the 1965 Dominican crisis, see José A. Moreno, *Barrios in Arms: Revolution in Santo Domingo* (Pittsburgh, Pa., 1970), 85–97.

34. For a published report on one contact with Fernández Domínguez, see the interview with Javier Castillo, Secretary General of the PRSC, published in Santiago, Chile, in a report issued by the Organización Demócrata Cristiana de América in 1966. See also *Listín Diario* (February 7, 1966).

35. See Martin, *Overtaken by Events*, 644, and J. I. Quello (*sic*) and N. Isa Conde, "Revolutionary Struggle in the Dominican Republic and Its Lessons," *World Marxist Review* (December 1965; December 1966).

36. See Quello (*sic*) and Isa Conde "Revolutionary Struggle in the Dominican Republic."

37. See the issues of *El Popular* and *El 1J4* for the first few months of 1965, as well as the special leaflets released by the 1J4 and the MPD on February 20 and by the PSP on March 9 and 16. For selected quotations in translation from these documents see Martin, *Overtaken by Events*, 640–643, and Quello (*sic*) and Isa Conde, "Revolutionary Struggle in the Dominican Republic."

38. See, for instance, the statements of Stormy Reynoso and César Roque criticizing the Pact of Rio Piedras (*Ahora!*, March 27, 1965). See also the article published in *Listín Diario* on April 22, 1965, by Thelma Frías de Rodríguez, PRD Vice-President of the Senate under Bosch, who argued that "no one is authorized to guide a people to its own destruction through the paths of violence" in a thinly veiled protest against Bosch's strategy. Also among PRD leaders favoring elections were Virgilio Mainardi Reyna and Casimiro Castro.

39. A typical expression of this view was *La Información*'s editorial of March 25, 1965, favoring a "return to constitutionality through elections . . . The position of Professor Bosch is very ethical and we understand it perfectly, but within the present conditions it is impractical. The return to constitutionality is the aim; to reach it through or without elections is a question of means. The important thing is the end. And that end should not be risked through a tactical error."

40. Colonel Caamaño indicated in several interviews that this was his own position until he was convinced personally, in a meeting with Reid Cabral days before April 24, that Reid had no intention of permitting elections. See *El Tiempo* (New York, January 27, 1966).

41. *Listín Diario* (April 10, 1965).

42. *Ahora!*, the Dominican Republic's leading weekly magazine, reported on March 20, for instance, that "people are noting that the election campaign is scheduled to begin in 71 days and still the Central Electoral Board has not said anything." "Could this be," *Ahora!* wondered, "because the Electoral Board does not believe in the elections it is supposed to guarantee?" On April 22, just two days before he fell, Reid Cabral told a press conference that he saw "no reason to vary his attitude about the return of Bosch and Balaguer." See *Listín Diario* (April 23, 1965).

3. THE DECISION TO INTERVENE

1. Imbert, a civilian given the honorary rank of Brigadier General in order to resolve a political crisis in 1962, has been a central figure in Dominican affairs for several years. One of the two known surviving members of the group which assassinated Trujillo in 1961, Imbert was appointed to the seven-man Council of State which took office in January 1962. During the Coun-

cil's tenure, Imbert had charge of police affairs, and he has since retained close ties with leading officers of the National Police as well as with personal followers in the Armed Forces. Imbert has been an active, not to say inveterate, participant in Dominican conspiratorial politics, his contacts ranging up to and including the extreme left. For information on Imbert's dealings with Dominican Communists, see Virginia Prewett, *Washington Daily News* (June 16, 1965), and Norman Gall, *Washington Post* (June 17, 1965).

2. "CRITIC" is the State Department's designation for very urgent messages which are given the highest priority in transmittal and decoding. A "CRITIC" cable may be expected to reach American officials in Washington within a few minutes of being filed from the embassy abroad.

3. In a political situation as complicated as the 1965 Dominican crisis, even the choice of terms to designate the various factions is very difficult.

Rather than call the pro-Bosch forces "constitutionalists" and the anti-Bosch forces "loyalists"—as they called themselves—I have decided it would be simpler and somewhat more accurate to call the pro-Bosch forces the "rebels"—as they were labeled in the U.S. press—and to call their opponents the "anti-Bosch" or "antirebel" faction. I do not mean thereby to deny that some of those in the pro-Bosch group were motivated by the desire to reinstate constitutional government nor do I intend to imply that none of those who opposed the coup in April 1965 were acting out of loyalty to the incumbent regime.

4. The "Dominican Republic Task Force" was to continue in being on a twenty-four-hour basis from this moment until June 4, 1965.

5. See "Dominican Action: Intervention or Cooperation?" *Special Report #2* (Center for Strategic Studies, Georgetown University, 1966), 15.

6. This was the nineteenth time since 1961 that the Caribbean Ready Group had been exercised; not all these cases involved the Dominican Republic.

7. What actually happened is still unclear. Fabio Herrera, a high-ranking bureaucrat with a recognized capacity for surviving political change who was then serving as Reid's Secretary of the Presidency, has claimed that Reid asked him to arrange

with PRD leaders for an orderly transfer of power to them. There is little doubt that Herrera did arrange to have a group of PRD officials, including Fernández Mármol, meet early that morning at the home of Nicolás Mogen (a European resident of Santo Domingo known to have close ties then with the Triumvirate, with Bosch's group, and with the American embassy) to discuss the terms of a transfer of power from Reid. Reid never acted on this possibility, however, and has subsequently denied ever having suggested this. It is possible that Herrera had acted on his own. It seems equally possible that Reid considered the idea but later rejected it, perhaps under pressure from General Montás and others.

8. *Listín Diario* and *El Caribe* (April 26, 1965).

9. *Listín Diario* (April 26, 1965). The commanders at Santiago, like others in the interior, hedged their bets and successfully kept their options open by refusing to pass out arms to pro-Bosch civilians; they were encouraged in this decision by the U.S. consul and also by a commission of local notables who visited the Army, Air Force, and police regional headquarters and pleaded for calm and order. The Bishop of Santiago, Monseñor Hugo Polanco Brito—one of those who visited the bases—demonstrated similar acumen with a series of radio statements calling for peace and declaring that the people had made clear their wish for "constitutional government"; he did not clarify whether this meant that a return to the elected regime was necessary or whether new elections would suffice.

10. It is not clear how close Bosch came to leaving for Santo Domingo that Sunday or in the next few days, nor is it entirely certain why he did not. Bosch has intimated and some observers have alleged outright that American officials impeded Bosch's departure from San Juan, but there does not appear to be any evidence that the U.S. government did any more than maintain FBI surveillance of Bosch. Critics of Bosch, even among his erstwhile supporters, have charged that Bosch demonstrated a lack of physical courage by failing to return, but they tend to ignore his record of bravery in the anti-Trujillo movement and to underestimate the logistical difficulties of landing in the Dominican Republic after the Dominican Air Force had closed the international airport and controlled all the others.

I believe that the only realistic chance for Bosch to return was before mid-afternoon on Sunday, when the anti-Bosch Air Force–CEFA faction strafed the Palace and asserted its willingness to fight to keep Bosch out. A Puerto Rican friend of Bosch who spent part of that afternoon with him asserts that Bosch was expecting to return to Santo Domingo triumphantly in an official plane, and that his supporters in Santo Domingo encouraged him by telephone to believe that this was a possibility. Friendly Puerto Rican political leaders who might have advised Bosch to return at once, or who might have facilitated his communications with American officials about the crisis, were preoccupied that day with arranging the funeral of Independentista hero Pedro Albizu Campos—which was expected to provoke violent demonstrations—and they were not in touch with Bosch.

11. The record (notes on Connett's telephone conversation with the Operations Center) indicating that Connett advised at this time against an attempt by the U.S. government to impede Bosch's return is an ambiguous and fragmentary piece of evidence. It is not clear to me whether Connett volunteered this view or whether his opinion was solicited, nor do I know whether Connett's view was recorded with respect to a specific suggestion that Bosch's departure from San Juan be prevented.

12. In previous crises Air Force planes had buzzed various military and civilian installations and had even strafed rival military camps, but this was the first time that Dominican planes had strafed Dominican civilians.

13. Colonel Jacinto Martínez Aranha, a veteran Army officer who a few days later was to be named Army Chief of Operations to direct the antirebel offensive, retreated from the Palace on Sunday afternoon into hiding at the home of a friend, for instance. The Air Force and the CEFA were just beginning to act, but the Dominican Army was already divided and in disarray.

14. See "Testimony of Brigadier General Elías Wessin y Wessin," *Hearings before the Internal Security Subcommittee of the Committee on the Judiciary,* U.S. Senate, 89th Congress, 1st session (October 1, 1965), 156–161.

15. Bosch asserts that "the bombing was specially and specifically ordered by the American military mission," and rebel sympathizers in the Dominican Republic often refer to a supposed tape recording which allegedly proves that the attachés "ordered" the Dominican Air Force to "bomb" the city. See Juan

Bosch, *Pentagonism: A Substitute for Imperialism* (New York, 1968), 107. See also *New York Times* (May 7, 1965).

When a rebel leader played for me what he claimed as "the" tape recording, however, it proved to be of various conversations, over open radio lines, between the attachés and Dominican military leaders on Tuesday morning. The conversations related to the embassy's desire that the planned antirebel attack on the city not threaten the evacuation of U.S. citizens nor interfere with Ambassador Bennett's imminent return; it also included the discussions, in which the attachés served as communication links, as to whether and where negotiations between rebel and antirebel leaders could be arranged. Although these recordings show that the embassy knew the plans of the antirebel faction on Tuesday morning, this does not in any way prove that the attachés ordered the anti-Bosch leaders to bomb the city on Sunday.

Some rebel sources contend, however, that there exists another tape recording which substantiates their claim. That may be, but it seems fair to suggest that if such damaging evidence of American actions existed, it would be in someone's interest to produce it; my extensive efforts to find the supposed "other" recording proved fruitless.

16. Although some American officials may have feared that these attacks were part of a communist-organized attempt to intimidate all nonleftist parties, embassy officers seem to have perceived (correctly, it appears) that the only pattern unifying the attack on the parties and on several businesses was that the objects of attack were identified as leading *golpistas,* key proponents of the 1963 coup.

17. *El Caribe* (April 26, 1965).

18. Ibid.

19. For an analysis of the reasons for the popular Dominican uprising, focusing directly on the importance of the military's strafing as the precipitant of violent response, see Bryant Wedge "The Case of Student Political Violence: Brazil, 1964, and Dominican Republic, 1965." *World Politics* (January 1969), 183–206, esp. 196 ff. See also José A. Moreno, *Barrios in Arms: Revolution in Santo Domingo* (Pittsburgh, Pa., 1970).

20. The four PRD leaders were Secretary General Antonio Martínez Francisco, National District Committee Chairman

Máximo Lovatón Pittaluga, former Ambassador to the United States Enriquillo del Rosario, and Santiago businessman S. Antonio Guzmán, Bosch's Minister of Agriculture.

21. See Philip Geyelin, *Lyndon B. Johnson and the World* (New York, 1966), 247. Frederick Richman, relying on notes of an interview by Geyelin with McGeorge Bundy, asserts that President Johnson instructed Bennett to set up a military junta and to work for a cease-fire, but not to permit a "second Cuba." See Frederick Richman, "The Dominican Intervention: A Case Study in American Foreign Policy," (Honors thesis, Department of Government, Harvard University, April 1967), 42.

22. See Richman, "The Dominican Intervention," 45. Richman relies here on the testimony of Charles Roberts, a White House reporter.

23. *Listín Diario* (April 27, 1969).

24. For information on the U.S. role in this propaganda battle, see note 36 below.

25. I rely for this estimate upon information which I cannot verify, supplied me by a CIA official, but it seems unlikely to me that he would have exaggerated the percentage of the station's reports dealing with Communist involvement in the crisis.

26. This was to become the first 82nd Airborne Division alert since World War II to be followed by deployment into a combat situation.

27. There is no doubt that American officials, especially in Washington, were genuinely frightened by the Hotel Embajador incident at first, but the incident soon became more significant as a means of discrediting the pro-Bosch movement than as a source of genuine concern. Secretary Rusk (in May) and President Johnson (in June) later spoke of the Hotel Embajador incident as if it had occurred on Wednesday, immediately before the decision to land the Marines. See *Department of State Bulletin* (June 14, 1965, 942, and July 5, 1965, 20).

28. Captain James Dare, the Commander of the Caribbean Ready Group, refers to this movement of the Group as a "show of force." See James A. Dare, "Dominican Diary," *U.S. Naval Institute Proceedings* (December 1965), 41.

29. See *Public Papers of the Presidents of the United States: Lyndon B. Johnson, 1965* (Washington, D.C., 1966), Book I, 449–457.

30. Charles Roberts, *LBJ's Inner Circle* (New York, 1965), 203.

31. Lieutenant Colonel Montes Arache was Commander of the Navy's elite "Frogman" unit, which joined him in supporting the rebel cause. A fearless combatant with a history of exploits —including participation in Trujillo's attempt to assassinate Rómulo Betancourt, it is said—Montes Arache came to play a leading role in the rebel command structure.

32. See Dare, "Dominican Diary," 43.

33. See Roberts, *LBJ's Inner Circle*, 203.

34. By his own account, Aristy has participated in almost every political movement of significance in the Dominican Republic since Trujillo's death. Prior to the fall of Reid, Aristy's most recent public stance was as an official of Luis Amiama Tió's Partido Liberal Evolucionista (PLE), the national convention of which he addressed on April 17, 1965. (See *El Caribe,* April 18, 1965.) When pro-Bosch sympathizers attacked PLE headquarters on Sunday, April 25, because of the *golpista* origins of the party, Aristy chose to switch sides. By Tuesday afternoon he was at Caamaño's side, where he remained throughout the crisis. Early in May, presidential envoy John Bartlow Martin suggested that the U.S. government consider seriously the possibility that Aristy might be a deep-cover Communist agent, trained in Eastern Europe. Intensive investigation produced no evidence of any such ties, and no U.S. official I interviewed seems now to believe that Aristy was anything other than an ambitious political entrepreneur.

35. *El Caribe* did so only in an inset on the front page, the rest of which emphasized the apparent defeat of the pro-Bosch movement and the asylum of many of its principal leaders.

36. Senator Joseph Clark stated in September 1965 that the Benoit junta was established "at the instance of the CIA," and there is reason to believe that the CIA immediately provided the junta with augmented communications facilities. See *Congressional Record* (September 17, 1965), 24242.

The official view that the U.S. government remained neutral in the Dominican power struggle is dramatically refuted by the actions taken to influence the relative effectiveness of the radio stations available to the competing factions. While U.S. agencies were reportedly augmenting the communications facilities of the antirebel forces, the Army Security Agency eventually used a total of twenty-eight jamming devices—from ships, aircraft, and ground locations—to interfere with rebel broadcasts until opposition to jamming within the U.S. government forced the Army to abandon these efforts late in May. No electronic interference was directed against the antirebel broadcasts by any U.S. government agency.

37. See Tad Szulc, *Dominican Diary* (New York, 1965), 44–45. Marine "Pathfinders" had already landed at Haina the previous day to establish control of the pier and access area there and to assist in the evacuation of American citizens. See Dare, "Dominican Diary," 41.

38. Senator Fulbright, whose access to the classified record on this point was probably more complete than mine, stated that "this request was denied in Washington and Benoit was thereupon told that the United States would not intervene unless he said he could not protect American citizens present in the Dominican Republic." See J. W. Fulbright, "The Situation in the Dominican Republic," *Congressional Record* (September 15, 1965), 23857. Senator Joseph Clark, another member of the Senate Foreign Relations Committee, has told essentially the same story. See Joseph Clark, *Congressional Record* (September 17, 1965), 24243.

I have not been able independently to verify the Fulbright-Clark report that Washington explicitly suggested the second cable, but it plausibly explains the sequence of recorded events.

39. Dare, "Dominican Diary," 41.

40. "Statement by President Johnson, May 2, 1965," *Department of State Bulletin* (May 17, 1965), 744.

41. Geyelin, *Lyndon B. Johnson and the World*, 252.

42. See Roberts, *LBJ's Inner Circle*, 252. Senator Russell stated some months later that the president called him before authorizing the Marine landing and that their discussion focused on the possibility of a Communist takeover, not on the supposed threat to American lives. As Russell recalled the incident: "I asked him if there were any indications of a definite Communist influence in the so-called rebel forces. He stated there was little doubt that there was a definite Communist influence there, and I told him that, in my opinion, he had no alternative other than to proceed to send the Armed Forces to Santo Domingo to avoid

another Cuba." See Richard Russell, "The Situation in the Dominican Republic: Tribute to Ambassador William Tapley Bennett, Jr.," *Congressional Record* (September 21, 1965), 24558.

43. Dare, "Dominican Diary," 42.

44. See John Bartlow Martin, *Overtaken by Events: The Dominican Crisis from the Fall of Trujillo to the Civil War* (New York, 1966), 657.

45. See Barnard Collier, "Nothing But Thunder" (unpublished manuscript cited with the author's permission), chap. xi, 9. Collier bases this quotation on information supplied him by persons present at the meeting.

46. See *Congressional Record* (September 15, 1965), 23862.

47. Roberts, *LBJ's Inner Circle*, 207; Rowland Evans and Robert Novak, *Lyndon Johnson: The Exercise of Power* (New York, 1966), 518.

48. A further indication that the embassy still hoped on Wednesday night that a massive military intervention would be unnecessary was the attempt to get PRD Secretary General Antonio Martínez Francisco to win popular acceptance of a cease-fire and of a junta plus elections solution. José Moreno reports that Martínez Francisco was compelled to make his radio statement by U.S. intelligence agents, among others. See Moreno, *Barrios in Arms*, 31–32.

49. David Shoup, "The New American Militarism," *The Atlantic Monthly* (April 1969), 54.

50. Although there were many incidents of violence during these hectic days, including clashes between civilians and police, these seem to have been similar to the phenomena experienced during the urban explosions suffered in the United States in the 1960's. Despite the intensive efforts of American officials after the fact to find evidence to substantiate allegations made at the time, there does not seem to be any credible indication that political executions or even planned and premeditated acts of violence took place in Santo Domingo during the first days of the 1965 crisis. It seems likely, in retrospect, that more atrocities were committed by the antirebel forces after the U.S. intervention than by the rebels before the Marines had landed. See Tenth Meeting of Consultation of Ministers of Foreign Affairs, Organization of American States, *Report on Atrocities Committed in Santo Domingo, Dominican Republic* (July 11, 1965; Washing-

ton, D.C.) and Anna P. Schreiber and Philippe S. Schreiber, "The Inter-American Commission on Human Rights in the Dominican Crisis," *International Organization* (Spring 1968), 508–528.

51. The two Europeans who appeared at Caamaño's side were soon publicly identified as Illo Capozzi, an Italian, and André Riviere, a Frenchman. Each had a long military career in a variety of causes, most of them anti-Communist. Capozzi had fought for Fascist Italy; Riviere had served with the French in Indo-China and with the Foreign Legion. Each man had been in the Dominican Republic for some time. Capozzi had been hired by Trujillo to help train the Dominican Navy's "frogmen," whom he still advised in 1965. Riviere had come in 1963, reportedly to seek sunken treasure off the Dominican coast.

Exact details about these somewhat shadowy figures are hard to find, especially because both were killed during the Dominican crisis. It seems fair to state, however, that if there were any possibility that these men were actually Communist agents, American officials anxious to defend the intervention would have made this claim by now; they do not do so, even privately.

It seems likely, in retrospect, that these two men were individual adventurers and treasure seekers in a long Caribbean tradition. Among the other foreigners who joined the rebel cause in 1965 were several others who seem to fit this description, including Venzeno Lovasto and Angelo Brunaldi, Italians brought to Santo Domingo by Trujillo for a variety of assignments, and William Bailes, an American airplane pilot who broadcast English-language propaganda for the rebel radio. Another such case was Michel Merjanov, a French merchant who served as Caamaño's interpreter for a time in 1965. Merjanov, according to Dominican press accounts in 1968, took this opportunity to remove from Dominican government files a number of documents related to criminal charges against him for commercial practices in 1964. Accused by Dominican immigration authorities in 1968 of links to the "international Mafia," Merjanov left the Dominican Republic at once. See *Listín Diario* (November 7–9, 1968).

52. Roberts, *LBJ's Inner Circle*, 208.

53. Robert F. Barry, ed., *Power Pack* (Portsmouth, Va.), 33.

4. DEPLOYING THE TROOPS

1. John Bartlow Martin, *Overtaken by Events: The Dominican Crisis from the Fall of Trujillo to the Civil War* (New York, 1966), 661.

2. Martin presents this passage as a direct quotation, presumably on the basis of notes he took at the time. See Martin, *Overtaken by Events*, 661.

3. Charles Roberts, *LBJ's Inner Circle* (New York, 1965), 209. Roberts mistakenly reports this incident as having taken place on Thursday afternoon.

4. Martin, *Overtaken by Events*, 661.

5. Ibid.

6. Ibid., 661, 662.

7. R. McC. Tompkins, "Ubique," *United States Marine Corps Gazette* (September 1965), 37.

8. It is unclear whether General York signed the cease-fire agreement. This embassy reported that he did; York told General Palmer, on the latter's arrival, that he had not.

9. See Martin, *Overtaken by Events*, 666–670, upon which part of this summary is based. Martin suggests (note 7, 670) that he still does not know who controlled the electric plant at this time. See also Tompkins, "Ubique," 38.

10. Martin, *Overtaken by Events*, 670.

11. Tompkins, "Ubique," 38. It is not clear whether the order to proceed with this linkup had been previously cleared with officials outside the Department of Defense.

12. Martin, *Overtaken by Events*, 676.

13. Such errors are apparently not as rare as one might expect or hope. In June 1967—according to Joseph Goulden's account—a key message directed at the *U.S.S. Liberty* was missent first to a Naval Communications Station in the Philippines, then to the National Security Agency in Maryland, and finally to another Naval Communications Station in Morocco; the result apparently contributed to the Israeli attack on the *Liberty*, in which 34 men died, 75 were wounded, and the Defense Department at first suspected a Soviet attack. Similar communications snafus plagued the *Pueblo* on its final mission in 1968. See Joseph Goulden, *Truth Is the First Casualty: The Gulf of Tonkin Affair—Illusion and Reality* (New York, 1969), 102–104.

5. EXPLAINING THE DOMINICAN INTERVENTION

1. See Appendix II for an annotated review of the main literature on the Dominican intervention. See also Howard Wiarda, "The Dominican Revolution in Perspective: A Research Note," *Polity* (Fall 1968), 114–124.

2. Among the major published items which reflect the "official line," I would include Jay Mallin's *Caribbean Crisis*; "Dominican Action: Intervention or Cooperation?" a report published in 1966 by the Center for Strategic Studies, Georgetown University; Thomas C. Mann's speech "Correcting Some Misconceptions," published in the *Department of State Bulletin* (November 8, 1965); and numerous public statements by administration officials then and since, many of them conveniently found in various issues of the *Department of State Bulletin*. Former Secretary of State Dean Rusk has consistently adhered to the official line in a number of speeches and statements to various audiences since he left the government.

3. Ellis O. Briggs, *Anatomy of Diplomacy: The Origin and Execution of American Foreign Policy* (New York, 1968), 188; Center for Strategic Studies, Georgetown University, "Dominican Action: Intervention or Cooperation?" *Special Study Report* #2 (Washington, D.C., 1966).

4. Among the main writings which best reflect the radical approach, I would mention: Fred Goff and Michael Locker, "The Violence of Domination: U.S. Power and the Dominican Republic," in Irving Louis Horowitz, Josué de Castro, and John Gerassi, eds., *Latin American Radicalism* (New York, 1969); John Gerassi, "Intervention in Santo Domingo," *Liberation* (June-July 1965); Victor Perlo, *Marines in Santo Domingo* (New Outlook Press, June 1965); James Petras, "The Dominican Republic; Revolution and Restoration," *New World Quarterly* (Cropover 1967); and Samuel Shapiro, "The Dominican Dilemma," *New Politics* (Spring 1965). A particularly well-stated exposition of this approach, included in a comprehensive review of postwar U.S. foreign policy, is chap. 8 in Richard T. Barnet's *Intervention and Revolution: America's Confrontation with Insurgent Movements Around the World* (New York, 1968).

Many foreign accounts of the 1965 Dominican crisis share

the radical view. Of these, perhaps the most interesting is an analysis by two leading Dominican Communists. See J. I. Quello (*sic*) and N. Isa Conde, "Revolutionary Struggle in the Dominican Republic," *World Marxist Review* (December 1965; January 1966).

5. Shapiro, "The Dominican Dilemma."

6. See, for example, Barnet, *Intervention and Revolution.*

7. Most of the literature published in the United States on the 1965 Dominican crisis fits essentially into the "liberal" category, although individual authors incorporate aspects of one or both of the other approaches. Of particular influence have been the various articles of Theodore Draper, compiled and reissued in 1968 by *Commentary* under the title *The Dominican Revolt: A Case Study in American Policy;* Draper's work combines elements of the "liberal" and the "radical" approaches. Other main items I would list as liberal analyses include Jerome Slater, *Intervention and Negotiation: The United States and the Dominican Revolution* (New York, 1970); Tad Szulc, *Dominican Diary* (New York, 1965); Dan Kurzman, *Santo Domingo: Revolt of the Damned* (New York, 1965); and Senator J. William Fulbright's Senate address on "The Situation in the Dominican Republic," published in the *Congressional Record* (September 15, 1965). Although he served as an official envoy during the crisis, John Bartlow Martin adopted the liberal approach in reviewing this period subsequently as part of his memoir, *Overtaken by Events* (New York, 1966). Chapters on the Dominican crisis in several general accounts of the Johnson period also reflect mainly the liberal critique; these include Philip Geyelin's, *Lyndon B. Johnson and the World* (New York, 1966); Rowland Evans and Robert Novak, *Lyndon B. Johnson: The Exercise of Power* (New York, 1966); and Charles Roberts, *LBJ's Inner Circle* (New York, 1965).

8. Kurzman, *Santo Domingo: Revolt of the Damned,* 298.

9. Mann, "Correcting Some Misconceptions," 731.

10. Mann contends, for instance, that "the action taken by Washington on the evening of April 28 (landing the Marines) had as its purpose the protection and evacuation of unarmed civilians." See Mann, "Correcting Some Misconceptions," 734. Secretary of State Rusk, testifying in closed-door session to members of the Senate Foreign Relations Committee late in

May 1965, reportedly said the decision to send in the troops "was ninety-nine percent the problem of protecting American and foreign nationals." See Haynes Johnson and Bernard Gwertzman, *Fulbright, the Dissenter* (Garden City, N.Y., 1968), 213.

11. "It was not until the evening of the 29th," Mann states, "that a decision had to be made on whether the Communist elements in the rebel camp presented a clear and immediate peril to the freedom of the Dominican nation," it was determined that such a peril did exist. See Mann, "Correcting Some Misconceptions," 735.

12. Center for Strategic Studies, *Dominican Action*, 1–2.

13. Philip Geyelin, *Wall Street Journal* (June 25, 1965).

14. Draper, *The Dominican Revolt*, 61.

15. Jerome Slater asserts, for instance, "that U.S. hostility to Juan Bosch was not part of a larger distaste for the democratic left in Latin America can be easily demonstrated by the considerable evidence that the U.S. has strongly supported the democratic left elsewhere in Latin America and in the Dominican Republic itself before and since 1965." Slater, *The United States and the Dominican Revolution*, 221–222.

16. Kurzman, *Santo Domingo: Revolt of the Damned*, 22. Cf. Senator Fulbright's conclusion that "the principal reason for the failure of American policy in Santo Domingo was faulty advice given to the President by his representatives at the time of acute crisis." See Fulbright, "The Situation in the Dominican Republic," 23855.

17. See Jerome Slater, *The United States and the Dominican Revolution*, 220.

18. This is essentially the argument Theodore Draper advances. See Draper, *The Dominican Revolt*, 5–10. Kalman Silvert refers to the Dominican intervention as "accidental" in the sense that the combination of United States leaders involved took an action 'inevitable' for them, but probably remote for other leaders." See Kalman Silvert, "Latin America and Its Alternative Futures," *International Journal* (Summer 1969), 407.

19. Evans and Novak, *Lyndon B. Johnson*, 82.

20. Johnson and Gwertzman, *Fulbright, the Dissenter*, 210–212.

21. Paul Bethel, *Washington Daily News* (June 21, 1965).

22. Szulc, *Dominican Diary*, 68–73.

23. *Chicago Tribune* (May 1, 1965).

24. "Statement by President Johnson, April 30, 1965," *Department of State Bulletin* (May 17, 1965), 742.

25. Graham Allison, "Conceptual Models and the Cuban Missile Crisis: Rational Policy, Organizational Process, and Bureaucratic Politics," *RAND Memorandum P-3919* (August 1968), 1. Cf. Allison's earlier discussion in "Policy, Process, and Politics: Conceptual Models and the Cuban Missile Crisis" (Ph.D. dissertation, Harvard University, 1968).

26. Without pretending to acknowledge or even to know all the sources of my approach to foreign policy formation, as outlined in the next few paragraphs, I should mention particularly the writings of Roger Hilsman, Richard Neustadt, Ernest May, Samuel Huntington, Warner Schilling, Paul Hammond, Charles Lindblom, and Harold Wilensky, in addition to Allison's previously mentioned writings. All are cited fully in the Bibliography.

27. On the concept of "satisficing," see James March and Herbert Simon, *Organizations* (New York, 1958), 140–141.

28. See, for example, Leslie Gelb's analysis of the massive American intervention in Vietnam which suggests that one of the reasons for the escalation of American participation in 1965 was that "after years of effort, the U.S. conventional forces were big enough and ready enough to intervene." Leslie Gelb, "Vietnam: Some Hypotheses about Why and How," Paper prepared for delivery at the 66th Annual Meeting of the American Political Science Association (Los Angeles, Calif.; September 8–12, 1970), 34.

29. Kenneth Glazier points out, for instance, that the proposed Allied guarantee to Japan that the Emperor would not be eliminated if Japan surrendered, a guarantee which might well have ended the war before the devastations of Hiroshima and Nagasaki, was "dropped primarily because of bureaucratic politics within the American government. The two strongest supporters of the proposal to clarify the surrender terms—Stimson and Grew—were, despite their titles, two of the weakest possible advocates for any policy in terms of influence wielded. They received no support from the military leaders,

each of whom naturally preferred to see his own military solution used for what they all saw as a military problem." See Kenneth M. Glazier, Jr., "The Decision to Use Atomic Weapons Against Hiroshima and Nagasaki," *Public Policy* (Summer 1970), 463–516.

30. See Roger Hilsman, *To Move a Nation* (New York, 1967), 3–16, 541–564.

31. As Raymond Bauer puts it, speaking more generally, "the student of policy tends to think of 'the problem' . . . In fact, there is no unity with respect to the problems people actually have, the way in which they perceive the problem or . . . their interests and values. Furthermore, since the policy process has a time dimension, each of these elements changes over time." See Raymond Bauer and Kenneth J. Gergen, eds., *The Study of Policy Formation* (New York, 1968), 14.

32. Allison, "Policy, Process, and Politics," 420.

33. Cf. Theodore Sorensen's observation that "Presidents rarely, if ever, make decisions—particularly in foreign affairs . . . The basic decisions which confine their choices have all too often been previously made." Theodore Sorensen, "You Get to Walk to Work," *New York Times Magazine* (March 19, 1967).

34. See Gabriel Almond, *The American People and Foreign Policy* (New York, 1950); Dexter Perkins, *The American Approach to Foreign Policy* (Cambridge, Mass., 1952); William Appleman Williams, *The Tragedy of American Diplomacy* (New York, 1962); and Stanley Hoffman, *Gulliver's Troubles, or the Setting of American Foreign Policies* (New York, 1968).

35. See Frederick Merk, *Manifest Destiny and Mission in American History: A Reinterpretation* (New York, 1963).

36. See David Potter, *The People of Plenty* (Chicago, 1953).

37. See Louis Hartz, *The Liberal Tradition in America* (Boston, 1955); Daniel Boorstin, *The Genius of American Politics* (Chicago, 1953); George Kennan, *American Diplomacy, 1900–1950* (Chicago, 1953); Hans Morgenthau, *In Defense of the National Interest* (New York, 1951) and numerous other writings; Reinhold Niebuhr, *The Children of Light and the Children of Darkness* (New York, 1960); Robert Osgood, *Ideals and Self-Interest in America's Foreign Relations* (Chicago, 1953).

38. See Samuel Huntington, *Political Order in Changing Societies* (New Haven, 1968).

39. See Arthur Whitaker, *The Western Hemisphere Idea; Its Rise and Decline* (Ithaca, N.Y., 1954), 1.

40. See Barnet, *Intervention and Revolution* . . . as well as his forthcoming study of "national security managers" since 1945. See also Herbert K. Tillema, "United States Military Intervention in the Era of Containment" (Ph.D. dissertation, Harvard University, 1969), and Alexander George, "The 'Operational Code': A Neglected Approach to the Study of Political Leaders and Decision-Making" (RAND Memorandum 5427, September 1967).

41. See Herbert Dinerstein, *Intervention Against Communism* (Baltimore, 1967), and James C. Thomson, Jr., "How Could Vietnam Happen?" *Atlantic* (April 1968), 47–53.

42. Security restrictions and bureaucratic self-protection being what they are, it is impossible for the outsider to prove conclusively the inaccuracy of American intelligence reports during the Dominican crisis. It is even difficult to establish exactly what those reports were at the time, as distinct from what was said in retrospect or in justification after the intervention began. One knows, for instance, that President Johnson declared on May 2 that "what began as a popular democratic revolution . . . very shortly moved and was taken over and really seized and placed in the hands of a band of Communist conspirators," but one cannot be absolutely sure that the president had before him reports which might have suggested this conclusion. Only inference and interdepartmental sniping are available so far to suggest that there were intelligence reports —received with skepticism by several of the president's advisers and by some relevant government departments, but which the president decided to credit, whatever his reasons—which provided a basis for the president's statement.

On the basis of the information one can piece together, I think it is fair to state not only that the president's statement could not be supported (despite considerable efforts by the administration to do so) but also that there is considerable positive evidence that American civilian and military intelligence officials seriously exaggerated the role and influence of Dominican Communists in the 1965 crisis, as well as their degree of connection with foreign Communist powers.

It appears, for instance, that every specific report of actual foreign Communist involvement on the rebel side turned out to be unsubstantiated, apart from information about the prior training of a score of Dominican Communists and about the public encouragement given to the rebels by Radio Havana broadcasts. In addition to the story repeated on April 25 that telephone calls between Molina Ureña and Castro Cuba had been intercepted, these reports include suggestions that the Europeans at Caamaño's side might be Communist agents, that the rebels were using Chinese Communist-manufactured grenades, that an unidentified ship in the harbor at Santo Domingo might have been used to bring weapons in to the rebels, that the rebels had been supplied by a "minisubmarine" operated from Cuba, and even that Ché Guevara had been put ashore to help the rebel cause!

Second, it is clear that many of the specific intelligence reports which were passed on to the White House and leaked to the press during the first days of the crisis were erroneous. Among these were the cases of key rebel appointees—including Luis Homero Lajara Burgos and Alfredo Conde Pausas—misidentified as Communist sympathizers, mistaken reports that Rafael Bonilla Aybar and other anti-Bosch leaders had been killed by the rebels, false statements that various specific businesses (including the branches of international banks) had been sacked, and a completely fictitious claim that Dominican Communist leaders had met with Caamaño, Peña Gómez, and other rebel leaders early in the crisis and reached various agreements with them. Statements by Ambassador Bennet and intelligence sources that Dominican Communists had been working closely with the PRD before the crisis began were never substantiated, and exactly the reverse actually seems to have been the case. Perhaps most important, the reports by American intelligence officials as of April 30 (and presumably earlier as well) that "no civilian PRD leaders of any significance remain with the rebels" were very much mistaken; José Francisco Peña Gómez, Manuel Ferández Mármol, Rafael and Emmanuel Espinal, Ramón and Manuel Ledesma Pérez and Luis Lembert Peguero were among the civilian PRD leaders with the rebel military leaders at this point.

American intelligence reports that Dominican Communists were actively supporting the rebel cause—agitating crowds, mimeographing announcements, distributing arms, establishing command posts and the like—were undoubtedly largely accurate, but there does not appear to be any credible evidence to support the public statements by President Johnson, Secretary Rusk, Ambassador Stevenson, and others that the rebel movement was "really seized and placed in the hands of a band of Communist conspirators," that the "Communists had captured the revolution according to plan" and that they were "decisively influencing the political leadership of the rebellion." (See various issues, May and June 1965, of the *Department of State Bulletin*). Even if communications intelligence or other highly sensitive sources so far undisclosed should reveal that some Dominican Communists *thought* they were in control of the revolution or shortly would be, there does not seem to be any credible indication that they actually were.

43. The phrase is Roger Hilsman's. See Roger Hilsman, *To Move a Nation* (New York, 1967), 548. Cf. Warner Schilling, "The H-Bomb Decision: How to Decide Without Actually Choosing," *Political Science Quarterly* (March 1961) and Gelb, "Vietnam: Some Hypotheses."

44. See Townsend Hoopes, *The Limits of Intervention* (New York, 1969), 7, 16, 21, 72.

45. See, for instance, Hilsman, *To Move a Nation*, 26–39, and Arthur Schlesinger, Jr., *A Thousand Days*, 219–278.

46. See Richard Neustadt, *Alliance Politics* (New York, 1970), 67; John Steinbruner, "The Mind and Milieu of Policy-Makers: A Case Study of the MLF" (Ph.D. dissertation, Massachusetts Institute of Technology, 1968); and Jeffrey Race, "American Intervention Abroad: Systematic Distortion in the Policy-Making Process," Paper prepared for delivery at the 66th Annual Meeting of the American Political Science Association (Los Angeles, Calif.; September 8–12, 1970).

47. See Dean Pruitt, "The Definition of the Situation as a Determinant of International Action," in Herbert Kelman, ed., *International Behavior* (New York, 1965).

48. See Else Frankel-Brunswik, "Tolerence of Ambiguity as an Emotional and Perceptual Personality Variable," *Journal of Personality* (1949), 108–183, as cited in Robert Jervis, "Cognitive Consistency and Cognitive Distortion," Paper prepared for delivery at the 66th Annual Meeting of the American Political Science Association (Los Angeles, Calif.; September 8–12, 1970).

49. See Smith Simpson, *Anatomy of the State Department*

(Boston, 1967) and Chris Argyris, "Some Causes of Organizational Ineffectiveness within the Department of State," *Occasional Paper #2,* Center of International Systems Research, Department of State (Washington, 1966).

50. See Thomson, "How Could Vietnam Happen?"

Bibliography

The Bibliography lists selected general works on the making of American foreign policy as well as all the literature on the 1965 Dominican intervention which I have consulted and which may be cited. A number of other documents, notes, and manuscripts were also used but remain classified or are otherwise restricted.

Substantially all the works on the history of United States–Dominican Republic relations which I consulted are cited in the Notes to Chapter 1 and are not repeated in the Bibliography.

Major works I have used on the history of Dominican politics before 1965 are cited in the notes to my essay "The Dominican Republic: The Politics of Chaos" in *Reform and Revolution: Readings in Latin American Politics*, edited by Arpad von Lazar and Robert Kaufman. More complete bibliographies on the history of Dominican politics are Howard J. Wiarda, *Política y gobierno en la República Dominicana, 1930–1966* (Santiago, Dominican Republic, 1968), and Deborah S. Hitt and Larman Wilson, *A Selected Bibliography of the Dominican Republic: A Century After the Restoration of Independence* (Washington, 1968).

I also read an extensive set of newspapers and periodicals published in the Dominican Republic during the period from September 1964 to July 1966, including: *Ahora!, El Caribe, El*

1J4, Diálogo, Dominican-North American Common Sense: Interchange of Ideas, La Hoja, La Información (Santiago), *Listín Diario, La Nación, Patria, El Popular, Pum!, Reconstrucción, Unidad, La Voz de la OEA,* and *La Voz de la Zona de Seguridad.*

I. GENERAL LITERATURE ON FOREIGN POLICY-MAKING

Allison, Graham T., Jr. "Conceptual Models and the Cuban Missile Crisis," *American Political Science Review* (September 1969).

———. "Policy, Process and Politics: Conceptual Models and the Cuban Missile Crisis." Ph.D. dissertation, Harvard University, 1968.

Almond, Gabriel. *The American People and Foreign Policy.* New York, 1950.

Argyris, Chris. "The Individual and Organization: Some Problems of Mutual Adjustment," *Administrative Science Quarterly* (June 1957).

———. "Some Causes of Organizational Ineffectiveness Within the Department of State," *Occasional Paper #2,* Center for International Systems Research (November 1966).

Banfield, Edward C. *Political Influence.* New York, 1961.

Barnet, Richard J. *Intervention and Revolution: America's Confrontation with Insurgent Movements Around the World.* New York, 1968.

Bauer, Raymond A., and Kenneth J. Gergen, eds. *The Study of Policy Formation.* New York, 1968.

Beichman, Arnold. *The "Other" State Department.* New York, 1968.

Braybrooke, David, and Charles Lindblom. *A Strategy of Decision.* Glencoe, Ill., 1963.

Briggs, Ellis O. *Anatomy of Diplomacy: The Origin and Execution of American Foreign Policy.* New York, David McKay, 1968.

Brown, Seyom. *The Faces of Power: Constancy and Change in U.S. Foreign Policy from Truman to Johnson.* New York, 1968.

Dinerstein, Herbert. *Intervention Against Communism.* Washington, D.C., 1967.

Dror, Yeheskel. "Muddling Through—'Science' or Inertia?" *Public Administration Review* (September 1964).

Fox, William, ed. *Theoretical Aspects of International Relations*. Notre Dame, Ind., 1959.

George, Alexander L. *The "Operational Code": A Neglected Approach to the Study of Political Leaders and Decision-Making*. Santa Monica, Calif., 1967.

Goulden, Joseph. *Truth Is the First Casualty: The Gulf of Tonkin Affair—Illusion and Reality*. New York, 1969.

Hammond, Paul. "Foreign Policy-Making and Administrative Politics," *World Politics* (July 1965).

———. "Super Carriers and B-36 Bombers" in Harold Stein, ed. *American Civil–Military Decisions*. Birmingham, Ala., 1963.

Hilsman, Roger. "Congressional-Executive Relations and the Foreign Policy Consensus," *American Political Science Review* (September 1958).

———. "The Foreign Policy Consensus: An Interim Report," *Conflict Resolution* (December 1959).

———. *To Move a Nation*. New York, 1967.

Hirschman, Albert O., and Charles Lindblom. *Economic Development, Research and Development, Policy Making: Some Converging Views*. Santa Monica, Calif., 1961.

Hoffman, Stanley, ed. *Contemporary Theories of International Relations*. Englewood, N.J., 1960.

———. *Gulliver's Troubles, or The Setting of American Foreign Policy*. New York, 1968.

Hoopes, Townsend. *The Limits of Intervention*. New York, Wiley, 1969.

Huntington, Samuel P. *The Common Defense: Strategic Programs in National Politics*. New York, 1961.

Institute for Defense Analysis, International and Social Studies Division. *The National Security Process*, vols. I and II. Arlington, Va., 1968.

Johnson, Haynes, and Bernard Gwertzman. *Fulbright, the Dissenter*. Garden City, N.Y., 1968.

Katzenbach, Edward L., Jr. "The Horse Cavalry in the Twentieth Century: A Study on Public Response," *Public Policy* vol. 8 (1958).

Kurth, James R. "To Govern Sovereigns: Hegemony in International Relations." Ph.D. dissertation, Harvard University, 1967.

Lindblom, Charles. *Bargaining: The Hidden Hand in Government*. Santa Monica, Calif., 1955.

———. *The Policy-Making Process*. Englewood, N.J., 1968.

Liska, George. *Imperial America: The International Politics of Primacy*. Baltimore, Md., 1967.

March, James G., ed. *Handbook of Organizations*. Chicago, 1965.

March, James G., and Herbert A. Simon. *Organizations*. New York, 1958.

May, Ernest R., "American Imperialism: A Reinterpretation," in *Perspectives in American History* vol. 1 (1967).

———. "The Nature of Foreign Policy: The Calculated versus the Axiomatic," *Daedalus* (Fall 1962).

Morgenthau, Hans J. *A New Foreign Policy for the United States* New York, 1969.

Neustadt, Richard E. *Alliance Politics*. New York, 1970.

———. *Presidential Power*. New York, 1960.

Paige, Glenn D. *The Korean Decision*. New York, 1968.

Ripley, Randall. "Interagency Committees and Incrementalism: The Case of Aid to India," *Midwest Journal of Political Science* (May 1964).

Rivera, Joseph de. *The Psychological Dimensions of Foreign Policy*. Columbus, Ohio, 1968.

Rosenau, James N. "The Concept of Intervention," *Journal of International Affairs* vol. 22 (1968).

———. *International Politics and Foreign Policy*. Glencoe, Ill., 1961.

———. "Pre-theories and Theories of Foreign Policy," in R. Barry Farrell, ed. *Approaches to Comparative and International Politics*. Evanston, Ill., 1966.

Rourke, Francis E. *Bureaucracy, Politics and Public Policy*. Boston, 1969.

———. "Bureaucracy in Conflict: Administrators and Professionals," *Ethics* (April 1968).

Sapin, Burton M. *The Making of United States Foreign Policy*. Washington, D.C., 1966.

Schilling, Warner R. "The H-Bomb Decision: How to Decide Without Actually Choosing," *Political Science Quarterly* (March 1961).

Simon, Herbert. *Administrative Behavior.* New York, 1957.
Snyder, Richard, H. W. Brack, and Burton Sapin. *Foreign Policy Decision-Making.* Glencoe, Ill., 1962.
Sorensen, Theodore. *Decision-Making in the White House.* New York, 1963.
————. "You Get to Walk to Work," *New York Times Magazine* (March 19, 1967).
Steel, Ronald. *Pax Americana.* New York, 1968.
Steinbruner, John. "Model Four and the MLF." Unpublished memo to the Public Policy Program, Harvard University (September 29, 1969).
————. "The Mind and Milieu of Policy-Makers: A Case Study of the MLF," Ph.D. dissertation, Massachusetts Institute of Technology, 1968.
Thomas, Hugh. *Suez.* London, 1966.
Thomson, James C., Jr. "How Could Vietnam Happen?" *Atlantic* (April 1968).
Tillema, Herbert. "United States Military Intervention in the Era of Containment." Ph.D. dissertation, Harvard University, 1968.
Weintal, Edward, and Charles Bartlett. *Facing the Brink: An Intimate Study of Crisis Diplomacy.* New York, 1967.
Whiting, Allen. *China Crosses the Yalu.* New York, 1968.
Wilensky, Harold. *Organizational Intelligence.* New York, 1967.
Wohlstetter, Roberta. *Pearl Harbor: Warning and Decision.* Stanford, Calif., 1962.
Yarmolinsky, Adam. "American Foreign Policy and the Decision to Intervene," *Journal of International Affairs* vol. 22 (1968).
Young, Oran R. "Intervention and International Systems," *Journal of International Affairs* vol. 22 (1968).

II. LITERATURE ON THE DOMINICAN INTERVENTION

A. Published Sources

Alba, Víctor. *Los sumergidos.* Mexico, 1965.
Alexander, Robert J. "U.S. Must Back Dominican Revolution," *New America* (June 18, 1965).
Baeza Flores, Alberto. "La crisis dominicana y el dilema de América Latina," *Política* (June–July 1965).

Baron, Dona. "The Dominican Republic Crisis of 1965: A Case Study of the Regional vs. the Global Approach to International Peace and Security," in Andrew Cordier, ed. *Columbia Essays in International Affairs*. New York, 1968.

Barry, Robert F., ed. *Power Pack*. Portsmouth, Va., 1965.

Bender, J. B. [pseud.]. "Dominican Intervention: The Facts," *National Review* (February 6, 1966).

Benoit, Pedro B. "Carta al redactor," *El Tiempo* (New York, July 22, 1965).

Berdle, Adolf A. "A Stitch in Time," *Reporter* (May 20, 1965).

Bernheim, Roger. "Drama in the Caribbean," *Swiss Review of Public Affairs* (July 1965).

Berrellez, Robert. "Dominican Revolt Still Confusing," *Los Angeles Times* (April 24, 1966).

Betancourt, Rómulo. "La dramática experiencia dominicana," in *Golpes de estado y gobiernos de fuerza en América Latina*. Caracas, 1966.

Bethel, Paul. "Dominican Intervention: The Myths," *National Review* (February 6, 1966).

Bogen, David S. "The Law of Humanitarian Intervention: United States Policy in Cuba (1898) and the Dominican Republic (1965)," *Harvard International Law Club Journal* (Spring 1966).

Bonsal, Philip W. "Open Letter to an Author," *Foreign Service Journal* (February 1967).

Bosch, Juan. "Comentarios al libro de un dominicano honesto," *Ahora!* (February 13, 1965).

———. "Communsm and Democracy in the Dominican Republic," *Saturday Review of Literature* (August 6, 1965).

———. "The Dominican Revolution," *New Republic* (July 24, 1965).

———. *Pentagonism: A Substitute for Imperialism*. New York, 1968.

———. "A Tale of Two Nations," *New Leader* (June 21, 1965).

———. *The Unfinished Experiment: Democracy in the Dominican Republic*. New York, 1965.

Breisky, Arthur E. "Favoring 'The Martin Approach.'" Letter to the Editor, *Foreign Service Journal* (July 1967).

Brugal Alfau, Danilo. *Tragedia en Santo Domingo: Documentos para la historia*. Santo Domingo, 1966.

Caamaño Deñó, Francisco A. "El reloj de la historia se detiene, pero no se atrasa," *Juventud Rebelde* (Havana, April 25, 1966).

Calamandrei, Mauro. "Santo Domingo: A People's War," *Atlas* (translation from *L'Espresso*, Rome), July 1, 1965.

Cárdenas, Florángel. "On-the-Spot Report from Santo Domingo," *San Juan Review* (May 1966).

———. "Three Coups: One Successful, One Aborted, One Yet to Come," the *San Juan Review* (February 1964).

Carlos, Newton. *Santo Domingo: La guerra de América Latina.* Buenos Aires, 1965.

Casals, Pedro Manuel. "How the U.S. Subverted the Dominican Revolt," *New America* (July 25, 1965).

———. "Inside the Dominican Revolution," *Independent* (August 1965).

Casals, Pedro Manuel, and Taña de Gómez. "Dominican Prospects," *Liberation* (March 1966).

Center for Strategic Studies, Georgetown University. "Dominican Action: Intervention or Cooperation?" *Special Study Report* #2 (Washington, D.C., 1966).

Clark, Rev. James A. *The Church and the Crisis in the Dominican Republic.* Westminster, Md., 1967.

———. "The Church and the Dominican Crisis," *Thought* vol. 41. (Spring 1966).

———. "Religion and Revolution in the Dominican Republic." *American Ecclesiastical Review* (January 1967).

Clingham, James H. "All-American Teamwork," *Army Digest* (January 1967).

Clos, Max. "Santo Domingo's Activist Adventurers," *Reporter* (June 17, 1965).

Connell-Smith, Gordon. "The OAS and the Dominican Crisis," *World Today* (June 1965).

Conte Agüero, Luis. *Cuba en Santo Domingo.* Miami, 1965.

Cordero, Michel. "The Dominican Revolution," *Progressive Labor* (December 1965).

Cuello, J. I., and N. Isa Conde. "Revolutionary Struggle in the Dominican Republic and Its Lessons," *World Marxist Review* (December 1965 and January 1966).

Dare, James A. "Dominican Diary," *U.S. Naval Institute Proceedings* (December 1965).

Dennis, Lloyd B. "Dominican Dilemma," *Editorial Research Reports* (April 13, 1966).

"Dice Wessin Sólo Rugía en Madriguera," *El Caribe* (November 25, 1965).

Dodd, Senator Thomas J. "Vietnam and the Dominican Republic," *Congressional Record* (May 4, 1965).

———. "The Story of the Dominican Uprising and the Division in the American Press," *Congressional Record* (August 23, 1965).

———. "A Reply to Senator Fulbright on the Dominican Republic," *Congressional Record* (August 24, 1965).

"The Dominican Invasion," *Political Affairs* (June 1965).

Draper, Theodore. "A Case of Defamation: U.S. Intelligence versus Juan Bosch," *New Republic* (Part I, February 19, 1966; Part II, February 26, 1966).

———. "A Case of Political Obscenity," *New Leader* (May 9, 1966).

———. "The Dominican Crisis: A Case Study in American Policy," *Commentary* (December 1965).

———. *The Dominican Revolt: A Case Study in American Policy.* New York, Commentary, 1968.

———. Letter to the Editor, *New Republic* (March 5, 1966).

———. "The New Dominican Crisis," *New Leader* (January 31, 1966).

———. "The Roots of the Dominican Crisis," *New Leader* (May 24, 1965).

Dreier, John C. "New Wine and Old Bottles: The Changing Inter-American System," *International Organization* (Spring 1968).

Dubois, Jules. "Exclusive—Washington Tries a Bribe," in David Brown and W. Richard Bruner, eds. *How I Got That Story.* New York, 1967.

Dudman, Richard. "Conflict Between Mann and Bundy Was Factor in Apparent U.S. Vacillation on Dominican Crisis," *St. Louis Post-Dispatch* (June 13, 1965).

Espaillat, Leopoldo A. "Carta al director," *Listín Diario* (September 18, 1969).

Estrella, Julio C. *La revolución dominicana y la crisis de la OEA.* Santo Domingo, 1965.

Evans, Rowland, and Robert Novak. *Lyndon B. Johnson: The Exercise of Power.* New York, 1966.

Fenwick, Charles. "The Dominican Republic: Intervention or Collective Self-Defense," *American Journal of International Law* (January 1966).

Ferreras, Ramón A. *Cárcel.* Santo Domingo, 1967.

———. *Guerra Patria.* Santo Domingo, 1965.

Fixx, James. "Report from Santo Domingo," *Saturday Review of Literature* (June 12, 1965).

Fougerolle, X. de. "République Dominicaine: Quatre Années de crises," *Révue de Défens Nationale* (July 21, 1965).

Franco, Franklin J. *República Dominicana: Clases, crisis y comandos.* Havana, 1967.

Frankel, Max. "Secret U.S. Report Details Policy Shift in the Dominican Crisis," *New York Times* (November 14, 1966).

Frente de Acción de la Juventud Reformista (FAJURE). "A los Reformistas y al pueblo en general," *Listín Diario* (April 27, 1966).

Fulbright, Senator J. William. "The Situation in the Dominican Republic," *Congressional Record* (September 15, 1965).

Gerassi, John. "Intervention in Santo Domingo," *Liberation* (June–July 1965).

Geyelin, Philip. *Lyndon B. Johnson and the World.* New York, Praeger, 1966.

Gilmore, Kenneth O. "The Truth About Santo Domingo," *Reader's Digest* (May 1966).

Girbau León, Vicente. "Imperalism in the Dominican Republic," *Monthly Review* (September 1965).

Goff, Fred, and Michael Locker. "The Violence of Domination: U.S. Power and the Dominican Republic," in Irving Louis Horowitz, Josué de Castro, and John Gerassi, eds. *Latin American Radicalism.* New York, 1969.

Goodman, Martin. "Numbers Game," *Columbia Journalism Review* (Summer 1965).

Halper, Sam. "The Dominican Upheaval," *New Leader* (May 16, 1965).

Hernando Ramírez, Miguel Angel. "Carta al redactor," *Ahora!* (May 2, 1966).

"How Latin America Sees It," *Christian Century* (June 23, 1965).

Institute for International Labor Research. *The Dominican Republic: A Study in the New Imperialism.* New York, 1965.

Klein, Major William E. "Stability Operations in Santo Domingo," *Infantry* (May–June 1966).

Kopkind, Andrew. "The Outlook for Bosch," *New Republic* (May 21, 1966).

Kurzman, Dan. *Santo Domingo: Revolt of the Damned.* New York, G. P. Putnam's Sons, 1965.

"Leader Abandons Caamaño Group," *El Mundo* (San Juan, August 3, 1965).

Lens, Sidney. "Lovestone Diplomacy," *Nation* (July 5, 1965).

————. "Santo Domingo: The Unfinished Revolution," *Nation* (May 2, 1966).

Lewine, John L. "The Politics of Metternich," *New Politics* (Spring 1965).

Llano Montes, Antonio, *Santo Domingo: Barricadas de odios.* Mexico, 1966.

"Logistics for Stability Operations," *Military Review* (September–October 1966).

Lowenthal, Abraham F. "The United States and the Dominican Republic to 1965: Background to Intervention," *Caribbean Studies* (July 1970).

————. "The Dominican Intervention in Retrospect," *Public Policy* (Fall 1969).

————. "The Dominican Republic: The Politics of Chaos," in Arpad von Lazar, and Robert Kaufman, eds. *Reform and Revolution.* Boston, 1969.

————. "Foreign Aid as a Political Instrument: The Case of the Dominican Republic," *Public Policy* vol. 14 (1965).

————. "The Limits of American Power—The Lesson of the Dominican Republic," *Harper's* (June 1964).

Maldonado, A. W. *San Juan Star Sunday Magazine* (June 6, 1965).

Mallin, Jay. *Caribbean Crisis: Subversion Fails in the Dominican Republic.* New York, 1965.

Manigot, Leslie F. "La Crise dominicaine," *Révue Française de Science Politique* (December 1965).

Mann, Thomas. "Speech Prepared for Delivery Before the Annual Meeting of the Inter-American Press Association," *Department of State Bulletin* (October 1965).

Marder, Murray. "Crisis Under the Palms," *Washington Post* (June 27, 1965).

Martin, John Bartlow. *Overtaken By Events: The Dominican Crisis from the Fall of Trujillo to the Civil War.* New York, Doubleday, 1966.

————. "The Struggle to Bring Together Two Sides Torn by Killing," *Life* (May 28, 1965).

Martínez, Julio César. "Revolution and Counter-Revolution in the Dominican Republic," *New Politics* (Spring 1965).

McGaffin, William, and Erwin Knoll. *Anything But the Truth: The Credibility Gap—How the News Is Managed in Washington.* New York, 1968.

Meeker, Leonard. "The Dominican Situation in the Perspective of International Law," *Department of State Bulletin* (July 12, 1965).

Meléndes, Darío. *Paso a la libertad.* Santo Domingo, 1965.

Miller, Linda B. "Regional Organization and the Regulation of Internal Conflict," *World Politics* (July 1967).

Miolán, Angel. "Carta a Juan Bosch," *Listín Diario* (January 15, 1966).

————. "Mi postura frente a la revolución de abril," *Listín Diario* (November 29, 1965).

Mockler, Tony. "Santo Domingo: Labyrinth of Policy," *Nation* (February 7, 1966).

Morley, Lorna. "Invasion and Intervention in the Caribbean Area." *Editorial Research Reports* (July 22, 1959).

Moskos, Charles C., Jr. "Grace Under Pressure—The U.S. Soldier in the Dominican Republic," *Army* (September 1966).

Moulis, Lieutenant Colonel Wallace J., and Major Richard Brown. "Key to a Crisis," *Military Review* (February 1966).

"Las Negociaciones: Una necesidad del momento," *El Popular* (Santo Domingo, July 19, 1965).

Niedergang, Marcel. *La Révolution de Saint Dominique.* Paris, 1966.

"The OAS in Action," *Americas* (September 1965).

O'Brien, W. V. "International Law, Morality, and American Intervention," *Catholic World* (September 1965).

Odena, Isidro J. *La intervención ilegal en Santo Domingo.* Buenos Aires, 1965.

Oglesby, J. C. M. "The Prospects for Democracy in the Dominican Republic," *International Journal* (Toronto, vol. 21, 1966).

Palmer, Lieutenant General Bruce, Jr. "The Army in the Dominican Republic," *Army* (November 1965).

———. "XVIII Airborne Corps Leads the Way," *Army Digest* (January 1967).

———. "Lessons from the Dominican Stability Operation," *Army* (November 1966).

Partido Comunista Dominicano. "El partido y la insurrección de abril: Auto-crítica del Comité Central," *El Popular* (August 16, 1965).

Peña Gómez, José Francisco. "Dominican Revolutionary Leader Replies to U.S. White Paper on Dominican Intervention," *New America* (November 25, 1965, and December 18, 1965).

———. "Versión acerca movimiento militar constitucionalista," *La Nación* (May 8, 1965).

Perlo, Víctor. *Marines in Santo Domingo.* New York. 1965.

Petras, James. "The Dominican Republic: Revolution and Restoration," *New World Quarterly* (Cropover, 1967).

Plank, John. "The Caribbean: Intervention, When and How," *Foreign Affairs* (October 1965).

Ranstead, Donald R. "The Dominican Crisis," *New Republic* (May 27, 1965).

"Un relato de la lucha de resistencia anti-yanqui," *Bohemia* (Havana, January 14, 1966).

"Reservists in Crisis," *Air Reservist* (July 1965).

Rettie, John. "A Hungary in the Caribbean," *New Statesman* (May 7, 1965).

"La revolución que convirtió en guerra la última invasión norteamericana," *Ahora!* (April 29, 1968).

Roberts, Charles. *LBJ's Inner Circle.* New York, Delacorte Press, 1965.

Roberts, T. D., ed. *Area Handbook for the Dominican Republic.* Washington, D.C., 1966.

Rodman, Selden. "A Close View of Santo Domingo," *Reporter* (July 15, 1965).

———. "Why Balaguer Won," *New Republic* (June 18, 1966).

Ross, Stanley. "El hombre que pidió la ayuda norteamericana cuenta la historia," *El Tiempo* (New York, July 10, 1966).

―――. "Pancho Aguirre: Segundo jefe de la República Dominicana," *El Tiempo* (December 12, 1964).

Roucek, Joseph S. "The Dominican Republic in Geopolitics," *Contemporary Review* (June 1965).

Rovere, Richard. "Letter from Washington," *New Yorker* (May 15, 1965, and June 12, 1965).

Sánchez Cabral, Eduardo. "Declaraciones exclusivas de Juan Bosch sobre los problemas nacionales," *Ahora!* (January 16, 1965).

―――. "El movimiento constitucionalista: La más bella revolución dominicana," *Ahora!* (September 25, 1965).

Schreiber, Anna P. and Philippe. "The Inter-American Commission on Human Rights in the Dominican Crisis," *International Organization* (Spring 1968).

Selser, Gregorio. *Aquí, Santo Domingo! La tercera guerra sucia.* Buenos Aires, 1966.

Sevareid, Eric. "The Final Troubled Hours of Adlai Stevenson," *Look* (November 30, 1965).

Shannon, William V. "The Marines Have Landed," *Commonwealth* (May 21, 1965).

Shapiro, Samuel. "The Dominican Dilemma," *New Politics* (Spring 1965).

―――. "Santo Domingo: Can We Withdraw?" *Nation* (May 24, 1965).

Shereff, Ruth. "How the CIA Makes Friends and Influences Countries," *Viet-Report* (January-February 1966).

Slater, Jerome. "Democracy vs. Stability: The Recent Latin American Policy of the United States," *Yale Review* (Winter 1966).

―――. *Intervention and Negotiation: The United States and the Dominican Revolution.* New York, Harper & Row, 1970.

―――. "The Limits of Legitimization in International Organizations: The Organization of American States and the Dominican Crisis," *International Organization* (Winter 1969).

―――. *The OAS in United States Foreign Policy.* Columbus, O., Ohio State University Press, 1967.

―――. "The United States, the Organization of American

States, and the Dominican Republic, 1961–1963," *International Organization* (Spring 1964).

Stebbins, Richard P. *The United States in World Affairs, 1965.* New York, 1966.

Stone, I. F. "The Dominican Republic as Lyndon Johnson's Hungary," *I. F. Stone's Weekly* (May 31, 1965).

Szulc, Tad: *Dominican Diary.* New York. 1965.

———. "When the Marines Stormed Ashore in Santo Domingo," *Saturday Evening Post* (July 31, 1965).

Thackray, John. "Schizophrenia in Santo Domingo," *New Statesman* (July 30, 1965).

Thomas, A. J., Jr. "The Dominican Republic Crisis 1965— Legal Aspects," *The Ninth Hammerskjöld Forum.* The Association of the Bar of the City of New York, 1966.

Tompkins, Major General R. McC. "Ubique," *Marine Corps Gazette* (September 1965).

"The Truth about Santo Domingo," *Young Socialists* (July-August 1965).

"U.S. Policy Toward Communist Activities in Latin America: Pro and Con," *Congressional Digest* (November 1965).

Volman, Sacha: "¿Quién impondrá la democracia?" *Panoramas* (July-August 1965).

Wagenheim, Karl. "Juan Bosch: Man on a Tightrope," *San Juan Review* (May 1966).

———. "Talking with Juan Bosch," *New Leader* (February 28, 1966).

Walsh, Frank, ed. *Dominican Crisis 1965–66.* Alexandria, Va., 1966.

Wells, Henry. "The Dominican Republic: Aftermath of Despotism," *Current History* (January 1966).

———. "The Dominican Search for Stability," *Current History* (December 1966).

———. "The OAS and the Dominican Elections," *Orbis* (Spring 1963).

Wiarda, Howard J. "The Changing Political Orientation of the Catholic Church in the Dominican Republic," *Journal of Church and State* (Spring 1965).

———. "The Development of the Labor Movement in the Dominican Republic," *Inter-American Economic Affairs* (Summer 1966).

————. ed. *Dominican Republic: Election Factbook* (Institute for the Comparative Study of Political Systems, June 1966).

————. *The Dominican Republic: Nation in Transition.* New York, 1969.

————. "The Dominican Revolution in Perspective: A Research Note," *Polity* (Fall 1968).

————. "From Fragmentation to Disintegration: The Social and Political Effects of the Dominican Revolution," *América Latina* (April-June 1967).

————. "The Politics of Civil-Military Relations in the Dominican Republic," *Journal of Inter-American Studies* (October 1965).

————. "The U.S. and the Dominican Crisis: Background to Chaos," *Caribbean Monthly Bulletin* (July 1965).

Wilson, Larman. "The Dominican Policy of the United States: The Illusions of Economic Development and Elections," *World Affairs* (July-September 1965).

————. "Estados Unidos y la guerra civil dominicana," *Foro Internacional* (vol. VIII #2, Mexico, October-December 1967).

————. "The Monroe Doctrine, Cold War Anachronism—Cuba and the Dominican Republic," *Journal of Politics* vol. 28 (May 1966).

————. "The United States and the Dominican Republic: A Post-Election Assessment," in Eugenio Chang-Rodríguez, ed. *The Lingering Crisis: A Case Study of the Dominican Republic.* New York, 1969.

Wood, Bryce. "Letter to the Editor, *New York Times* (June 13, 1965).

Wyckoff, Don P. "An American Peacekeeping Force," *Marine Corps Gazette* (September 1965).

B. *Public Documents*

Constitution of the Dominican Republic, 1962.

Constitution of the Dominican Republic, 1963.

Gaceta Oficial, Gobierno Constitucional. May 20–August 31, 1965.

Gaceta Oficial, "Número Especial Extraordinario." May 4, 1965.

————. Ad Hoc Committee, *First General Report of the Ad Hoc*

Committee, Tenth Meeting of Consultation of Ministers of Foreign Affairs (July 17, 1965).

————. Ad Hoc Committee, *Second General Report of the Ad Hoc Committee,* Tenth Meeting of Consultation of Ministers of Foreign Affairs (September 24, 1965).

Organization of American States, *Annual Report of the Secretary-General* (Fiscal year 1964–65).

————. *Annual Report of the Secretary-General* (Fiscal year 1965–66).

————. Comisión de Asistencia Técnica. *Informe sobre atroci dades cometidas en Santo Domingo* (July 7, 1965).

————. Comisión Inter-Americana de Derechos Humanos, *Situación de los derechos humanos en la República Dominicana: Informe preliminar.* OAS Series L/V /II: 12 (June 23, 1965).

————. *Minutes of Tenth Meeting of Foreign Ministers, Plenary Sessions* (1965–66).

————. *Minutes of Tenth Meeting of Foreign Ministers, Sessions of General Committee* (1965–66).

————. *Report of the Secretary-General of the Organization of American States Regarding the Dominican Situation: Activities from April 29, 1965, until the Installment of the Provisional Government* (November 1, 1965, Document 405).

————. Tenth Meeting of Consultation of Ministers of Foreign Affairs (MFM), *Official Documents* (OAS Series, F/ii, 10, 1965–66).

United Nations. *Annual Report of the Secretary- General* (June 16, 1964–June 15, 1965).

————. *Annual Report of the Secretary-General* (June 16, 1965–June 15, 1966).

U.S. Congress. Senate, Committee on the Judiciary, *State Department Security: The William Wieland Case.* 87th Congress, 1st session. Washington, 1962.

————. Committee on the Judiciary, Subcommittee to Investigate the Administration of the Internal Security Act and Other International Security Laws. *Castro's Network in the United States.* 87th Congress, 1st session. 88th Congress, 1st session. Washington, 1963.

————. *Communist Threat to the United States Through the*

Caribbean: Testimony of Brigadier General Elías Wessin y Wessin (October 1, 1965). 89th Congress, 1st session. Washington, 1965.

————. *Documentation of Communist Penetration in Latin America.* 89th Congress, 1st session. Washington, 1966.

————. *Testimony of Juan Isidro Tapia Adames and Alfonso L. Tarabochia* (December 9, 16, 1965). 89th Congress, 1st session. Washington, 1966.

————. Committee on Foreign Relations. *Background Information Relating to the Dominican Republic.* 89th Congress, 1st session. Washington, 1965.

U.S. Department of State. *Department of State Bulletin,* 1960–1965.

————. *The Dominican Crisis: The Hemisphere Acts.* Washington, 1965.

C. *Unpublished Sources*

Alpert, Richard. "Intervention: The United States and the Dominican Republic," Paper submitted at Harvard University (December 1966).

Bennett, W. Tapley, Jr. "Address on Receipt of 'Big Beef' Award at Dinner Sponsored by Professional Groups Active in Journalism and Public Relations" at Atlanta, Ga. (September 17, 1965).

Benoit, Pedro. "Aclaraciones que hace el Coronel Pedro Bartolomé Benoit, F.A.D. al periodista Sr. José Juárez Núñe_." Mimeographed. (March 26, 1967).

Bosch, Juan. Interview on *Face the Nation,* CBS Radio anc Television (May 2, 1965).

————. "Letter to Sacha Volman." Mimeographed. (November 25, 1964).

Bundy, McGeorge. "Transcript of a Discussion with Bundy at Harvard," Harvard University Archives (June 14, 1965).

Burt, Al. "Remarks on the Dominican Crisis," University of Florida (November 1965).

Collier, Barnard L. "Nothing But Thunder." Uupublished manuscript (August 1965).

"Comunicado de las Fuerzas Armadas Dominicanas." Mimeographed. (April 25, 1965).

"Exhortaciones del Monseñor Hugo E. Polanco Brito, Obispo de Santiago." Mimeographed. (April 25–27, 1965).

Free, Lloyd A. "Attitudes, Hopes and Fears of the Dominican People," Institute for International Social Research. Princeton, N.J., 1962.

Heinl, Robert D. "Revolt in Santo Domingo." Unpublished typescript (Summer 1965).

Hombres de Trabajo. "Llamado al pueblo dominicano." Mimeographed. Santiago, Dominican Republic (August 10, 1965).

Hoon, Mok Chung. "The 1963 Coup d'Etat in the Dominican Republic." Paper submitted at University of Pennsylvania (1966).

Horowitz, Irving L. "The Dominican Crisis in Perspective," Address at St. Louis Teach-In (May 16, 1965).

"La juventud católica dominicana y su participación en la vida política." Mimeographed. (June 1966).

Littig, David. "Student Activity in the Dominican Republic, 1962–64." Report. 11th International Student Conference.

"Los obispos dominicanos hablan al pueblo, a los bandos en lucha, a todos los dirigentes responsables de nuestra nación." Mimeographed. (May 22, 1965).

Lowenthal, Abraham F. "The Dominican Intervention of 1965: A Study in U.S. Policy." Center for International Affairs, Harvard University (February 2, 1967).

Mensajes del Santo Padre Paulo VI a los Dominicanos, Abril 1965–Abril 1966.

Moreno, José "The Emergence of Leadership in a Revolutionary Setting." Center for International Affairs, Harvard University (March 30, 1967).

———. "Sociological Aspects of the Dominican Revolution." Ph.D. dissertation, Cornell University (June 1967).

Moses, Carl. "U.S. Intervention in the Dominican Republic: Its Implication for the Inter-American System." Meeting of Southern Political Science Foundation, Gatlinburg, Tenn. (November 10–12, 1966).

Needler, Martin. "The Dominican Crisis of 1965 and United States Policy." Mimeographed. (March 23, 1967).

Partido Demócrata Cristiano. "El Caso Dominicano: Los sucesos del 24 de abril—sus antecedentes y consecuencias." Mimeographed. (August 4, 1965).

"Pacto intervenido entre el Dr. Antonio Martínez Francisco, Secretario General del Partido Revolucionario Dominicano y la Junta Militar de Gobierno que integran el Coronel Pedro Benoit, Fuerzas Aéreas Dominicanas, el Coronel Apolonar Enrique Casada Saladín, Ejército Nacional, y el Capitán de Navío Olgo Manuel Santana Carrasco, Marina de Guerra." Mimeographed (April 28, 1965).

Partido Revolucionario Social Cristiano. "Manifiesto al pueblo dominicano." Mimeographed. (May 21, 1965).

————. Memorándum a la Comisión Ad Hoc de la Organización de los Estados Americanos; Asunto: Opinión del Partido Revolucionario Social Cristiano (PRSC) sobre su propuesta de fecha 18 de junio de 1965 "para la solución de la crisis dominicana" (July 5, 1965).

Palmer, Lieutenant General Bruce A. "The Dominican Republic." Address to Pan-American Society of New England (November 1966).

————. "U.S. Stability Operations in the Dominican Republic." Speech to Association of the U.S. Army. Washington, D.C. (October 11, 1966).

Ray, Talton F. "Obstacles to a Settlement of the Dominican Crisis: April 24–May 26, 1965." Paper presented to seminar on Inter-American Affairs, Columbia University (May 1967).

Reid Cabral, Donald. "Revolución dominicana fue planeada por comunistas." Speech at National Press Club, Washington, D.C. (July 22, 1965).

Richman, Frederick. "The Dominican Intervention: A Case Study in American Foreign Policy." Undergraduate Honors thesis, Department of Government, Harvard University (April 1967).

Rosario, Antonio. "Los Social Cristianos y la revolución dominicana." Mimeographed. (May 1965).

Slater, Jerome. "The OAS and Political Change in the Dominican Republic." Center for International Affairs, Harvard University (March 30, 1967).

————. "The United States and the Dominican Revolution." Unpublished manuscript (June 1969).

Volman, Sacha. "Significance of Sale of Juan Bosch Book in the Dominican Republic." Mimeographed. (February 1965).

Wedge, Bryant. "Communism and the Development of the Dominican Revolutionary Movement: An Interpretative Analysis." Unpublished manuscript (December 1965).

Wiarda, Howard J. "The Aftermath of the Trujillo Dictatorship: The Emergence of a Pluralist Political System in the Dominican Republic." Ph.D. dissertation, University of Florida (June 1965).

―――. "The Context of U.S. Policy Toward the Dominican Republic: Background to the Revolution of 1965." Center for International Affairs, Harvard University (December 8, 1966).

―――. "Trujillo's Dominican Republic: The Legacy of Dictatorship." Southwestern Political Science Association, Dallas, Tex. (March 23, 1967).

Wilson, Larman. "The United States and the Dominican Civil War: The Challenge to Inter-American Relations." Lecture at the School of International Affairs, Columbia University (November 1966).

―――. "The United States Dominican Intervention of 1965: Illicit or Licit Exercise of Force?" Paper prepared for Institute of World Polity, Georgetown University, Washington, D.C. (1966).

―――. "U.S. Military Assistance to the Dominican Republic, 1916–1967," Center for International Affairs, Harvard University (April 26, 1967).

Index

239

Ball, George, 103, 106, 111, 118; and presidential announcement, 105; and OAS, 117
Banana industry, 46
Barnet, Richard, quoted, 152
Batista y Zaldivar, Fulgencio, 24
Bay of Pigs invasion, 26, 160
Benítez, Jaime, vii, 114, 123, 148
Bennett, W. Tapley, Jr., vii, 3, 31, 49, 70, 82, 95, 99, 104, 108, 110, 111, 118, 122, 130, 135, 137, 143; appointed ambassador, 16; cables request for Marines, 100–101; ceasefire stances, 124, 129; confers with papal nuncio 121–122; conflicting accounts of crisis meeting, 93–94; and presidential announcement, 105–106; refuses Bosch negotiations, 92–93, 157; to resume charge of embassy, 85–86; supports Reid, 44–47; troop-landing recommendation, 102–103; walkie-talkie request, 97–98, 100, 157
Benoit, Pedro, 77, 107; asks U.S. assistance, 99; cites Communists in requests for troops, 101–102; establishes junta, 76, 99–100; incapable of advancing, 119, 120; letter promising restraint, 119–120; requests military aid, 100–101, 118–119; U.S. help to, 3; U.S. urges constraint by, 118–119
Betancourt, Rómulo, 114, 117, 148; seen as possible crisis resolver, 124
Bonnelly, Rafael F., 41
Bordas, Diego, 36
Bosch, Juan, 3, 31, 38, 45, 48, 49, 68, 120, 123, 143, 157, 159; apparent takeover by supporters of, 72–81; com-

munications link with White House, 114; *La crisis . . .*, 51–52; courts middle class, 50–51; movement to reseat, 41–42, 55–58; negotiation proposal rebuffed by Bennett, 92–93; overthrown, 35–38; and "radical view" of intervention, 132–133, 134–135, 139–140; reasserts control of PRD, 50; return ruled out, 70–71, 79–81; strengthens military ties, 52–54; urged to take anti-Communist measures, 27–28; U.S. view of, 136, 140–142, 156; wants Molina as provisional president, 74–75
Bowdler, William, 64
Boxer (U.S.S.), 92, 97, 98, 101, 104, 110
Brito Mata, Miguel Angel, 51
Brookings Institution, ix
Bundy, McGeorge, 3, 100, 103, 130, 159; attitude on sending troops, 101; and presidential announcement, 105
Bunker, Ellsworth, 4; calls OAS Council meeting, 114

Caamaño, Fausto, Jr., 122
Caamaño Deñó, Francisco, 43, 91, 93, 95, 96, 101, 109, 123, 143, 144; consolidates hold on city, 98–99; on coup, 74; described, 125–126; meeting with U.S. representatives, 125–126
Cabral, Severo A., 41
Cacao trade, 39, 46
Cáceres, Ramón, 21; arrested, 74
Calderón, Juan, 109
Campagna, Aníbal, 51
Cantina Nacional, 42–43
Caribbean Ready Group (U.S. Navy), 70, 71, 106, 110; helicopter landings, 103;

La Vega garrison, 67
Leoni, Raúl, 117; on intervention, 116
Listín Diario, 99
Long, Russell, 105
Lora, Francisco Augusto, 41, 58, 76
Lovatón, Pittaluga, Máximo, 88; at U.S. embassy, 94

McCain, John, Jr., quoted, 138
McClean, Malcom, 63
McCone, John, 96
MacMichael, David C., quoted, 19
McNamara, Robert, 82, 103, 111, 116; concern for troop strength, 107, 110
Mann, Thomas, C., 70, 72, 82, 86, 103, 117, 121, 143, 156, 159; attitude on sending troops, 101; and presidential announcement, 105; requests written statement from Benoit, 104; and walkie-talkie requests, 98
Manzanillo Bay, 19
Marines, U.S., 1, 3, 71, 110, 111, 124, 134; all available troops landed, 110–111; alleged "pathfinder" landing, 101; arrival, 103–104; casualties, 120; compete with Army, 107; immediate landing called for, 102–103; *1916* invasion, 9; troops available, 116–117; *1,200* requested, 100–101
Martin, John Barlow, 3, 16, 31, 114, 115, 116, 127, 148; and "Castro-Communist" threat, 27–28; first meeting with rebel leadership, 125–126; to help Bennett, 117–118; and *1962* election, 13; opposes troop use in mid-city, 128–129; *Overtaken by Events*, 15; to Santo Domingo for "facts," 119, 122–123; works

to strengthen cease-fire, 123–124
Martínez, Francisco, 92–93; at U.S. embassy, 94
Masterson, K. S., 106, 111, 115, 118, 122; advises Washington on troop needs, 129–130
Medrano Ubiera, Colonel, 76
Mella (yacht), 91
Military assistance advisory group, U.S. (MAAG), 13, 15, 63, 98, 99, 102, 108
Miolán, Angel, 50, 59
Molina Ureña, José Rafael, 15, 36, 50, 53, 86, 88, 92, 122, 143; conference at U.S. embassy, 93–94, 144; proposed "provisional presidency," 74–75, 76; sworn in as provisional president, 77; willing to compromise with anti-Bosch leaders, 91
Monroe, James, 20
Monroe Doctrine, Roosevelt corollary, 6
Montás Guerrero, Salvador Augusto, 43, 69, 73, 107, 143; argues for U.S. help, 119; forms junta, 71, 72; joins rebel movement, 68; military setback, 96; moves toward city, 92
Montes Arache, Manuel R., 96, 144
Mora, José A., 114, 120
Morales Carrión, Arturo, 11
Moscoso, Teodoro, 28, 117
Movimiento Popular Dominicano (MPD), 40, 73, 101, 108; pro-Bosch stand, 56
Moyers, Bill, 114; and presidential announcement, 105
Muñoz Marín, Luis, 114, 148

National Police, Dominican, 27, 65, 67, 69; Reid's reform of, 43
National Police Palace, 65
Navy, Dominican: alleged

Navy (*cont.*)
plans to attack capital, 89, 90, 91; bombardment by, 76, 93
Navy, U.S., Task Force to Dominican coast (*1961*), 11, 26. *See also* Caribbean Ready Group; Marines, U.S.
Neustadt, Richard, 160
New York Times, 5, 11
Nicaragua, 23
Nivar Seijas, Neit, 55; organizes coup plot, 58

Okinawa (U.S.S.), 117
Organization of American States (OAS), 129, 130; approves troop-positioning plan, 130–131; asked to arbitrate, 122; Council called into session, 114–115; and free elections, 7; and *1962* election, 13; president's desire to involve, 117; role in Dominican crisis, 4; Special Committee, 124, 148; and Trujillo regime, 6, 10, 24; and unilateral intervention, 1, 2
Ornes, Horacio J., 41
Ozama Fortress, 65, 108, 115

Palmer, Bruce, Jr., vii, 121; assigned to Santo Domingo, 116; on cease-fire, 123; lost message from Wheeler, 129–130, 149; suggests "cordon," 127–128
Papal nuncio, 117, 148; meeting with rebel leadership, 125–126; seeks cease-fire, 120–121
Partido Reformista (PR), 41
Partido Revolucionario Dominicano (PRD), 30, 31, 36, 37, 38, 45, 64, 66, 70, 71, 87, 92, 94, 135, 138, 141, 144, 157; alleged takeover agreement with Reid, 72; anticoup measures (*1963*), 35; Bosch reasserts control of (*1964*), 50; leaders at U.S. embassy, 83; moves to reseat Bosch, 41–42; opposition to Reid, 41, 58–60; and Rio Piedras Pact, 52
Partido Revolucionario Social Cristiano (PRSC), 37, 38; and Rio Piedras Pact, 52; supports Bosch, 35–36
Partido Socialista Popular (PSP), 40, 108; pro-Bosch stand, 56
Peace Corps, 4, 14
Peguero Guerrero, Belisario, 43, 55, 102; joins revolt, 69
Peña Gómez, José Francisco, 36, 50, 53, 58, 64, 88, 127, 137; announces Reid downfall, 61, 64; radio speeches, 55; seeks CIA help, 94
Peña Taveras, Mario, 61, 66, 68, 91, 92; leftist friends, 78
Peru, Cooperación Popular, 47
Polk, James, 20
Puerto Rico, 6, 90; Bosch activities in, 45, 52; imports from, 43

Raborn, William, 64, 110, 111, 143; reports Communists in rebel movement, 104–105
Race, Jeffrey, 160
Radio, stations compete during crisis, 86–87
Radio Comercial, 64
Radio Havana, 102
Radio Santo Domingo, 64, 65, 66, 67; "Castro flavor" of broadcasts, 97; recaptured by pro-Bosch activists, 74
Radio San Isidro, 99, 100, 122
Read, Benjamin, 66, 105
Red Cross, Dominican, 122
Reid Cabral, Donald J., 109, 138, 140, 157; arrested, 74; and attacks on Triumvirate, 40–41; crisis meeting with Connett, 70–71; economic